With gratitude [illegible]
journey to re-discover your inner strength!
Christina Lynne HorsePlay HP2 [illegible]

INSIGHT PUBLISHING
SEVIERVILLE, TENNESSEE

Published in the United States by
INSIGHT PUBLISHING
647 Wall Street • Sevierville, Tennessee • 37862
www.insightpublishing.com

Publisher's Disclaimer: This book is a compilation of ideas from numerous experts who have each contributed a chapter. As such, the views expressed in each chapter are of those who were interviewed and not necessarily of the interviewer or Insight Publishing.

ISBN 978-1-60013-292-6

10 9 8 7 6 5 4 3 2 1

TABLE OF CONTENTS

A Message from the Publisher...

I've faced many challenges in my life and I know what it means to struggle. I sure wish I'd had this book during those times. We handpicked some of the most successful people we know who have had to learn how to discover their inner strength. The authors I interviewed for this book have the experience and knowledge that will help everyone learn a little more about this vital component for success—inner strength.

This book is custom designed for those who want to increase their skills and knowledge. Self-development is vital to success. One author made this poignant observation: "Self-development tends to fall to the bottom of the priority list for most people and they are not the only ones to suffer for this choice. Their family suffers. Their coworkers suffer. Their employees suffer. All of the crucial relationships in their life suffer because they are not being the absolute best they could truly be."

If you strive for excellence and want valuable information about how some of the most successful people in business today have found their inner strength and achieved success, this book is the resource you need. People who want to hone their skills to cope with life's challenges will learn from what these authors have to say. I know that I did and I believe you will too.

Interviews Conducted by:
David E. Wright, President
Insight Publishing & International Speakers Network

Chapter 1

AN INTERVIEW WITH...

ANN ROULAC

DEVELOPING PERSONAL MASTERY

DAVID WRIGHT (WRIGHT)

Today we are talking with Ann Roulac, visionary, author, and speaker who serves as a catalyst for change, inspiring and empowering people to transform their personal and professional lives. Ann is nationally recognized for her strategic advice, and, as a trusted advisor, she has enabled thousands of entrepreneurs and executives to achieve extraordinary wealth. Through her research and working with clients, she has discovered the qualities and thinking that distinguish highly successful individuals—those she describes as pursuing the path to personal mastery.

She designed Personal Mastery Programs to support entrepreneurs and small business owners who are committed to creating highly successful businesses. Her mission is to empower her clients to actualize their authentic visions—

visions that are energizing and spirit-enhancing—to achieve personal, professional, and financial freedom.

Ann, welcome to *Discover Your Inner Strength.*

ROULAC

Thank you David, it is a pleasure speaking with you today.

DAVID WRIGHT (WRIGHT)

What is the secret to developing personal mastery?

ROULAC

During the last thirty years, I've had the privilege of working with countless successful men and women who lead balanced lives and make enormous contributions to their companies and communities. And yet, even though a number of them are among the wealthiest people in the world, many of them—like many of us—are not truly in touch with their own mastery and power.

Success is not the result of a particular level of intelligence or education. While a quality education and being very smart make the journey a little easier, they are not the main prerequisites for greatness. Some people make it look effortless, as though they had tapped into some magic or secret formula. The reality is that they have achieved personal, professional, and financial freedom by following their own convictions, personal truths, and authentic vision.

In my work with entrepreneurs, I have observed unique characteristics in those who are advancing on what I call the "path of personal mastery." They have developed and embody certain qualities that allow them to make healthy changes in their lives and a positive difference in the lives of others. This development of mastery is not an event but a journey. It's a process of deepening your vision to achieve your goals and purpose.

Everyone's path to mastery is unique and we all have different lessons along the way. It's unlikely that we will eliminate personal challenges that we need to deal with, but each problem presents an opportunity to learn and grow. Sometimes it's necessary to stand still and reflect on where we're going and what we're learning. But other times it's better to be in action, even if it means making mistakes, so we can bring about change.

Maryann Williamson said, "Our deepest fear is not that we are inadequate. Our deepest fear is that we are powerful beyond measure. It is our light, not our darkness, that most frightens us." The path toward mastery requires risk-taking and a leap of faith. It requires an act of courage and heroics to move forward in a new direction. It also demands that we release our addiction to instant gratification, the dream of winning the lottery, or quick solutions. Fast, temporary relief—whether we're dealing with an illness, a weight-loss program, a life plan, or a new business strategy—produces only disappointment, not long-lasting results and well-being.

By developing personal mastery, you will access higher levels of inspiration and learn to consciously control your life in accordance with your desires, life purpose, and vision.

The only limitations to a fulfilling and rewarding life come from within. We are the sole impediment to our own mastery.

WRIGHT

How did you become interested in personal growth and mastery?

ROULAC

My fascination with the concepts of personal mastery began over twenty-five years ago when I started my first entrepreneurial endeavor. I had been working for a large bank as a lender to real estate developers and had developed expertise in a form of financing so complex that very few banks understood the process or even how they could benefit. I taught banks how to structure these transactions in a way that also benefited my Real Estate clients. From that initial idea, we expanded our services to meet the needs of our clients, which eventually included economic advice, marketing strategies, and management consulting and coaching.

My parents were real estate developers so I've always been interested in this field. Additionally, the complexity of development was attracting the best and the brightest from the most prestigious business schools in the country. This made my work challenging, exciting, and a lot of fun.

After several years, I began to notice that some executives were continually successful and others were not. I was fascinated by what they had in common and what differentiated them. They all came from solid middle-class backgrounds, had graduated from top business schools, were bright and creative thinkers, and were attractive and personable. Yet some excelled and became the leaders in their industry, and others failed miserably.

Clearly, what set these two groups apart was a set of personal principles, beliefs, and perspectives held by most of those who were successful—what I define as "personal mastery." In my book *Power, Passion & Purpose,* I identified the qualities of powerful people. The seven key characteristics that my most successful clients had in common are that they:

- Know who they are, what they want, where they are going, and with whom they want to spend time,
- Are aware of their strengths, gifts, unique qualities, and what's "right" for them,
- Do what they say they are going to do and are clear about their priorities and values,
- Stay in the present, neither dwelling on the past nor worrying about the future,
- Believe in the power of something greater than themselves and/or feel guided or supported by God,
- Have a strong sense of self but are not self-centered (i.e., life does not revolve around their needs and wants), and
- Are passionate about making a difference in the world and giving to others.

WRIGHT

What is the value in pursuing and developing personal mastery?

ROULAC

We live in complex times. Every day presents innumerable ways to lose our balance and sense of control. Our busy lives leave little time for solitude or reflection, and whatever time we do have is usually spent seeking some kind of relief. Many feel they have no control over their daily lives, let alone their destiny and future. This sense of powerlessness can lead to disillusionment with their careers, stress-related diseases, transient relationships, and a general confusion of purpose.

When we experience the present as chaotic and the future as unpredictable, it's easy to become befuddled and cautious about moving forward. In a climate of uncertainty, when we aren't in touch with our purpose and our personal power, we become vulnerable to the well-meaning opinions of others—family, friends, neighbors, gurus and therapists, even the local newscaster. This is especially true in times of transition, when we're stressed out and overwhelmed. Unconsciously, we may give away our power until there isn't much left.

Joseph Campbell said, "The world is full of people who have stopped listening to themselves or have listened only to their neighbors to learn what they ought to do, how they ought to behave, and what the values are that they should be living."

The development of mastery is a process of moving toward our highest potential and the discipline of clarifying and deepening our personal vision. Peter Senge said, "People with a high level of personal mastery approach their life as an artist would approach a work of art. They do that by becoming committed to their own lifelong learning."

Like a story, we are each a unique work of art. And because the tale is never finished, we all have the capacity to re-envision our lives in ways that help us achieve our dreams.

Wright

So do you believe that anyone can achieve success and personal mastery?

Roulac

I believe that we each have a specific and important mission to fulfill in this lifetime, and that when we are not on track with our mission and purpose, we feel drained of energy, life, and spirit. When we develop a strong sense of who we are and when we begin to access our own personal power and inner wisdom, we will begin to manifest our deepest visions and dreams.

My lifework is anchored in a conviction that we all possess a unique genius. My passion is to support individuals to achieve their highest potential. Through my study of personal mastery disciplines and work with clients, I have discovered that as we become more aware of our true nature, our capacity to experience life-affirming shifts increases.

Anyone can attain higher levels of success through personal mastery, but you need a guide, a coach, or trusted advisor. One of the key aspects of successful entrepreneurs is that they ask for advice, and they're always learning. Few people seem to have the insight and discipline to get there on their own. It's difficult, if not impossible, to become an astute observer of oneself—that's why people hire coaches. I began working with one when I started my business twenty-five years ago and that was a wise decision.

A study of Fortune 1000 companies showed that coaching programs returned nearly six times the original investment. It's become common now for senior managers and executives to have coaches, and many public companies I work with are providing coaching for all of their employees. Numerous courses offered via the Internet provide coaching through teleseminars and webinars at affordable prices. You have to do your homework, however, to make sure you're engaging someone with the knowledge and skills to benefit you. Internet marketing has made this a greater challenge, I believe, because some coaches advertise guidance services, but their main talent is nothing more than brilliant marketing.

Wright

Why do you believe understanding power is the foundation for creating personal mastery?

Roulac

Most cultures identify powerful individuals as those with the greatest amount of control over others. Political and business leaders certainly qualify, but the phenomenon of power isn't limited to people in obvious positions of influence. It applies to anyone who claims a superior position due to race, education, net worth, physical strength, physical beauty, position of authority, or accumulation of assets. But *true* power comes from within. Those who are in touch with their own true power have a presence and a quality that affect the people around them. They impress, not because they want to, but because of the energy they radiate, which often has nothing to do with material accomplishment or career success.

Unfortunately, many of us feel power-*less* and unable to change our lives or make a difference in the world. When we feel power-less we don't feel power-

full. We desire what we think we don't have, which we view as external to us. This is one of the reasons we emulate the lifestyles of those we perceive as having "made it." We focus our attention—sometimes to the point of obsession—on pursuing the things they have: more money, more beauty, more toys, more authority. If we could just get a bit more of *that*, we could control our lives and feel safe and secure.

But these are only *symbols* of power. Real power is not about control or looking good or having more. Real power is about getting in touch with your strengths, skills, talents, and gifts—your unique purpose and contribution to the greater whole. To reclaim your power, you must let go of your fears of making mistakes and leaving your comfort zone, stop worrying about what others think, and open yourself to the constant flow of ideas, opportunities and energies that are available to every one of us, all of the time.

The tendency to look outside oneself for answers is largely a product of our materialist culture, spinning at breakneck speed. We're addicted to the adrenaline rush of a 24/7 lifestyle, constantly responding to crisis and chaos with hardly any time to reflect on what we're actually doing. And yet its dizzying pace makes us feel important and worthy. We've come to believe that if our time is in demand every minute of the day, if our days and nights are filled with activities, then we must be doing something right. These distractions and perceptions can lead to some very disempowering beliefs and habits.

WRIGHT

How can our readers reclaim their personal power?

ROULAC

The source of your personal power—your passion and life purpose—is what energizes you, enables you to create an extraordinary life, and allows you to tap into the wisdom of geniuses. When you are clear about your life's vision, it will serve as a guidepost for all of your personal and business decisions and enable you to live with greater clarity and ease.

Those with a clear life purpose are not as vulnerable to workplace stress and the pressures of day-to-day living. They are able to see the big picture and observe how the decisions they make either contribute—or not—to their own personal growth, the life they want to lead, and the impact they want to make on the world around them. When you integrate power, passion, and purpose—the essence of personal mastery—you can accomplish great things.

Materialism and the quest for more money and possessions are motivating factors for many, but such goals are not life-sustaining. Achieving them provides only temporary satisfaction; they don't feed the soul. I believe this is the main reason why many people who attain a high level of financial comfort and/or career success resort to mood-altering drugs to alleviate depression. In spite of their wealth and accomplishments they still feel empty, as if something is missing, and the pain of that realization is too much to bear.

Power is the ability to get things done—to take action and realize your goals and dreams. Personal power is the ability to create what you want in life. When you reach a greater understanding of who you are, it gives you power. The more self-knowledge you have, the easier it becomes to create what you want, rather than settling for less. If you don't have the self-knowledge, you don't have the power. If you don't have the power, you can't create what you want in life.

The process to regain power over your life is not for the timid. Taking the necessary steps requires a life-altering shift in your worldview. But why remain powerless when you can get in touch with who you are and gain a sense of your own personal purpose and passions—what truly makes you happy. When you align yourself with change and flow with the pace and energy of the universe, realignment occurs. You need only to strengthen your will to live life more fully.

And so instead of turning your life's decisions over to others, commit to your own empowerment and to symbols of inspiration and guidance that *you choose* to follow. The challenge for each of us is to find that "missing" piece, to embrace our gifts and put them in service to a grander vision of who we can become and how we can contribute.

WRIGHT

What are the disciplines that can support people to attain personal mastery?

ROULAC

George Leonard, a pioneer in the human potential movement, said that taking up a regular practice or discipline—anything from aikido to gardening to Zen—can help heal us of our addiction to instant gratification. There are many disciplines that can access your higher levels of vitality and creativity and enable you to live in greater harmony and balance. But I believe it's important to find the ones that best fit your lifestyle and personality, and then create an approach that is uniquely yours.

For example, I've studied the basics of tai chi with more than half a dozen teachers. When I follow someone else's discipline, I usually get caught up in doing it their way—precisely and perfectly. In my own practice, however, I just move and allow the energy to flow through me. Sometimes my practice resembles tai chi, and sometimes it resembles an ancient Middle Eastern dance. Although we shouldn't become sloppy in our applications, especially in the beginning, I believe there is always room for improvisation if that feels right to your unique body.

All transformation and change require an understanding of the principles of energy. The state of our personal energy affects all of our decisions, careers, relationships, investments, and health choices. We all have the capacity to tune in and access the most optimal choices and decisions that will lead us toward greater happiness, health, harmony, and a heightened state of awareness and insight.

Daily practices designed to increase, manage, and balance personal and collective energies were a routine part of life for many of our distant ancestors. These practices are still around today, offering numerous benefits to anyone who wants more control over his or her health and more wisdom for making the right decisions. Instruction in yoga, tai chi, feng shui, and meditation is now available in most major cities and towns. The basics are easy—even modest practice can provide great benefits—and most of them can be done by people of any age.

The more you understand the concepts of energy and how you are affected in both positive and detrimental ways by its movement and quality, the easier it will be for you to change your environment, relationships, and the health of your body. When you incorporate energy practices into your daily life, you will come to view what is sometimes called "miraculous healing" as logical and understandable, and not some kind of magic or mystery. Personal mastery and change need not be difficult or complex; it only takes a commitment to integrate energy practice into your daily routine.

Wright

Do you provide coaching for corporate employees or entrepreneurs?

ROULAC

My commitment is to help individuals achieve personal, professional, and financial freedom, so there's a greater possibility of that happening if you work for yourself rather than for someone else. J. Paul Getty, oil tycoon and once the richest man in America, said, "There is only one way to make a great deal of money; and that is in a business of your own." Besides, I have a lot more fun working with entrepreneurs than with corporate employees, and having fun is one of my guiding principles.

I spent more than fifteen years employed within corporate America as an executive and was hired specifically for my mastery as a rainmaker. In my industry, everyone had great technical skills, but what differentiated my ability to produce extraordinary results was my commitment to learning and personal mastery.

While corporate employees certainly benefit from coaching, entrepreneurs can't afford not to have a coach. If your business is not large enough to have an advisory board, you risk being overwhelmed by the pressure of daily decisions. The isolation can become very lonely.

I serve more as a trusted advisor and catalyst than a coach. There are many great professionals who are highly skilled at coaching, but may lack a technical business background, which I believe is an important element. My diverse experience in economics, finance, entrepreneurial strategies, as well as personal mastery knowledge and disciplines, enable me to help my clients achieve their highest potential.

The foundation of my own business has been to provide strategic advice to business owners who are committed to becoming leaders in their industry. My counsel has enabled them to create extraordinary wealth and achieve personal freedom. We're currently expanding our training programs to incorporate what author Margaret Lobenstine described as "Renaissance Souls."

WRIGHT

What is a Renaissance Soul and why is this your current focus?

ROULAC

In her book, *The Renaissance Soul,* Margaret Lobenstine describes this personality as one who continually pursues multiple passions and prefers variety to concentrating on just one activity. The fact that these people do not follow a linear path, are in touch with their emotions, and are masters at multitasking may equip them to thrive in our volatile economy. In a world where adaptability and creativity are fundamental to success, they may have the necessary skills to become future business leaders. In fact, I believe that if you don't acquire the skills of a Renaissance Soul, you won't succeed as an entrepreneur.

I consider myself a Renaissance Soul, so I can easily relate to the challenge that creative types have in staying focused. We're currently offering Personal Mastery Programs that teach people how to think like Renaissance Entrepreneurs, but also help them to clarify and focus their vision.

Clearly a sea of change is occurring, since many emerging business leaders exhibit some of the characteristics of Renaissance Souls. They have learned to harness their energy and talents to achieve their vision and become successful Renaissance Entrepreneurs. Renaissance Entrepreneurs who have created enormously successful ventures include Sir Richard Branson, business magnate and founder of The Virgin Group; the late Anita Roddick, activist and founder of The Body Shop; and Michael Dell, philanthropist and founder of Dell, Inc.

Some of the key qualities that distinguish highly successful Renaissance Entrepreneurs include:

- They are visionaries with exceptional focus who know how to call future possibilities into being.
- They continually reinvent themselves in order to respond to changing market cycles and economic shifts.
- They are masters at marketing and understand how to utilize both dynamic and magnetic manifestation strategies.
- They appreciate the importance of staying inspired and energized and have mastered being fully engaged in life.

I believe that entrepreneurs who possess the attributes of a Renaissance Soul and who can create and actualize a clear, authentic vision for their business and life will emerge as future leaders.

WRIGHT

What is the key to finding balance and creating life success in these turbulent times?

ROULAC

Finding balance amid the chaos is an art, not a science, and there are no singular solutions. Yet, when you learn how to become more focused and balanced, you can make wise decisions and the right choices. The real key is maintaining internal balance and drawing from the principles of energy and the power of thought to change your reality. Whenever you take the time to evaluate your reactions, feelings, or responses in a challenging situation, you accelerate your growth on the path of mastery.

The more observant and conscious you become, the more you increase and expand your energy. When you begin to do this consistently, you will attract the right opportunities and people. And when you accept others, understanding that they are exactly where they need to be in their life work and process, you further energize your own growth.

The biggest challenge for entrepreneurs is the relentless demand to bring in more business and obtain new buyers for their products and services. In traditional business development models and marketing training programs, it is commonly believed that a start-up business will require that owners devote up to 75 percent of their time and energy on marketing. This would be true for those who have not honed their personal mastery skills. Old paradigm thinking will cause you to work longer hours and receive a lower return for your efforts. I've observed that many of the marketing programs currently being offered leave people exhausted and frustrated.

The speeding up of the world that we all struggle with also means that the dynamics of cause and effect—the maxim that every action creates an equal and opposite reaction—have also accelerated. The result: it's getting easier and easier to manifest what you want in life when you use the right tools, but the impacts of wrongful actions are also more evident.

Individuals who have achieved a high level of personal mastery display the following traits:

1. They are selective in their activities and relationships and know how to release those that distract from their goals and drain them of energy.
2. They are continually reinventing themselves in order to respond to changing market cycles and economic shifts.
3. They are masters at marketing and know how to utilize both dynamic and magnetic marketing strategies.
4. They understand how to be of service to others and are clear about the contributions they make to their clients.
5. They understand the importance of staying inspired and energized and have developed mastery in being fully engaged in life.

When you learn how to slow down, simplify your life, and create an environment that nourishes your spirit, your life will be more balanced, harmonious, and fulfilling. When you become more centered, focused, and balanced, you can make wise decisions. You'll then be able to discover the nature of your own particular genius, stop trying to conform to other people's models, and learn to be your authentic, individuated self.

WRIGHT

So what do you believe is the foundation of achieving higher levels of success and attaining personal mastery?

ROULAC

Through my work with thousands of clients, including highly compensated business leaders and executives, what I know for sure is this:

- When you identify your personal strengths—your unique genius—you can accomplish your goals with greater ease.
- When you understand the source of your personal power, connect with your passion, and identify your purpose, you will produce extraordinary results.
- The secret of successful individuals is to be fully engaged—mentally, emotionally, physically, and spiritually.
- The only limitation to achieving life success is the extent to which you are committed to your own personal growth and mastery.

Having spent most of my business career in the fast lane, I know that I am as susceptible as anyone to loss of perspective and the stress that follows. I've also come to know that I have the capacity to balance myself and to make wise choices, to create a state of being where I'm in control more than out of control. This enables me to concentrate on more important life commitments without the discomfort and distraction of physical, emotional and psychological distress.

In fact, from my own experiences, observations and interviews with truly successful people, I know it is possible to work, live and even thrive in this hectic world of ours without compromising our health and principles. More importantly, I believe that by developing our "shape-shifting/shamanic" potential—the ability to change and control our state of being—we tap into a deeper source of balance and wisdom that can profoundly impact how we see ourselves and the purposes we choose to follow.

Successful people appear to manifest what they want in life with very little effort. And because it seems effortless, we believe it's the result of long hours, advanced degrees, or a high level of mental intelligence. Ultimately, however, success, power, and the ability to manifest do not originate from such efforts or talents; they fall into the category of *otherworldly*, as they cannot truly be explained with any degree of accuracy or depth by the measures of a material world.

We live in a time when it has never been easier to initiate change or nurture creative ideas into existence. We have the power to alter our actions, our beliefs, and our lives *instantaneously* and for the better; we have merely forgotten that we possess these skills. They are part of our heritage, part of our DNA. We are the only impediment to our own mastery. We are the only limitation to living a fulfilling and rewarding life.

ABOUT THE AUTHOR

AS A VISIONARY, SPEAKER, AND AUTHOR, Ann Roulac acts as a catalyst for change, empowering people to transform their personal and professional lives. Roulac has provided strategic advice to entrepreneurs and executives throughout the world enabling them to develop highly profitable businesses. She served as a Principal and national director of Arthur Andersen and as a division president of Bank of America Mortgage and International Realty Corporation.

Ann's experience as an entrepreneur, background as a corporate executive, and teacher of personal mastery disciplines give her a unique ability to support people to achieve their highest potential. Her sense of adventure and quest for knowledge have led her to the jungles of Guatemala, the mountain ranges of Nepal and Peru, and the pyramids of Egypt.

Roulac is the author of *Power, Passion & Purpose*, and *How To Create the Life You Want*. She is a co-author of *Community Building: Renewing Spirit and Learning in Business.* These books have been published and distributed internationally and have sold in excess of 40,000 copies.

ANN ROULAC
Inspiring Visions and Strategies
709 Fifth Avenue
San Rafael, CA 94901
Ann@AnnRoulac.com
www.AnnRoulac.com

AN INTERVIEW WITH...

DR. KEN BLANCHARD

ATTITUDE IS EVERYTHING

DAVID WRIGHT (WRIGHT)

Few people have created a positive impact on the day-to-day management of people and companies more than Dr. Kenneth Blanchard. He is known around the world simply as Ken, a prominent, gregarious, sought-after author, speaker, and business consultant. Ken is universally characterized by friends, colleagues, and clients as one of the most insightful, powerful, and compassionate men in business today. Ken's impact as a writer is far-reaching. His phenomenal best-selling book, *The One Minute Manager*®, coauthored with Spencer Johnson, has sold more than thirteen million copies worldwide and has been translated into more than twenty-five languages. Ken is Chairman and "Chief Spiritual Officer" of the Ken Blanchard Companies. The organization's focus is to energize organizations around the world with customized training in bottom-line business strategies based on the simple, yet powerful principles inspired by Ken's best-selling books.

Dr. Blanchard, welcome to *Discover Your Inner Strength.*

DR. KEN BLANCHARD (BLANCHARD)

Well, it's nice to talk with you, David. It's good to be here.

DAVID WRIGHT (WRIGHT)

I must tell you that preparing for your interview took quite a bit more time than usual. The scope of your life's work and your business, the Ken Blanchard Companies, would make for a dozen fascinating interviews.

Before we dive into the specifics of some of your projects and strategies, will you give our readers a brief synopsis of your life—how you came to be the Ken Blanchard we all know and respect?

BLANCHARD

Well, I'll tell you, David, I think life is what you do when you are planning on doing something else. I think that was John Lennon's line. I never intended to do what I have been doing. In fact, all my professors in college told me that I couldn't write. I wanted to do college work, which I did, and they said, "You had better be an administrator." So I decided I was going to be a Dean of Students. I got provisionally accepted into my master's degree program and then provisionally accepted at Cornell because I never could take any of those standardized tests.

I took the college boards four times and finally got 502 in English. I don't have a test-taking mind. I ended up in a university in Athens, Ohio, in 1966 as an Administrative Assistant to the Dean of the Business School. When I got there he said, "Ken, I want you to teach a course. I want all my deans to teach." I had never thought about teaching because they said I couldn't write, and teachers had to publish. He put me in the manager's department.

I've taken enough bad courses in my day and I wasn't going to teach one. I really prepared and had a wonderful time with the students. I was chosen as one of the top ten teachers on the campus coming out of the chute!

I just had a marvelous time. A colleague by the name of Paul Hersey was chairman of the Management Department. He wasn't very friendly to me initially because the Dean had led me to his department, but I heard he was a great teacher. He taught Organizational Behavior and Leadership. So I said, "Can I sit in on your course next semester?"

"Nobody audits my courses," he said. "If you want to take it for credit, you're welcome."

I couldn't believe it. I had a doctoral degree and he wanted me to take his course for credit—so I signed up.

The registrar didn't know what to do with me because I already had a doctorate, but I wrote the papers and took the course, and it was great.

In June 1967, Hersey came into my office and said, "Ken, I've been teaching in this field for ten years. I think I'm better than anybody, but I can't write. I'm a nervous wreck, and I'd love to write a textbook with somebody. Would you write one with me?"

I said, "We ought to be a great team. You can't write and I'm not supposed to be able to, so let's do it!"

Thus began this great career of writing and teaching. We wrote a textbook called *Management of Organizational Behavior: Utilizing Human Resources.* It came out in its eighth edition October 3, 2000, and the ninth edition was published September 3, 2007. It has sold more than any other textbook in that area over the years. It's been over forty years since that book first came out.

I quit my administrative job, became a professor, and ended up working my way up the ranks. I got a sabbatical leave and went to California for one year twenty-five years ago. I ended up meeting Spencer Johnson at a cocktail party. He wrote children's books—a wonderful series called *Value Tales® for Kids.* He also wrote *The Value of Courage: The Story of Jackie Robinson* and *The Value of Believing In Yourself: The Story of Louis Pasteur.*

My wife, Margie, met him first and said, "You guys ought to write a children's book for managers because they won't read anything else." That was my introduction to Spencer. So, *The One Minute Manager* was really a kid's book for big people. That is a long way from saying that my career was well planned.

Wright

Ken, what and/or who were your early influences in the areas of business, leadership, and success? In other words, who shaped you in your early years?

BLANCHARD

My father had a great impact on me. He was retired as an admiral in the Navy and had a wonderful philosophy. I remember when I was elected as president of the seventh grade, and I came home all pumped up. My father said, "Son, it's great that you're the president of the seventh grade, but now that you have that leadership position, don't ever use it." He said, "Great leaders are followed because people respect them and like them, not because they have power." That was a wonderful lesson for me early on. He was just a great model for me. I got a lot from him.

Then I had this wonderful opportunity in the mid-1980s to write a book with Norman Vincent Peale. He wrote *The Power of Positive Thinking*. I met him when he was eighty-six years old; we were asked to write a book on ethics together, *The Power of Ethical Management: Integrity Pays, You Don't Have to Cheat to Win*. It didn't matter what we were writing together; I learned so much from him. He just built from the positive things I learned from my mother.

My mother said that when I was born I laughed before I cried, I danced before I walked, and I smiled before I frowned. So that, as well as Norman Vincent Peale, really impacted me as I focused on what I could do to train leaders. How do you make them positive? How do you make them realize that it's not about them, it's about who they are serving? It's not about their position—it's about what they can do to help other people win.

So, I'd say my mother and father, then Norman Vincent Peale. All had a tremendous impact on me.

WRIGHT

I can imagine. I read a summary of your undergraduate and graduate degrees. I assumed you studied Business Administration, marketing management, and related courses. Instead, at Cornell you studied Government and Philosophy. You received your master's from Colgate in Sociology and Counseling and your PhD from Cornell in Educational Administration and Leadership. Why did you choose this course of study? How has it affected your writing and consulting?

BLANCHARD

Well, again, it wasn't really well planned out. I originally went to Colgate to get a master's degree in Education because I was going to be a Dean of Students over men. I had been a Government major, and I was a Government major because it was the best department at Cornell in the Liberal Arts School. It was exciting. We would study what the people were doing at the league of governments. And then, the Philosophy Department was great. I just loved the philosophical arguments. I wasn't a great student in terms of getting grades, but I'm a total learner. I would sit there and listen, and I would really soak it in.

When I went over to Colgate and got into the education courses, they were awful. They were boring. The second week, I was sitting at the bar at the Colgate Inn saying, "I can't believe I've been here two years for this." This is just the way the Lord works: Sitting next to me in the bar was a young sociology professor who had just gotten his PhD at Illinois. He was staying at the Inn. I was moaning and groaning about what I was doing, and he said, "Why don't you come and major with me in sociology? It's really exciting."

"I can do that?" I asked.

He said, "Yes."

I knew they would probably let me do whatever I wanted the first week. Suddenly, I switched out of Education and went with Warren Ramshaw. He had a tremendous impact on me. He retired some years ago as the leading professor at Colgate in the Arts and Sciences, and got me interested in leadership and organizations. That's why I got a master's in Sociology.

The reason I went into educational administration and leadership? It was a doctoral program I could get into because I knew the guy heading up the program. He said, "The greatest thing about Cornell is that you will be in the School of Education. It's not very big, so you don't have to take many education courses, and you can take stuff all over the place."

There was a marvelous man by the name of Don McCarty who eventually became the Dean of the School of Education, Wisconsin. He had an impact on my life; but I was always just searching around.

My mission statement is: to be a loving teacher and example of simple truths that help myself and others to awaken the presence of God in our lives. The reason I mention "God" is that I believe the biggest addiction in the world is the human ego; but I'm really into simple truth. I used to tell people I was trying to get the B.S. out of the behavioral sciences.

WRIGHT

I can't help but think, when you mentioned your father, that he just bottom-lined it for you about leadership.

BLANCHARD

Yes.

WRIGHT

A man named Paul Myers, in Texas, years and years ago when I went to a conference down there, said, "David, if you think you're a leader and you look around, and no one is following you, you're just out for a walk."

BLANCHARD

Well, you'd get a kick out of this—I'm just reaching over to pick up a picture of Paul Myers on my desk. He's a good friend, and he's a part of our Center for FaithWalk Leadership where we're trying to challenge and equip people to lead like Jesus. It's non-profit. I tell people I'm not an evangelist because we've got enough trouble with the Christians we have. We don't need any more new ones. But, this is a picture of Paul on top of a mountain. Then there's another picture below that of him under the sea with stingrays. It says, "Attitude is everything. Whether you're on the top of the mountain or the bottom of the sea, true happiness is achieved by accepting God's promises, and by having a biblically positive frame of mind. Your attitude is everything." Isn't that something?

WRIGHT

He's a fine, fine man. He helped me tremendously. In keeping with the theme of our book, *Discover Your Inner Strength,* I wanted to get a sense from you about your own success journey. Many people know you best from *The One Minute Manager* books you coauthored with Spencer Johnson. Would you consider these books as a high water mark for you or have you defined success for yourself in different terms?

BLANCHARD

Well, you know, *The One Minute Manager* was an absurdly successful book so quickly that I found I couldn't take credit for it. That was when I really got on my own spiritual journey and started to try to find out what the real meaning of life and success was.

That's been a wonderful journey for me because I think, David, the problem with most people is they think their self-worth is a function of their performance plus the opinion of others. The minute you think that is what your self-worth is, every day your self-worth is up for grabs because your performance is going to fluctuate on a day-to-day basis. People are fickle. Their opinions are going to go up and down. You need to ground your self-worth in the unconditional love that God has ready for us, and that really grew out of the unbelievable success of *The One Minute Manager.*

When I started to realize where all that came from, that's how I got involved in this ministry that I mentioned. Paul Myers is a part of it. As I started to read the Bible, I realized that everything I've ever written about, or taught, Jesus did. You know, He did it with the twelve incompetent guys He "hired." The only guy with much education was Judas, and he was His only turnover problem.

WRIGHT

Right.

BLANCHARD

This is a really interesting thing. What I see in people is not only do they think their self-worth is a function of their performance plus the opinion of others, but they measure their success on the amount of accumulation of wealth, on recognition, power, and status. I think those are nice success items. There's nothing wrong with those, as long as you don't define your life by that.

What I think you need to focus on rather than success is what Bob Buford, in his book *Halftime,* calls "significance"—moving from success to significance. I think the opposite of accumulation of wealth is generosity.

I wrote a book called *The Generosity Factor* with Truett Cathy, who is the founder of Chick-fil-A. He is one of the most generous men I've ever met in my life. I thought we needed to have a model of generosity. It's not only your *treasure,* but it's your *time* and *talent.* Truett and I added *touch* as a fourth one.

The opposite of recognition is service. I think you become an adult when you realize you're here to serve rather than to be served.

Finally, the opposite of power and status is loving relationships. Take Mother Teresa as an example—she couldn't have cared less about recognition, power, and status because she was focused on generosity, service, and loving relationships; but she got all of that earthly stuff. If you focus on the earthly, such as money, recognition, and power, you're never going to get to significance. But if you focus on significance, you'll be amazed at how much success can come your way.

WRIGHT

I spoke with Truett Cathy recently and was impressed by what a down-to-earth, good man he seems to be. When you start talking about him closing his restaurants on Sunday, all of my friends—when they found out I had talked to him—said, "Boy, he must be a great Christian man, but he's rich." I told them, "Well, to put his faith into perspective, by closing on Sunday it costs him $500 million a year."

He lives his faith, doesn't he?

BLANCHARD

Absolutely, but he still outsells everybody else.

WRIGHT

That's right.

BLANCHARD

According to their January 25, 2007, press release, Chick-fil-A was the nation's second-largest quick-service chicken restaurant chain in sales at that time. Its business performance marks the thirty-ninth consecutive year the chain has enjoyed a system-wide sales gain—a streak the company has sustained since opening its first chain restaurant in 1967.

WRIGHT

The simplest market scheme, I told him, tripped me up. I walked by his first Chick-fil-A I had ever seen, and some girl came out with chicken stuck on toothpicks and handed me one; I just grabbed it and ate it; it's history from there on.

BLANCHARD

Yes, I think so. It's really special. It is so important that people understand generosity, service, and loving relationships because too many people are running around like a bunch of peacocks. You even see pastors who measure their success by how many are in their congregation; authors by how many books they have sold; businesspeople by what their profit margin is—how good sales are. The reality is, that's all well and good, but I think what you need to focus on is the other. I think if business did that more and we got Wall Street off our backs with all the short-term evaluation, we'd be a lot better off.

WRIGHT

Absolutely. There seems to be a clear theme that winds through many of your books that has to do with success in business and organizations—how people are treated by management and how they feel about their value to a company. Is this an accurate observation? If so, can you elaborate on it?

BLANCHARD

Yes, it's a very accurate observation. See, I think the profit is the applause you get for taking care of your customers and creating a motivating environment for your people. Very often people think that business is only about the bottom line. But no, that happens to be the result of creating raving fan customers, which I've described with Sheldon Bowles in our book, *Raving Fans*. Customers want to brag about you, if you create an environment where people can be gung-ho and committed. You've got to take care of your customers and your people, and then your cash register is going to go ka-ching, and you can make some big bucks.

WRIGHT

I noticed that your professional title with the Ken Blanchard Companies is somewhat unique—"Chairman and Chief Spiritual Officer." What does your title mean to you personally and to your company? How does it affect the books you choose to write?

BLANCHARD

I remember having lunch with Max DuPree one time. The legendary Chairman of Herman Miller, Max wrote a wonderful book called *Leadership Is an Art*.

"What's your job?" I asked him.

He said, "I basically work in the vision area."

"Well, what do you do?" I asked.

"I'm like a third-grade teacher," he replied. "I say our vision and values over, and over, and over again until people get it right, right, right."

I decided from that, I was going to become the Chief Spiritual Officer, which means I would be working in the vision, values, and energy part of our business. I ended up leaving a morning message every day for everybody in our company. We have twenty-eight international offices around the world.

I leave a voice mail every morning, and I do three things on that as Chief Spiritual Officer: One, people tell me who we need to pray for. Two, people tell me who we need to praise—our unsung heroes and people like that. And then three, I leave an inspirational morning message. I really am the cheerleader—the Energizer Bunny—in our company. I'm the reminder of why we're here and what we're trying to do.

We think that our business in the Ken Blanchard Companies is to help people lead at a higher level, and to help individuals and organizations. Our mission statement is to unleash the power and potential of people and organizations for the common good. So if we are going to do that, we've really got to believe in that.

I'm working on getting more Chief Spiritual Officers around the country. I think it's a great title and we should get more of them.

WRIGHT

So those people for whom you pray, where do you get the names?

BLANCHARD

The people in the company tell me who needs help, whether it's a spouse who is sick or kids who are sick or if they are worried about something. We've got over five years of data about the power of prayer, which is pretty important.

One morning, my inspirational message was about my wife and five members of our company who walked sixty miles one weekend—twenty miles a day for three days—to raise money for breast cancer research.

It was amazing. I went down and waved them all in as they came. They had a ceremony; they had raised $7.6 million. There were over three thousand people walking. A lot of the walkers were dressed in pink—they were cancer victors—people who had overcome it. There were even men walking with pictures of their wives who had died from breast cancer. I thought it was incredible.

There wasn't one mention about it in the major San Diego papers. I said, "Isn't that just something." We have to be an island of positive influence because all you see in the paper today is about celebrities and their bad behavior. Here you have all these thousands of people out there walking and trying to make a difference, and nobody thinks it's news.

So every morning I pump people up about what life's about, about what's going on. That's what my Chief Spiritual Officer job is about.

Wright

I had the pleasure of reading one of your releases, *The Leadership Pill.*

Blanchard

Yes.

Wright

I must admit that my first thought was how short the book was. I wondered if I was going to get my money's worth, which by the way, I most certainly did. Many of your books are brief and based on a fictitious story. Most business books in the market today are hundreds of pages in length and are read almost like a textbook.

Will you talk a little bit about why you write these short books, and about the premise of *The Leadership Pill?*

Blanchard

I really developed my relationship with Spencer Johnson when we wrote *The One Minute Manager*. As you know, he wrote, *Who Moved My Cheese*, which was a phenomenal success. He wrote children's books and is quite a storyteller.

Jesus taught by parables, which were short stories.

My favorite books are *Jonathan Livingston Seagull* and *The Little Prince.* Og Mandino, author of seventeen books, was the greatest of them all.

I started writing parables because people can get into the story and learn the contents of the story, and they don't bring their judgmental hats into reading. You write a regular book and they'll say, "Well, where did you get the research?" They get into that judgmental side. Our books get them emotionally involved and they learn.

The Leadership Pill is a fun story about a pharmaceutical company that thinks they have discovered the secret to leadership, and they can put the ingredients in a pill. When they announce it, the country goes crazy because everybody knows we need more effective leaders. When they release it, it outsells Viagra.

The founders of the company start selling off stock and they call them Pillionaires. But along comes this guy who calls himself "the effective manager," and he challenges them to a no-pill challenge. If they identify two non-performing groups, he'll take on one and let somebody on the pill take another one, and he guarantees he will outperform that person by the end of the year. They agree, but of course they give him a drug test every week to make sure he's not sneaking pills on the side.

I wrote the book with Marc Muchnick, who is a young guy in his early thirties. We did a major study of what this interesting "Y" generation—the young people of today—want from leaders, and this is a secret blend that this effective manager uses. When you think about it, David, it is really powerful in terms of what people want from a leader.

Number one, they want integrity. A lot of people have talked about that in the past, but these young people will walk if they see people say one thing and do another. A lot of us walk to the bathroom and out into the halls to talk about it. But these people will quit. They don't want somebody to say something and not do it.

The second thing they want is a partnership relationship. They hate superior/subordinate. I mean, what awful terms those are. You know, the "head" of the department and the hired "hands"—you don't even give them a head. "What do I do? I'm in supervision. I see things a lot clearer than these stupid idiots." They want to be treated as partners; if they can get a financial partnership, great. If they can't, they really want a minimum of a psychological partnership where they can bring their brains to work and make decisions.

Then finally, they want affirmation. They not only want to be caught doing things right, but they want to be affirmed for who they are. They want to be known as individual people, not as numbers.

So those are the three ingredients that this effective manager uses. They are wonderful values when you think about them.

Rank-order values for any organization is number one, integrity. In our company we call it ethics. It is our number one value. The number two value is partnership. In our company we call it relationships. Number three is affirmation—being affirmed as a human being. I think that ties into relationships, too. They are wonderful values that can drive behavior in a great way.

Wright

I believe most people in today's business culture would agree that success in business has everything to do with successful leadership. In *The Leadership Pill*, you present a simple but profound premise; that leadership is not something you do to people; it's something you do *with* them. At face value, that seems incredibly obvious. But you must have found in your research and observations that leaders in today's culture do not get this. Would you speak to that issue?

Blanchard

Yes. I think what often happens in this is the human ego. There are too many leaders out there who are self-serving. They're not leaders who have service in mind. They think the sheep are there for the benefit of the shepherd. All the power, money, fame, and recognition move up the hierarchy. They forget that the real action in business is not up the hierarchy—it's in the one-to-one, moment-to-moment interactions that your frontline people have with your customers. It's how the phone is answered. It's how problems are dealt with and those kinds of things. If you don't think that you're doing leadership *with* them—rather, you're doing it *to* them—after a while they won't take care of your customers.

I was at a store once (not Nordstrom's, where I normally would go) and I thought of something I had to share with my wife, Margie. I asked the guy behind the counter in Men's Wear, "May I use your phone?"

He said, "No!"

"You're kidding me," I said. "I can always use the phone at Nordstrom's."

"Look, buddy," he said, "they won't let *me* use the phone here. Why should I let you use the phone?"

That is an example of leadership that's done *to* employees, not *with* them. People want a partnership. People want to be involved in a way that really makes a difference.

WRIGHT

Dr. Blanchard, the time has flown by and there are so many more questions I'd like to ask you. In closing, would you mind sharing with our readers some thoughts on success? If you were mentoring a small group of men and women, and one of their central goals was to become successful, what kind of advice would you give them?

BLANCHARD

Well, I would first of all say, "What are you focused on?" If you are focused on success as being, as I said earlier, accumulation of money, recognition, power, or status, I think you've got the wrong target. What you need to really be focused on is how you can be generous in the use of your time and your talent and your treasure and touch. How can you serve people rather than be served? How can you develop caring, loving relationships with people? My sense is if you will focus on those things, success in the traditional sense will come to you. But if you go out and say, "Man, I'm going to make a fortune, and I'm going to do this," and have that kind of attitude, you might get some of those numbers. I think you become an adult, however, when you realize you are here to give rather than to get. You're here to serve, not to be served. I would just say to people, "Life is such a very special occasion. Don't miss it by aiming at a target that bypasses other people, because we're really here to serve each other."

WRIGHT

Well, what an enlightening conversation, Dr. Blanchard. I really want you to know how much I appreciate all the time you've taken with me for this interview. I know that our readers will learn from this, and I really appreciate your being with us today.

Blanchard

Well, thank you so much, David. I really enjoyed my time with you. You've asked some great questions that made me think, and I hope my answers are helpful to other people because as I say, life is a special occasion.

Wright

Today we have been talking with Dr. Ken Blanchard. He is coauthor of the phenomenal best-selling book, *The One Minute Manager*. The fact that he's the Chief Spiritual Officer of his company should make us all think about how we are leading our companies and leading our families and leading anything, whether it is in church or civic organizations. I know I will.

Thank you so much, Dr. Blanchard, for being with us today.

Blanchard

Good to be with you, David.

ABOUT THE AUTHOR

FEW PEOPLE HAVE CREATED MORE of a positive impact on the day-to-day management of people and companies than Dr. Kenneth Blanchard, who is known around the world simply as "Ken."

When Ken speaks, he speaks from the heart with warmth and humor. His unique gift is to speak to an audience and communicate with each individual as if they were alone and talking one-on-one. He is a polished storyteller with a knack for making the seemingly complex easy to understand.

Ken has been a guest on a number of national television programs, including *Good Morning America* and *The Today Show*. He has been featured in *Time, People, U.S. News & World Report*, and a host of other popular publications.

He earned his bachelor's degree in Government and Philosophy from Cornell University, his master's degree in Sociology and Counseling from Colgate University, and his PhD in Educational Administration and Leadership from Cornell University.

DR. KEN BLANCHARD

The Ken Blanchard Companies
125 State Place
Escondido, California 92029
800.728.6000
Fax: 760.489.8407
www.kenblanchard.com

AN INTERVIEW WITH...

KIMBERLY ALYN

LEADERSHIP: YOUR VITAL INNER STRENGTH

DAVID WRIGHT (WRIGHT)

Today we're talking with Kimberly Alyn. Kim is a best-selling author and award-winning professional speaker. She speaks to groups and organizations all over the world on self-improvement issues such as leadership, conflict resolution, and team-building. Kim has written a variety of books on these topics and it is a pleasure to interview her today.

Kimberly Alyn, welcome to *Discover Your Inner Strength.*

KIMBERLY ALYN (ALYN)

Thank you, David.

WRIGHT

Kim, your background and education appears to focus on leadership. What has sparked your interest in this area?

ALYN

There are a number of reasons I have been drawn to the topic of leadership. First of all, I think it is one of the most prominent inner strengths that can be developed and yet one of the most neglected. Secondly, I didn't have the opportunity to grow up with many real examples of role model leadership, so I was curious as to what that looked like and what leadership really meant. Thirdly, I have made some bad decisions in my own life and reaped the consequences of those decisions, which made me realize the importance of stepping up to real leadership. Lastly, over the years I have noticed a decline in the quality of leaders who are represented in public and private organizations, and it has inspired me to focus on this area.

As I started conducting training seminars in different organizations, I noticed a plethora of "command and control" style of leaders. These people assumed that if they barked orders at others and held a position of authority, things would get done. But they couldn't understand why morale was low and turnover was high. As I interviewed managers and leaders, there appeared to be a prevalent attitude of "it's my way or the highway," and "if I want your opinion, I will give it to you."

One of the sectors I work closely with is the fire service. I noticed that this type of intimidating management style was pervasive in fire departments throughout the United States, as it is with a lot of organizations. One of the justifications I heard for this type of leadership was, "We are a paramilitary organization." Many of the managers in the fire service assumed there was no other way to get results other than using your title and position to force people to do what you wanted (a combination of positional and coercive power). After conducting countless leadership training classes in the fire service, it was obvious that there was a hunger and a need for better leadership. There are some fantastic leaders in the fire service who use their positive influence to get people to *want* to follow and my goal is to get more people to step up to that style of leadership.

WRIGHT

That makes sense. Well, that brings me to my next question on leadership. Do you think great leaders are born or made?

ALYN

Both. Leadership is all about influence and the ability to get people to work together toward common goals. I think there are people who are born with a natural tendency to influence others. However, if these people do not direct their abilities to influence in a positive direction, they will end up like Hitler. He was considered a leader. So was Saddam Hussein. But these types of leaders used coercive power to demand compliance from their followers instead of inspiring people with a positive vision and core values that call people to a higher moral ground and ethical behavior. I try to warn leaders that with the Hitler type of leadership, followers will undermine your leadership when you are not present, try to overthrow your leadership, or eventually try to kill you!

In my opinion, great leaders who leave a lasting legacy of leadership are more made than born. If leadership is "an ability" to influence people to achieve certain goals, then abilities can be developed. Researchers and leadership experts have differing ideas and opinions about what it really means to be a leader or what defines leadership. When I survey people about what leadership is and what describes great leaders, I often get differing answers, but there seems to be some pretty common themes. The main common themes are: people want leaders to be honest, to take initiative, to be competent, to inspire others, to get things done, to empower others, to show integrity, to serve others, and to be team players. These are all actions and behaviors that can be developed.

WRIGHT

So do most people embrace these types of leadership concepts as a way to develop their inner strengths or do they resist it?

ALYN

My experience has been very positive in this area. Most of the people I speak to and work with in the public and private sectors embrace these concepts. There are always a handful of people who want to cling to the pushy leadership style, and those people tend to resist my message. But for those who welcome it, real changes take place.

I met a manager at a conference where I was giving a keynote presentation on leadership—let's call him "Matt." Matt approached me after the presentation and admitted that he had been using a command and control style of leadership. He said that's what he grew up with and that's what his military father grew up with. He confided in me that he had convinced himself that this was the only way to get respect from his followers, otherwise, they might see him as weak and walk all over him.

Matt's belief system is not uncommon among some people in leadership positions. They think they have to *demand* respect from people when in fact, if they would exhibit the behaviors of positive leadership, they would *command* respect. When you garner this type of respect from followers, the respect is apparent in your presence and in your absence. As I discussed these very issues with Matt, he said he realized that he was definitely born with natural leadership ability and had always gravitated toward leadership positions. Matt had the natural ability to influence others, but he was the first to admit that he was influencing people in a manner that caused resentment when he left the room, and his actions hurt morale in the organization.

As Matt and I continued to discuss these leadership issues, he made a commitment to go back to his organization and start changing his behavior. Matt was going to attempt to choose different actions that would inspire people instead of intimidate them. He was going to go back and work on getting people to *want* to follow his lead.

I meet a lot of people at conferences and training seminars, and after some time goes by, I often forget about some of the conversations I've had. I had long put Matt out of my mind when an e-mail popped into my box seven months later. It was from Matt. He started out by refreshing my memory with where he had met me and what we had discussed. Our conversation came flooding back and I was anxious to see why Matt was contacting me. As it turned out, he wanted to let me know the incredible transformation that had taken place. He returned to his organization and began to focus on the needs of his followers (serving others), admitting his mistakes and being honest about things (showing integrity), following through on his commitments (taking initiative), and allowing the employees more input and decision-making ability (empowerment). Matt witnessed an incredible change. His followers started to trust his motives. They saw his effort and followed his lead by putting in more effort themselves. They became more committed to the team. Morale went up, grumbling went down, and he was being rated as a much better leader and manager.

Matt discovered something that leaders all over the United States are discovering: great leaders can be made by the actions they choose. So while some people are born with some natural leadership ability, *great* leaders are more made than born.

Wright

You mentioned "empowerment" as one of the common themes followers want in their leaders. Why do you think that is so important, and can you provide some examples of what that really looks like?

Alyn

Absolutely. Employees want to be empowered by leaders in a few key areas. One is the ability to provide input. Employees find it very difficult to carry out missions, visions, and strategic plans that they didn't help create. By giving followers the opportunity to give input into these major areas, what you create is an environment where people take ownership of those missions, visions, and strategic plans. Having things "dictated" to employees cultivates a resentful compliance when the leader is present, and a pervasive rebellion when the leader is absent.

Another area in which employees want to be empowered is decision-making. They want to be trusted to use their best judgment once they have been thoroughly trained in their jobs. When you train your employees to think and make decisions at the customer level, you create very satisfied customers! It is very frustrating for employees and customers to encounter a problem that cannot be solved without having to call for a manager. When employees are empowered to solve problems and make decisions, everyone wins.

The CEO of the Ritz Carlton understands this important aspect of leadership. He tours all his properties personally and asks the employees for input and suggestions on how to improve operations and customer service. He has empowered employees to make any decision up to $1,500 to solve a customer's problem. The employees feel empowered and guests feel valued. This CEO understands the importance of getting customers to come back. He communicates this importance to his employees by letting them know that every guest at the hotel potentially represents over $100,000 of lifetime business! You will never hear an employee at the Ritz Carlton say "I am sorry, there is just nothing I can do."

Leaders need to eradicate some of these common sayings from the vocabulary of their employees: "I will have to get a manager to approve that." "I am not authorized to do anything else." "That's just our policy." "There is nothing I can do to help you." "I am not the person to talk to about that." "That's not my job." All of these phrases demonstrate a lack of empowerment and poor leadership within the organization. Strong leadership is reflected when employees own the problems and create the solutions. They don't push it off to someone else or another department.

I work with a lot of organizations across the United States on leadership development. The lack of employee empowerment is a common issue. Too many leaders worry about empowering employees because they feel it will dilute their own power. The exact opposite holds true. When you empower your followers to think, make decisions, and solve problems, you increase your own power and productivity. It frees you up as a leader to work on big picture issues and ensure the organization is moving toward its mission, vision, and goals. Leaders who refuse to empower employees spend their time putting out fires and solving simple problems that force them to operate on a small picture level while the big picture issues are neglected.

When employees are empowered, they begin to discover their own inner strengths for creative problem-solving. Additionally, they begin to perceive the trust their leaders have in them.

WRIGHT

I think everyone appreciates it when employees can solve problems. I can see the importance of empowering others as a leader. Earlier you listed "taking initiative" as one of the important behaviors of a leader. Will you expand on that a little bit more?

ALYN

One of the traits of all great leaders throughout history is the ability to get things done. Christopher Hegarty once said, "Vision without action is nothing more than hallucination." It doesn't do anybody any good for leaders to create great vision if they don't take the initiative to make sure that vision becomes a reality. Followers need leaders who will get off their butt and make things happen. Additionally, followers who want to be considered leaders need to take initiative as well. Even leaders need to operate in the role of a follower at times and it is impossible to become a great a leader without being a great follower. Taking initiative is a critical element to both.

So what does taking initiative really look like? It is best depicted with a story I read several years ago: A father is working in the field one day when one of his sons asks, "Father, why is it that you give my brother more reward and more responsibility when I am the oldest?"

The father answered, "That is a great question son, and I will be happy to answer that for you. But first, I need you to do something for me. I need you to run over to the Johnson's farm and see if they have any geese for sale. We need to add to our stock."

So the son ran over to the Johnson's farm and returned quickly. "Yes Father, they have some geese they would be willing to sell."

"Excellent, son. Now please find out how many they would be willing to sell to us."

The son ran off again to the Johnson's farm and returned with the answer. "Father, they have ten geese they would be willing to sell to us."

"Wonderful!" the father beamed. "Now go and find out if they could deliver those geese tomorrow by 3:00 PM if we were to purchase them today."

Once again, the son jetted off to the Johnson farm. He returned out of breath saying, "They can deliver the geese tomorrow by 3:00 PM without a problem."

"Thank you for gathering that information son. Now I want you to stand here and watch and listen." The father called his younger son in a nearby field.

As the younger son approached the father said, "Son, I need you to run over to the Smith's farm and see if they have any geese for sale. We need to add to our stock."

The son dashed over to the Smith's farm and returned with his information: "Father, the Smiths have fifteen geese for sale. They want $10 a piece for them but if we buy all fifteen, they will reduce the price to $8 each. I told them to deliver all fifteen geese by tomorrow at noon unless they hear from us otherwise."

The father turned to the older son and said, "That is why your younger brother has more responsibility and more reward."

Taking initiative is not doing what you are asked or doing what is expected of you. It's doing what you are *not* asked to do and anticipating what would be expected of you. Leaders take the initiative to anticipate the needs of their followers and meet those needs. They anticipate what needs to be done and they get it done. Great followers anticipate the needs of their leaders and take the initiative to make things happen.

WRIGHT

That's a great story to demonstrate initiative. I want to go back to another characteristic of a good leader that you brought up. You mentioned "team player." I know that effective team-building is a challenge for every organization. What are some ways leaders can build better teams?

ALYN

You're right—teambuilding is a challenge for many organizations. There are a number of things leaders can do to create more effective teams. Let me share seven great ways to build better teams:

1. **Let team members have input into creating the vision and goals for the team** (part of the empowerment we talked about earlier). Leaders can also inventory the skills, talents, and interests of the team members to best utilize their abilities. Even some of the best employees tend to do a mediocre job at tasks they have no interest in or any of the skills necessary to perform the task. On the other hand, employees tend to excel at things they love and are skilled in doing. Too many leaders neglect this important aspect of team-building. They just assign tasks to employees and expect the employees to do a stellar job without providing an environment of inspiration or adequate training to develop skills. This is the process where leaders discover the inner strengths of their followers—it's vital!
2. **Provide constructive evaluation and positive feedback for the team members.** Employees need to know when they are off track, and they need to know when they are excelling at goals and expectations. When

leaders become too busy to provide this important element, morale suffers. Additionally, when leaders spend more time on correcting employees than giving positive feedback, employees become discouraged.

3. **Provide an environment where employees can be self-motivated.** I don't believe you can motivate people. Motivation is intrinsic and people have to motivate themselves. But what leaders can do is create an environment where employees can be self-motivated. Leaders do this by finding out what drives employees and gives them a sense of passion and purpose. Once you have that information, you can provide the tools, resources, and working environment where people can put their self-motivation to use.
4. **Facilitate an environment of open communication.** One of the major problems I see in organizations is the hoarding of information. There is always information that needs to free-flow up, down, and across the chain of command. What inevitably happens is someone receives information and decides to hoard it so he or she can feel more powerful. Now that person is "in the know" while others are in the dark. Hoarding information gives people a sense of one-upmanship against those they work with. This type of behavior hurts teams and creates animosity. Leaders need to set the example by providing open communication and encouraging others to do the same.
5. **Give Credit Away Freely to the Team.** Great leaders build better teams when they allow the team to share credit for successes. The leader doesn't feel the need to be in the limelight and get all of the attention. Instead, the glory is shared freely with the team where all members of the team can feel valued. When things go wrong, the leader steps up and takes responsibility for team failures. This takes guts and real leadership, and few people are willing to rise to this standard.
6. **Serve the Members of the Team.** People tend to look out for number one instead of looking out for what's in the best interest of the team as a whole. To build better teams, leaders need to start by serving the needs of the team. Great leaders understand that by helping the individuals of the team meet their needs and goals, the team members in turn want to contribute more to the team and exhibit a higher level of commitment.

7. **Let the Team Have Fun!** This is one of the most neglected aspects of team-building. Managers and leaders get so focused on the end result that they forget the importance of having fun. It's a physiological fact that stress and laughter cannot occupy the same space at the same time. Employees cannot be stressed while laughing. Some would also argue that they can't get things done while they are laughing or having fun. That is simply not accurate. Some managers seem to be on a mission to hunt down any resemblance of fun and beat the living hell out of it. When employees hate their jobs, they are less productive and they are less committed to the team. By allowing employees to have fun, you build stronger teams with a sense of camaraderie.

Well, that was a mouthful. Can you tell I feel strongly about the importance of building teams?

WRIGHT

Yes, I can see that! What advice would you have for a new leader or a leader coming into a new organization or team as far as building trust with employees?

ALYN

People who are newly promoted into a supervisor's position often feel the need to prove themselves or let people know they are the new "boss" with the new power. Margaret Thatcher once said, "Being in power is a lot like being a lady—if you have to tell people you are, then you aren't." When you have to go around telling people you are the one in charge, you are probably not doing a very good job of building trust and influencing people to want to follow your lead.

New leaders, or leaders in new positions, need to take the time to establish trust with employees. The best way to start this process is to meet with employees, interview them, and ask them what their goals, expectations, and needs are. Ask them what they believe would make the organization better and what would make their job more rewarding.

One of the best things you can do as a leader is learn to listen—I mean, really listen. Let followers share their concerns, their ideas, and their goals. Listen without interrupting or interjecting or making it about you. Ask for clarification.

Ask them to share more. Listen intently without judging, getting defensive, or jumping to conclusions. Listen without finishing their thoughts or sentences. Show an interest in what is being said by smiling and nodding and asking for more. Active listening takes practice and great leaders have learned the absolute importance of this vital skill. You would be amazed at the amount of trust you can build with followers just by truly listening to where they are coming from and where they want to go.

Another way for new leaders to build trust is to show a high level of dependability. Do what you said you will do when you say you will do it and in the manner you say it will be done. If followers can't depend on you to follow through on what you say you will do, a breech in trust occurs.

If leaders want to establish more trust with followers, they also need to tell them the truth. Don't lie to your employees and don't keep bad news from them. There's a great saying that "trust is a lot like fine China—once broken, it can be repaired, but it's never quite the same." The fastest way to erode trust with employees is to deceive them or keep pertinent information from them. Leaders need to openly communicate what is happening in the organization and what their thought processes are. Transparency in leadership is a huge trust-builder. This area takes us back to an earlier point of the importance of communication and making sure information is free-flowing in the organization.

Another huge trust-builder for employees is seeing the vulnerability and authenticity of their leaders. Followers have a difficult time trusting leaders who act like they are perfect and never make mistakes. As a leader, a surefire way to build trust is to admit your mistakes. Learn how to say these important phrases if you want to build trust: "I screwed up." "I am sorry." "Please forgive me." "What can I do to make this right?" "I have a lot to learn too." Projecting an image of infallibility does not build trust, but humility does.

Wright

Those are some great tips for building trust.

Let me ask you about another hot topic in leadership discussions—change. How important do you think it is to be open to change as a leader?

ALYN

I don't think it's enough to be open to change anymore. I think it's imperative to initiate the positive changes that are needed in every organization. Constantly looking for ways to improve is a sign of good leadership. Just to make myself clear, I am not talking about change for the sake of change. Not all change is positive. Some managers and leaders think they need to create change just to show they are "change agents." If change doesn't result in improvement, it was probably an unnecessary change. I am talking about productive change that results in improvement.

Unfortunately, a lot of employees and managers cling to the status quo. It's like a security blanket for people and it gets them stuck in a rut. People tend to convince themselves that if something didn't work before, it won't work now. I hear a lot of the same things: "We tried that before and it didn't work." "We don't have the budget for that." "No one around here would get behind that idea." "That's just the way we've always done it around here."

There are also employees who have stuck out their neck for change and gotten burned in the process. They tend to recoil and not want to try again. Leaders have a real challenge in overcoming this obstacle when it comes to change.

At one point in my childhood we had a Doberman pinscher. He was a huge dog with a lot of rebellion pent up inside. He had a bad habit of leaving our property and stalking the neighborhood poodles to use as chew toys. So we decided to put up a radio fence around the property to change his behavior. These radio fences come with a collar for the dog and are designed to "train" the dog to stay on the property. When the dog goes near the property line he receives a deterring shock. After a few of these shocks, the dog decides to stay clear of the property line. After a good amount of training, you can remove the collar from the dog and it won't try to test the boundaries of the property line again.

People are the same way. People tend to avoid repeating any potentially unpleasant experiences. So if employees get up the nerve to make suggestions for change or improvement and they get shot down, they clam up. If they put themselves out there and get burned, they avoid putting themselves out there again.

Mark Twain once said, "We should be careful to get out of an experience only the wisdom that is in it and stop there; lest we be like the cat that sits down on a hot stove lid. She will never sit on a hot stove lid again and that is well; but she will never sit down on a cold one anymore either." Leaders need to set the role model example of not becoming victim to this "hot stove effect." Then they need to slowly coax employees to test the stove top—it may be cold this time and easy to sit on!

Change takes risk and it requires leaders who are willing to take that risk while keeping the best interest of their followers in mind. Sometimes great leadership is taking your followers where they *need* to go and not necessarily where they *want* to go.

WRIGHT

I can certainly see the importance of change. We are a rapidly changing society! What role do you think technology will play in the future generations of leaders?

ALYN

Technology is advancing so fast, it will play a huge role in the future generations. It is estimated that more new, unique information will be generated worldwide this year alone than in the previous five thousand years combined. In a book titled *The Jobs Revolution: Changing How America Works*, the authors point out that as recently as 1991, less than 50 percent of all jobs in the United States required skilled workers. By the year 2015, it is estimated that 76 percent of jobs will require highly skilled employees who are comfortable with high technology. Former Secretary of Education Richard Riley asserted that the top ten jobs in demand in 2010 did not even exist in 2004. Future leaders will need to be skilled and knowledgeable about technology and how to use that technology to solve problems.

Additionally, our older generation of leaders will need to learn how to communicate with our incoming generation. I call the up and coming generation the "E" generation. The "E" stands for electronic and entitlement. This generation is born with iPods in their ears, cell phones in their hands, and computers on their laps. They also feel "entitled" to all of the luxuries and technological advancements that society has to offer. This generation communicates primarily through technology, whether it's text messaging, cell phones, instant messaging, or MySpace.

As a society, we are accepting this massive shift toward technology more and more each year. Willard R. Daggett EdD described it well when he said, "To achieve a 25 percent penetration rate in U.S. homes, it took thirty-five years for the telephone, twenty-six years for television, sixteen years for personal computers, seven years for the Internet, and three years for personal digital assistants (PDAs)." Technology is coming at us faster and faster and we are embracing it in record time as well.

When I conduct leadership presentations, I encourage leaders to become very proficient with technology. It's not going away and it's advancing at rates faster than we can keep up. The purpose of most of this technology is to improve the efficiency and effectiveness of communication. It has certainly improved efficiency—we can communicate faster and with anyone anywhere in the world within seconds. However, in my opinion, it has not improved effectiveness. We are communicating less and less face-to-face. Younger generations are not learning how to read body language, interpret facial expressions, or carry on meaningful conversations in person. Instead, they are relying on technology for their communication and this can be a detriment when they attempt to lead teams later in life.

Leaders today will need to be ready and willing to deal with this E generation and provide the training they will need to be better face-to-face communicators. Leaders will also need to stay on top of technology and the advancements we face or they will be left in the dust. Adaptability will be a critical skill for leaders as technology continues to change the way we communicate, do business, and operate as a global community.

Wright

Those are some amazing statistics on technology. We are advancing like crazy and I can see why leaders need to keep up.

Kim, do you think leaders have a higher accountability in any particular areas (other than keeping up on technology) than people who are not leaders?

Alyn

I actually do. There are a number of areas in which I feel leaders have a higher level of accountability than people who are not leaders. The first area is to set the role model example. You need to be the change you want to see in others. Be the leader you want to see in your team. Be the work ethic you desire in your followers.

The second area of higher accountability is supporting the mission, vision, and goals of the organization. This doesn't mean you agree with every single aspect of every goal or objective, but it means you support the general direction the organization is taking. Great leaders understand this important concept: if you don't like something, you try to change it. If you can't change it, you try to change the way you look at it. If you can't change the way you look at it, you change employers or careers. What you don't do is spread a cancer throughout the organization with your negative comments and criticisms. Great leaders go up the chain with their complaints and concerns, not down or across. If you can't support the general direction of the organization, you shouldn't be working there.

The third area is having a love and a passion for what you do. Leaders need to show followers that they love their job. It doesn't mean you have to love every aspect of your job, but it means you show a passion for the work you do. People want to be around people who love what they do. People want to do business with people who love what they do. People want to follow people who love what they do. When you love what you do, you tend to do it well.

There are aspects of my job that I don't love. In fact there are aspects of my job that I hate. I hate cancelled flights, and it happens a lot! I have to rent cars and drive for hours when an airline cancels the last leg of my flight. I have arrived at my hotel at 3:00 AM in the past only to have to get up at 6:00 AM to set up at 7:00 AM to do an all-day workshop starting at 8:00 AM. I hate showing up for a keynote and asking if the batteries are new in the lavalier microphone and being told they are, only to have it die on me after fifteen minutes. I hate overpriced airport food. I hate being told I can't carry certain items on an airplane only to go through airport security and then have the "opportunity" to buy some of that stuff in the airport and stick it in my bag! There are so many things I could do without; but I put up with all of the aspects I hate to be able to do what I love.

Too many people take a brush of disdain and paint it over their entire job or career because there are aspects of their jobs they don't like. If you don't love what you do, you need to do yourself and everyone around you a favor and get the heck out! Life is too short to spend such a large portion of your life doing something you hate.

Wright

I like the way you put that—you don't have to love every aspect of your job, but you should at least love what you're doing.

Okay Kim, I have one final question for you. What do you think is the biggest hindrance for people when it comes to discovering their inner strengths?

Alyn

I think the biggest hindrance is a lack of prioritization. People insist they don't have time to really evaluate their skills, talents, and strengths, much less work on developing them. I think we make time for what's important to us. We all have the same twenty-four hours in a day and yet some people seem to make time for this important area while others do not. Self-development tends to fall to the bottom of the priority list for most people and they are not the only ones to suffer for this choice. Their family suffers. Their coworkers suffer. Their employees suffer. All of the crucial relationships in their life suffer because they are not being the absolute best they could truly be.

You would be amazed at the amount of time you have available to work on these important areas if you cut out just a few of the time siphons in your life. The biggest time-waster is television. The A.C. Nielsen Company estimates that the average adult watches five hours of television a day. That may sound like a lot, but I challenge you to add yours up. Keep track of how often your television set is on—I think it will shock you. If you shifted some of that television time to discovering and developing your inner strengths, you could make some serious progress in improving yourself!

Another huge time-waster is "surfing the 'Net." There are appropriate times when you need to look something up and do some research, but that's not what I'm talking about. I'm talking about pulling up your browser to look something up and seeing that news story link you just have to click on or seeing that sports highlight clip calling your name. Before you know it you have wasted thirty minutes on something that didn't add any value to your life.

If you don't make a concerted effort to prioritize your time, life will just happen to you and before you know it, you'll be ninety years old wondering where all of the years went. It has taken me a long time to learn this valuable lesson, and I am so thankful I learned it before age ninety. My top priority is making sure my life aligns with the will of God. My next priority is my family. My next priority is making sure I develop the inner strengths, skills, and talents that God has blessed me with and figuring out what those are. In the process of doing that, I become a better person for my family, my friends, and the people I work with. This is a never-ending process that I hope to be continuing when I am ninety!

ABOUT THE AUTHOR

KIMBERLY ALYN IS A BEST-SELLING AUTHOR and an award-winning professional speaker. She delivers time-tested, progressive self-improvement concepts with laughter and insight—and audiences rave!

Kim is the author of ten books including the best-seller, *How to Deal With Annoying People* (with Bob Phillips, PhD), *101 Leadership Reminders, Pillars of Success,* and *It's Not Brain Surgery—Simple Tips on Getting a Grip on a More Successful Life.* Kim has also developed and produced numerous CD/DVD productions on a variety of topics.

Kim offers keynotes and longer presentations on topics such as leadership, success principles, team-building, dealing with annoying people, and giving butt-kicking presentations.

Kim has been an entrepreneur and successful business owner since the age of nineteen and possesses a contagious passion and enthusiasm for life that you just have to experience for yourself!

KIMBERLY ALYN

Best-Selling Author & International Professional Speaker

3591 Sacramento Drive, Suite 118

San Luis Obispo, CA 93401

800.821.8116

Kim@KimberlyAlyn.com

www.KimberlyAlyn.com

AN INTERVIEW WITH...

MARY LIPPITT

SEIZE OPPORTUNITIES, ELIMINATE PITFALLS, MOBILIZE ENERGY, & ACHIEVE RESULTS

DAVID WRIGHT (WRIGHT)

Today we're talking with Dr. Mary Lippitt, who is an award-winning author, consultant, trainer, and researcher. With more than twenty-five years of experience, she is an internationally recognized authority on leading for results, the successful execution of strategy, and capturing tangible benefits from building a high trust culture. Her results orientation and her focus on organizational priorities guide leaders as they set goals and implement plans. Unlike most leadership work that examines personal style or skill sets, Mary targets how leaders use information and adjust to new business circumstances. By applying this approach, leaders can recognize what needs to change to ensure both short- and long-term results. With a bias toward action, Mary spotlights a new aspect in leadership development—business results. A business framework offers immediate impact, captures opportunities, and avoids pitfalls. It is in stark contrast to the costly trial-and-error school of leadership. Her award-winning book, *The Leadership Spectrum: Six Business Priorities That Get Results,* makes the case that you must focus on results to get results.

Mary, welcome to *Discover Your Inner Strength.*

Mary Lippitt (Lippitt)

Well, thank you. It's a pleasure to be here.

Wright

You focus on business priorities in your work. How do you define a priority and why do you target them?

Lippitt

I define a priority as a leader's most desired goal or outcome, given the current situation. Too often the business context is omitted from the discussion of leadership. We are in a fast-changing world and the cycles—whether economic, technological, or product—impact what we can achieve.

There are several advantages to focusing on priorities. First, using priorities ensures that all the key information is fully vetted and weighed before decisions are made. Next, priorities provide a common language for communicating plans and expectations throughout the organization, aligning efforts and gaining support for action. Finally, no "translation" is needed. People understand these business terms right away since they are part of our business language.

The priority framework does not replace the two traditional approaches to leadership development—personal style and skill set. Instead, it adds the new dimensions of business decision-making and goal-setting to ensure solid results. If leaders want results, they must focus on them.

Wright

Of course, that's certainly a new way of looking at leadership. What led you to this new priority perspective?

LIPPITT

Many of my clients were asking for concrete guidance on how to adapt to the changing realties within their organizations and within the larger business world. They wanted a framework to assess what actions would produce the best results. The costs of not adapting are painfully high. The priorities framework helps leaders recognize when change is needed, stay well positioned for change, and communicate change for rapid implementation. The traditional leadership approaches are not outcome focused. Recent Wall Street failures reflect what happens when leaders don't fully examine options and assumptions.

The traditional leadership frameworks are not outcome focused. Style frameworks look at "who" is in front of you, while priorities look at "what" you are confronting. In the end, getting things done must be the prime leadership focus. When business situations shift, leaders must know how to read the internal and external signals and adjust accordingly. While skill development is important, it still does not address the "bottom line" of producing a desired outcome. Priorities equip leaders with the mindset to select the right skill sets for the situation. My clients wanted business impact, not just improved satisfaction with a leader's personal skills or competencies.

Put another way, leaders want guidance on what they must do to cope with changing realities. They want the business wisdom to make the best decision possible. Leaders are acutely aware that the cost of a poor decision is not only job loss, but also organizational failure.

WRIGHT

You talk and write a lot about business wisdom; would you tell our readers a little bit more about what you mean by "business wisdom"?

LIPPITT

Let's start with the U.S. financial crisis. It does not take a rocket scientist to know that the more mortgages you make, the more profit the organization has the potential to earn. However, how many financial institutions understood the risk of what could happen if a homeowner owes more than the house is worth? How many financial institutions saw the advantage of increasing their "leverage" by extending a loan, but did not see the potential problems with having to foreclose on homes when the homeowner could not pay the mortgage?

Wisdom means making a smart decision for short- and long-term. A wise leader knows it is crucial to ask all relevant questions, to weigh the information appropriately, and to make a choice that serves all key stakeholders.

Instead, banks seem to have "cloned" each other's business strategy and entered into either sub-prime loans or "liar loans" without really assessing the liabilities. Some leaders felt that since everyone was doing it, it must be okay. And we all know that this kind of thinking leads to problems, not excellence.

WRIGHT

So how can knowledge of the priority framework help leaders develop their business wisdom?

LIPPITT

I think it will help them plan. There's a saying that leaders never plan to fail but they do fail to plan. Without a grasp of key business priorities and how to balance them, crucial issues, variables, or assumptions are overlooked, resulting in distorted decisions. This happens to many leaders—those who make the headlines as well as those who do not.

Leaders tend to target one thing at a time. While I value the KISS, or Keep It Simple Stupid principle, our complex world is not easily simplified. That was a luxury for another time, and such simplistic thinking must stay in the past.

Priorities also serve as a checklist for key elements that must be factored into goal-setting and decision-making. They help to keep leaders "in tune" with the times.

We all know leaders who assume that persistence with a "vision" will eventually lead to success. While I value persistence, we live in a world of such complexity and speed that persistence is a vice as well as a virtue. I want leaders to persist wisely, having considered all of the relevant issues, factors, information, opportunities and potential consequences. Conviction without thorough analysis is dangerous. With knowledge of the full spectrum of key priorities, success is much more likely.

WRIGHT

Will you give our readers and listeners an example of how priorities helped a leader demonstrate wisdom?

LIPPITT

Yes. Let me tell you about a wise CEO. His organization was about to launch a new product line, which was widely assumed to help the firm become a market leader. Enthusiasm was high, the financial projections scrutinized and positive, and everyone was on board for what seemed like a slam-dunk for the firm.

The CEO called a meeting prior to making the final plunge. The leader asked his team, what are the risks if we implement today? After a long silence, it became evident that no one could identify any risk. Everyone had become fixated on the benefits. Many leaders might have taken that as a sign to move ahead full steam. This leader recognized that trap. He said, "If we do not know the risks, we do not understand the entire picture." He knew that only when they understood the potentially negative consequences would they have sufficient knowledge for solid decision-making.

In my opinion, that is an example of business wisdom. Many leaders would authorize the new venture, happy to have "everyone on board." Instead, he knew that no decision is entirely risk free. Their blind spot was dangerous and this executive recognized it, preventing problems in the future.

I think business wisdom is demonstrated when decisions are made by design rather than default, and when leaders ask the relevant questions instead of relying on a quick answer. Wisdom happens when leaders interpret all of the facts, trends, and opportunities to make an informed decision.

WRIGHT

I can see how overlooking some priorities threaten effective decision-making. Why are leaders prone to overlook key priorities?

LIPPITT

I think leaders believe that they must have *the* answer, and they must come up with it quickly, resulting in the proverbial silver bullet approach, where The Lone Ranger only needed one bullet to handle any desperado. It can also be called the "ready, fire" leadership school. An analogy would be the homeowner who believes that WD–40 is the answer to anything stuck, just as duct tape is the solution for anything broken. In our rush for action, we cling to what has worked before and skip over analysis. Critical thinking is not considered a key leadership function, when it really is the most important one. Only thinking, analysis, and judgment can help leaders cope with changing organizational situations and challenging business realities.

Let me offer an example of how a failure to consider context and a broad scope of priorities can derail executives. Consider new CEOs who are hired from outside the organization. These new CEOs tend to replicate what they did before, and fail to see that the context is different, so they flounder and frequently fail. This is what happened at Home Depot. Bob Nardelli was a highly successful GE executive who was considered Jack Welch's successor. When he did not get the top job, Nardelli became CEO of Home Depot and brought his GE practices with him. The practices that worked well in an established firm like GE did not work well in a rapidly growing firm.

This tendency to use what has worked in the past has also encouraged many executives to imitate successful CEOs like Welch. When Welch introduced a new policy or practice, many CEOs assumed that if it was good for Welch it would be good for them, too.

Celebrity CEOs do not face the same situation as every other leader, so their solutions are not guaranteed to work in every organization. Leaders need to make informed and balanced choices, and avoid believing that any "fad of the month" is the path to success.

In some organizations there is actually a parade of single solutions based on a Celebrity CEO or a recent best-selling management book, each lasting about six to twelve months. After each fails, it is discarded and another adopted. Then the workforce becomes skeptical and less likely to support the next initiative. What is lost in the tendency to replicate others is a balanced, comprehensive, and tailored approach to setting strategy and goals.

Wright

Those examples of the cost of focusing on one or two goals or priorities are compelling. I understand you conducted some research in this area. Was that tendency validated in your research?

Lippitt

Yes, it was. Our research indicates that 45 percent of the leaders we work with are using one priority, another 31 percent are using two, and 22 percent are using three priorities. When you tally those up, it means that 98 percent are using half of the six business priorities. Now, this does not necessarily mean that these leaders are making poor decisions. The critical question is whether the full spectrum of priorities was included in their deliberations before they selected the priorities that guided their actions. Knowing the priorities and how to weigh them for their situation helps leaders select the ones that will deliver success.

Let me briefly summarize the six key priorities in the framework. They are:

1. developing new products or services
2. gaining marketing share and retaining customers
3. designing systems and policies for internal excellence
4. improving efficiencies and quality
5. developing talent and a high performing culture
6. examining trends, assumptions, and new business models

(A more complete description can be found on my Web site.)

As you can see, these are business issues, and trying to balance all of them requires judgment. Leaders are known to ask that production be done "faster, cheaper, better." When employees ask, "Which one do you want done first?" a leader typically indicates which priority is most crucial. It would be better to make that decision before the workforce gets confused. Finding the right balance between the six priorities and then knowing when to adjust that balance as circumstances evolve is the hallmark of an outstanding leader.

Wright

I understand the attraction of the silver bullet or the single simple solution; we've all probably been a victim of this mentality. Applying a single solution must have a cost. Will you tell our readers about the cost?

Lippitt

The costs, as your question suggests, are quite high. We see it in a extremely high turnover rate in the C suite. However, there are hidden costs. We know from research that the success rate of new initiatives ranges between 11 and 33 percent and that means a huge investment loss. We also see it in failed mergers, where the goal of "economy of scale" overshadows other pressing needs. A "bet the ranch" approach is costly, yet it still has adherents. The allure of the brass ring keeps some leaders searching for *the* answer. It reminds me of the definition of insanity, which is doing what you have always done, but expecting different results.

WRIGHT

In a workshop I held the other day, one of our speakers said that practice does not make perfect, practice makes permanent.

LIPPITT

I like that very much, it's very true.

WRIGHT

Given my age I had to agree with him! Given those long odds against success, what can leaders do to successfully implement strategic change?

LIPPITT

One way, of course, is to use the priority framework. There is a second strategy too, which is to examine your assumptions about how to move from strategic planning into project management. Too many leaders want to develop a goal and then immediately start implementation. It is our action orientation and it rarely works.

The "ready, fire" mentality must be replaced with a "ready, aim, fire" practice. Aiming is a translation step, which I term "execution planning." The payoff is that people understand, accept, and are committed to implementation. Execution planning also fosters more cross functional approaches, creates clear progress measures for monitoring achievement, and enables mid-course corrections to keep the plan on track.

Mid-course corrections ensure that a leader achieves the intended goals. NASA reports that rockets are off target 80 percent of the time. However, with multiple mid-course corrections, the rockets arrive at the intended target. The same is true with organizations. Only with active monitoring and adjustment will any plan succeed.

WRIGHT

Tell me more about execution planning's role as the translation step between strategy and project planning.

LIPPITT

Let me say that strategic planning is comparable to looking at the future from 50,000 feet. It is lofty and far-reaching. What happens is that the big picture view rarely offers sufficient detail to guide project planning, where the rubber meets the road.

What is needed is something more at the 1,000 foot level that translates lofty goals into specific outcomes that can drive action. In addition, many leaders want the strategic plans to do more than guide decision-making, they want them to be inspiring. Clarity is rarely found in strategic plans. Execution planning is a process that bridges this gap to the development of project plans that position implementation for smooth sailing.

WRIGHT

What actions can leaders take to ensure successful change?

LIPPITT

To me, building a culture of trust is essential, and frequently overlooked. Drucker knew the power in culture and captured it with his statement that "culture eats strategy for breakfast." Our research and experience show that trust is critical to alignment, initiative, and collaboration. Few people think about culture in those terms. Too often culture is equated with dress codes, using first names in the hallway, attendance policies, and loyalty.

What I mean by culture is a composite of the organization's systems, practices, policies, and actions that foster personal behavior and practices. When there is a high level of organizational trust, it means that the workforce believes the organization is fair, that management walks its talk, and the organization is headed in the right direction. With low trust or worse, distrust, people drag their feet, actively resist, or wait to see if a new initiative has any sticking power. Too many adopt membership on the "B" team (i.e., I'll be here when it starts and I'll be here when it ends. I can wait it out until it passes. No reason to really get on board).

We need to recognize that organizational culture plays a substantial role in creating the way staff view management. Today, many see senior management as the "them" on the top floor who have low credibility at exactly the point in time when more is being asked of the workforce. Only high trust will enable an organization to move quickly, seize opportunities, and enter new markets.

I have seen a great deal of attention focused on individual trust, and that is valuable. The question is where you should focus first—on the organization's culture and top management or on frontline individuals? From my experience, I think you must start with senior management creating a high trust culture. The reason is that it is easier for an organization's culture to shape the frontline worker than it is for a frontline worker to shape an organization's culture.

WRIGHT

Well, you've certainly given us a lot of food for thought. What is the one thing that you want readers to take away from our discussion?

LIPPITT

I would like readers to know how critical it is to keep their eye on the prize—they need to keep their eye on the outcomes and results. They can do that with the priorities framework, since it focuses on results. In times of change, relying on the silver bullet mentality just will not work. Wise decision-making in the face of change is critical to leadership effectiveness. Not only will it produce results, but it also enables leaders to move from being the one "with all the answers" to asking the key priority questions. Socrates demonstrated the power of questions. Questioning spurs innovative as well as analytical thinking. It also develops personal judgment, while molding future leaders. While developing others may sound like a long-term payoff, there is also an immediate one—you get the results you want.

WRIGHT

What a great interview. I really appreciate all the time you've taken with me this afternoon to answer these questions. I have really learned a lot and you've given me a lot of things to think about.

LIPPITT

Thank you. I have enjoyed speaking with you.

WRIGHT

Today we've been talking with Dr. Mary Lippitt. Mary is the Founder and President of Enterprise Management Ltd. She is an internationally recognized authority, consultant, speaker, and writer on leadership, strategic execution, trust, and implementing change. Her book, *The Leadership Spectrum: Six Business Priorities That Get Results,* earned the Best Business Book Award and her firm won the Top Ten Training Product of the Year Award from *Human Resource Executive.* Mary provides exciting, cutting-edge ideas and practical tools to help clients get desired short- and long-term results.

Dr. Lippitt, thank you so much for being with us today on *Discover Your Inner Strength.*

LIPPITT

David it's been a pleasure. Thank you very much.

ABOUT THE AUTHOR

AS FOUNDER AND PRESIDENT of Enterprise Management Ltd., Dr. Mary Lippitt was in the forefront of recognizing the need to link leadership development to results. Armed with a doctorate in business administration, experience in the private and public sectors, and more than two decades in the field, Mary works with exceptional leaders to polish their business acumen and help them achieve the right results at the right time.

Her work has received award from the National Association of Counties and she is also the recipient of multiple awards from the American Society for Training and Development. He book and materials have also received national awards.

Finding teaching stimulating and a way to stay on the leading edge, Dr. Lippitt has taught at The George Washington, Georgetown, and St. Thomas Universities. Mary recently presented her research findings on leadership gender differences at Harvard University's John F. Kennedy School of Government alumni meeting. She served as an Executive in Residence at the HR Institute, where she worked on research studies on: The Future of Leadership, Quest for Innovation, and Strategic Execution.

In addition to consulting, speaking, and writing, she enjoys her community work, time with her two grandsons and crossing items off her "bucket list."

MARY LIPPITT

4531 Roanoak Way

Palm Harbor, FL 34685

727.934.9810

mlippitt@enterprisemgt.com

www.enterprisemgt.com

AN INTERVIEW WITH...

LIN SCHEIB

PUT *LIFE* IN YOUR LIFE!
7 SPARKS TO ALIVENESS

DAVID WRIGHT (WRIGHT)

Today we're talking with Lin Scheib. Lin is a certified personal and professional coach and is the owner of Lightning Life, LLC, where she specializes in coaching and consulting with executives and professionals. Her multi-faceted corporate career and coaching credentials give her unique insight into the challenges and opportunities faced by professional men and women.

Lin, welcome to *Discover Your Inner Strength.*

You had a very successful corporate career. What made you retire early—"graduate," as you call it—to start your own personal and professional coaching business?

LIN SCHEIB

Thank you, David. It is a pleasure to be talking with you today.

Yes, I did have a successful corporate career—beyond my wildest dreams. I grew up in poverty in a pretty dysfunctional family. I was the first and only member of my family to graduate from college. So, the fact that I enjoyed seven very unique careers in two corporations and worked all over the United States and in eleven other countries was quite amazing to me. Actually, when I started with IBM, I dreamed of being CEO someday. Of course, that was before I had any idea what it meant to be an executive in a global corporation. By the time I had enough experience and was included in the Executive Resource Program, I wasn't at all sure that it was what I wanted.

As I progressed in my career, I was exposed to more and more of the demands of a corporate culture. At one time, I wrote in my journal, "I have no friends, no life. My home is an airplane or hotel room, and my only friends are my professional colleagues." That was when I realized I was allowing my life to be usurped by my professional role. But, I was wrapped up in achieving the external and internal notions of success. I struggled with myself and learned as much as I could about claiming my own life. I began to study and later taught Stephen Covey's "seven habits of highly successful people." I drank in this material—to me it was like water to a dehydrated vagabond. It helped to stabilize me.

In 2004, I attended a coaching class. The class changed my life. I knew from the first moment that my purpose was to bring coaching to the lives of others. Over the next few years, as I completed the coaching training, certification, and leadership programs, the plan began to materialize. I worked with my own coach to clarify my dreams and to gain my new life. I coached professionals as part of my global leadership role. The more I coached and saw the impact it had on people's lives, the more I wanted to coach. It was infectious.

So, I made the very difficult decision in mid 2007 to leave my corporate career to begin my own business coaching and supporting other professionals. I termed my departure as "graduation." To me, the term signified that I was moving on to another exciting part of my life for which my experiences to date had prepared me well.

WRIGHT

You said that leaving your corporate career was a difficult decision. How did you manage to find the strength to make that decision?

SCHEIB

Well, it's like the experience I've heard other people relate—one day I just *knew.* It was a Monday morning in early 2007. My husband and I were taking a walk before work. I felt like I was tethered to something heavy that made any movement difficult. In my heart, I knew that the tether was to the financial security and very comfortable income level I had achieved. As tears ran down my face, I told my husband that the money wasn't worth another five years of the desolate life I was experiencing—it wasn't worth even one more year or one more day. With his support, I set about to make some changes.

I talked with my boss that very day. Over the next couple of weeks, we explored options like part-time work, leave of absence, etc. But my heart cried out that I needed to be brave and trusting enough to significantly sever my ties to the life that claimed me. I believe my courage came from listening to my inner self, from being unhappy enough, and from wanting something else badly enough. I had worked in transformation for most of my career, and I knew that change is never easy. But, I also knew that it is the only way to break old patterns and open ourselves up to discover our inner strength. I have never looked back.

WRIGHT

So, you have started your own coaching business, called Lightning Life. Why did you choose that name?

SCHEIB

The name is very consistent with the impact I want to have in the world. I want people to realize and claim the rich life that can be theirs. Lightning is powerful, beautiful, exciting, and cannot be ignored. When it flashes, nothing can stand in its way or dim its natural essence. I am passionate about helping people live their fullest lives. With that goal in mind, I developed the "7 Sparks to Aliveness."

WRIGHT

What are the "7 Sparks to Aliveness" and how does your company name relate to them?

SCHEIB

The "7 Sparks to Aliveness" are aimed at helping professional women reclaim their personal lives in the midst of corporate culture. Like lightning, they are powerful. They ignite energy and passion into a woman's life. I use the acronym, "ISPARCS" to talk about them because the verbalization of the acronym is "I spark." Using the acronym "ISPARCS," the following are the seven sparks:

I—Imagine the Possibilities
S—Live in Serenity
P—Claim your Personal Power
A—Awaken to New Beginnings
R—Release your Radiance
C—Act with Confidence
S—Soar with Synergy

WRIGHT

How did you identify the seven sparks?

SCHEIB

As I thought about my professional career and the women with whom I worked, I felt a void that needed to be filled. Personally, I had allowed my professional life to identify me to the point where I was performing but not really living. I knew from working with other women that they shared the same experience. It is not new. There is a phrase in the 1955 version of the Merle Travis song, "Sixteen Tons," that says, "I owe my soul to the company store." What is new is that women are assuming more and more of the professional roles and are struggling to preserve their true selves as they integrate into the corporate culture.

Women, by nature, are caring, giving, and nurturing. We also tend to carry the burdens of others on our shoulders and to be our own worst critics. The competitive environment of the corporate world positions one person against another on a daily basis. It is draining and counter to most women's inherent nature. Over time, if we aren't very careful, that demanding, competitive environment takes over our lives, leaving us flat. It isn't very fulfilling to live life like a flat line on an EKG monitor.

So, I thought, "What would I like to encourage in professional women so that they could more fully enjoy their lives while also performing in the corporate world?" (I am not suggesting that all women follow the path I did to leave the corporate world—I only want them to have the life of abundance, joy, and fulfillment that can be theirs.)

As I pondered this question, I was inspired by nature during a quiet, solo drive through the high plains of the western United States. I guess you could say that the universe spoke to me.

I saw the blue sky with gently floating clouds and I wished for women to caress the *serenity* of that scene. I noticed the bright sunshine and was moved by the *confidence* and stability exuded by its golden hue. I thought of a star-filled night and remembered as a child believing that *anything was possible*—all I had to do was wish upon a star. I recalled beautiful sunrises, washing the Earth with new light and life and knew that every moment could be a *new beginning.* I thought of a powerful thunderstorm and knew that each woman has her own *personal power* to claim. The sunset filling the horizon reminded me of the passion and *radiance* that lives within every woman. And, finally, the rainbow reminded me of the exquisite beauty that is achieved through harmony, balance, and *synergy*.

WRIGHT

Let's spend some time talking in more depth about each of the seven sparks. Let's start with "Imagine the Possibilities."

SCHEIB

Remember when you were a child and you really believed that anything was possible? Maybe you wished upon a star:

"Star light, star bright
First star I see tonight.
I wish I may, I wish I might,
Have the wish I wish tonight."

No holds barred—you asked for what you wanted. I'll bet you didn't think, "Is it practical, logical, doable, or reasonable?" You simply let your imagination work and asked for your wish.

The inspiration in nature for the "Imagine the Possibilities" ISPARC™ is a starlit night. It is about recalling and reclaiming our ability to dream, imagine, and wish with the unbridled faith of a child. I'm not sure when we begin to lose this ability, but I see it absent or hidden in many people. We get worn down by being told "no" and by conforming to a corporate environment. My, how we deprive ourselves when we bury that child-like openness and excitement and belief in possibilities.

There are ways to reignite the spark to "Imagine the Possibilities." One way is to brainstorm all the wishes you have for your life. Include a friend you trust and who will encourage you. Stop yourself when you begin to think about reality (practical, doable, reasonable, etc.). Just let your imagination play!

Do this daily at first, then as often as you feel compelled. If you get stuck, look up at Father Sky on a starlit night. Let it inspire you and remind you of the endless possibilities that reside in you. Wish upon a star. Be reminded of the unending and ever-present potential that is a part of your humanness.

Imagine the Possibilities—it will be fun!

Wright

I can see how keeping the dream alive is important. Now, tell me about "Live in Serenity."

Scheib

Life can be hectic, full of "to do," "not done," "wish I hadn't done," "if only." You could probably add more of your own. When we allow our lives to be dominated by all the "should'a," "would'a," "could'a," thoughts, we lose focus on the soul of our lives.

This challenge isn't unique to today's world. *The Serenity Prayer* was written over six decades ago and is equally relevant today.

"God, grant me the serenity
to accept the things I cannot change;
the courage to change the things I can;
and the wisdom to know the difference."
—Reinhold Niebuhr

Of the things we cannot change, one thing is certain—we cannot change anything that has happened in the past. No amount of regret, guilt, or worry will change past events. Another certainty is that we cannot change another person. Only that person has the will and power to make changes in his or her life.

However, we *can* change how we respond to people and events around us. This is a conscious decision to choose how we act in the world. It is about choosing to be grateful and living a life of abundance.

"Live in Serenity" is about adopting a gentle acceptance of our past mistakes and failures. It is about being comfortable in our humanness. It is also about choosing and deciding to focus on the impact we can have in the world—from this moment on—all the time honoring our uniqueness and gifts. Imagine lying in a lush meadow, gazing up into a blue sky, with white clouds gently moving with the breeze—this is nature's inspiration for serenity.

Here's a tip to gain more serenity in life: When you find yourself faced with a difficulty, ask yourself whether the situation is something you can change. Write down the situation and what needs to be changed. If you can truly do something about it and you choose to, put the paper in an obvious place for your action. If not, ceremoniously tear it up, throw it away, or burn it. Let it go.

Live in Serenity—it will add peace to your life.

Wright

That certainly sounds like something we could all take to heart. Tell me about "Claim Your Personal Power."

Scheib

The "Claim your Personal Power" portion of ISPARC reminds us that as human creatures, we have enormous personal power. We are gifted with the intellect to learn, reason, and choose our path. Most things we do are by choice, and realizing this makes us feel more in control in our own lives.

All too often, though, we give away our inherent power to people and circumstances in our lives. We tell ourselves, "I can't," or equally as disempowering, "I have to," or we blame others for the circumstances of our lives. In all cases, we give our power to another person. In effect, we are saying, "I have no control. I have no choice. I have no power."

In the book, *The 7 Habits of Highly Effective People,* Stephen Covey talks about responsibility by separating the components of the word: response-ability. He teaches that we all have the *ability to choose our response* to life's situations. The next time you're about to blame someone else for a circumstance, reconsider the role you played and the choices you have. Then, move forward from a place of choice, knowing your personal power.

Visualize the power released in a thunderstorm—the sharp glow of the lightning, followed by the rumble of thunder. This is truly power in action and is the inspiration for this ISPARC. As humans, we are no less powerful than the thunderstorm. We have *our* power to release to the world. It is a gift and a responsibility—choose to use it in ways that benefit yourself and others.

To claim your personal power, begin by noticing when you use words or have thoughts or beliefs that give away your personal power. Then, make a small change to reclaim your power, such as replacing the words "I have to" with "I choose to." This simple act will raise your awareness of your power to choose.

Claim Your Personal Power—it will give direction to your life

Wright

Wow! What powerful thoughts. Let's now discuss "Awaken to New Beginnings."

Scheib

What would it be like if every sunrise truly brought the dawn of a new day into our lives? Imagine what might be possible if we could know that we are truly beginning anew. This, in fact, is the reality. Every last day, every last moment, every last second has passed. The reality and the opportunity exist only in the *now!*

It's pretty easy to identify the obvious opportunities for new beginnings: a new year, marriage, divorce, birth, death, new location, new job, new school, or new career. These are significant life changes that can trigger the desire and dedication to make changes in our lives. We can look at all these and other major life events as new beginnings—the time to let go of unhealthy, disempowering habits and beliefs—and adopt the habits that bring us joy and happiness. Less obvious are the everyday opportunities to create new beginnings.

Sometimes we allow ourselves to get in a rut and the longer we stay there, the deeper it gets. Pretty soon, it's almost impossible to see the way out. The weeds of complacency take over where blossoms could thrive. Hope for something better is a distant memory.

I recently read an intriguing statement on hope in a newspaper article, "Hope remains, even when it's hidden by nagging doubts," by Bob Lively who is a teacher-in-residence at the First Presbyterian Church of Austin and serves on the adjunct faculty of Seton Cove Spirituality Center. He wrote,

"Hope is a fragile thing easily damaged by skepticism . . . and suffocated by cynicism . . .

". . . it is an amazing . . . power that is bequeathed to us when we need it most, especially in those dark nights of the soul when despair is poised to attack. And because its origin is pure love, it invariably comes to us gently, and silently it invites us to embrace its essence as the bedrock upon which one can build a new and beautiful life.

"Those who claim that 'hope is passion for the possible' are likely on target . . .."

Try this exercise: Stand with your weight firmly planted on both feet. Then, begin to release one foot, then the other, shifting your weight at an even pace. This reminds us of the ticking of time. It also reminds us that each moment brings the opportunity for a new beginning. The last moment is passed; the current moment is an opening for creation. It is as certain as the dawn of a new day, which is nature's inspiration for this spark.

Awaken to New Beginnings—it will bring hope to your life.

Wright

That's an exciting thought—that every moment is the opportunity for a new beginning. Let's move now to "Release Your Radiance."

SCHEIB

Do you remember a time when your world was filled with radiance? Perhaps it was when a child was born or you met a person whose presence filled the room. Perhaps it was when you observed a sunset that filled the horizon and touched the heavens. You couldn't help but notice.

Sunset is the inspiration for this element of ISPARC. It's about our not holding back and playing small. It's about letting our internal beauty shine forth in a way that cannot be overlooked. It's about knowing our impact and standing in it—full out!

The key to releasing our radiance is to know and appreciate our internal beauty. Here's a portion of a poem, called "Broaden Your Base of Beauty" by Patty Mayeux that says it all:

"Seek the beauty within;
Be bold and let it shine . . .

Embrace Beauty!
Not from without

But from within
And smile when you encounter it."

Releasing our radiance is about learning our authentic self and being true to ourselves. Sometimes there are so many expectations on us that it feels like life is squeezing us into an ever-smaller box, leaving no room for the real us.

To begin to recognize your internal radiance, write down all the gifts you bring to the world—yes, *all* of them. Focus on who you are (e.g., sincere, honest, trustworthy, generous), as well as what you do (e.g., run fast, lead people, manage projects). Vibrantly share your gifts with those around you. Add to your list as you discover more of your gifts.

Release Your Radiance—it will impact the world!

WRIGHT

The world could certainly be a brighter place. Next is "Act with Confidence." Tell me about that spark.

Scheib

You know confidence when you see it. It is often associated with standing tall, holding the head erect, and maintaining eye contact. Confidence is also associated with the clear and direct expression of thoughts and ideas. These actions send the message that people are sure of themselves and their position. But, what is really going on inside? Only the person knows. He or she may be feeling squirmish like a bowl of Jello or as strong as steel. In either case, the person is *projecting* a sense of confidence, which engenders confidence from others. The person is acting "as if" he or she is totally sure of his or her value and message.

People aren't born with confidence. We acquire it through recognizing our knowledge, skills, and value throughout life. And sometimes we have to fake it because inside we are as wobbly as a toddler. It doesn't matter. The perception of confidence is largely in the eyes of the beholder.

Try this exercise to increase your confidence: Spend time in front of a mirror. Examine your posture. Bring your shoulders down and back, spine erect, vertically aligned from head to toe. Practice breathing deeply and easily, while holding your abdominal muscles taut. Keep your hands at your side. Now, look yourself squarely in the eyes for two minutes. As you do so, notice the amazing person staring back at you. What an unbeatable pair! This will help confidence come more naturally the next time you need it.

Act with Confidence—it will boost yourself and others.

Wright

The last of the seven sparks is "Soar with Synergy." Tell me about that one.

Scheib

The word "synergy" dates from around 1660 and comes from the Greek word, *synergos,* meaning "working together." It refers to the phenomenon in which two or more discrete things act together to create an effect *greater than* that predicted by knowing only the separate affects of the individual things. It was originally a scientific term.

The opposite of synergy is antagonism, the phenomenon where two things in combination have an overall effect that is *less than* that predicted from their individual affects. In short, synergy occurs when the whole is greater than the sum of its parts. It is important to realize, however, that synergy is a *dynamic* state in which combined action is favored over the sum of individual actions. Synergy is achieved when the combined actions are in balance with priorities.

Visualize a rainbow, which is the inspiration for this ISPARC. Individually, each arc of a rainbow is beautiful. Joined in balance and harmony, the arcs unify into something truly magnificent. This is synergy. The "Soar with Synergy" element of ISPARC reminds us to pay attention to balance in our lives, with all aspects gently supportive of and contributing to the lives we wish to create.

Here is an exercise to examine the synergy in your life. Draw a circle and divide it into the aspects of your life (e.g., family, career, health, finances). Use names that are relevant to you. Taking the center of the wheel as zero and the outer edge as ten, rate your satisfaction with each aspect by drawing a line (ten is best). Notice where your satisfaction is low. Identify action plans to bring balance.

Soar with Synergy—it will add fullness to your life.

Wright

Let's talk more about the "7 Sparks to Aliveness." Is there a set pattern for women to follow as they develop these sparks?

Scheib

As I started working on the sparks, there was no set pattern. As I mentioned, I arranged them into the acronym ISPARCS because it was catchy and gave the message "I spark!" in a succinct way. As I have continued to develop them, however, I have recognized that there might be a pattern. That being said, I would encourage women to start with any of them and work with each in a way that resonates most with them.

Wright

Tell me more about the pattern that emerged.

Scheib

To make a change in life, we must first believe that it is possible. The first ISPARC, "Imagine the Possibilities," is about opening ourselves to that belief. A logical next step is to acknowledge what we can and can't control in the world.

Most of us spend a lot of time worrying or fretting over things that we can't control. The "Live in Serenity" ISPARC encourages us to accept the things we cannot change. By doing this, we release energy that we can devote to those things we can change. With renewed belief and energy, we can step fully into our power. The message of the "Claim Your Personal Power" ISPARC is to empower ourselves fully and rid ourselves of blame and self-doubt.

In doing so, we can embrace the notion that every moment holds the opportunity for a new beginning. So, with the dawn of each new day (new moment, in fact), we can "Awaken to New Beginnings." The "Act with Confidence" ISPARC encourages us to move boldly into each of those opportunities. By acting "as if," we can develop the confidence that is required to move into uncharted territories. The culmination is our ability to let our true light shine to the world; thus the "Release Your Radiance" ISPARC. Armed with the belief that anything is possible and that we have the power and confidence to make it happen, we no longer play small. We fully live our lives, radiating the strength and beauty that we possess.

Finally, the "Soar with Synergy" ISPARC is about finding the harmony and balance that is right for a particular time in our lives. Synergy is not static; it is a constant rebalancing of priorities. With conscious choice, we can achieve the synergy that makes the whole of our lives better than the sum of the parts.

Wright

It sounds like the seven sparks would be good for men, too. Are they applicable only to women?

Scheib

Well, I defined them based on my personal experience as a professional woman and on my interactions with other professional women. Many people have told me that they are also applicable to men, but I don't have direct experience with that! I do believe they are *important* to any man who lives with, works with, or knows a woman!

WRIGHT

So, let's assume that a professional woman wants the support of her corporation in developing the seven sparks we've talked about. What's in it for the corporation?

SCHEIB

Having incorporated the seven sparks into her life, a woman will be more creative, more focused, more productive, less risk-averse, a better public relations ambassador, better at getting results, and overall happier and more balanced. Any corporation would love those characteristics in their employees!

WRIGHT

How can women remember to incorporate the seven sparks into their lives?

SCHEIB

We are each responsible for the lives we create, no matter the circumstances that surround us. This might be a little hard to swallow at times, but it is ultimately the truth. We can't look to any other person or thing as responsible for the joy, or lack of it, in our lives. And, we could all use a little help.

I have mentioned the inspiration in nature for each of the sparks. Simply let these acts of nature remind you of the sparks. For example, on a beautiful sunny day, let the bright sunshine remind you to act with confidence. I have also designed jewelry as a reminder for each of the sparks. It is patterned after nature's inspiration and meant to be worn as a reminder. Pictures and more information on it and other products are available on my Web site. Finally, work with a coach or trusted advisor who supports your desire to live fully.

We must remember that this life is momentary and transient. I love the quote, "A lifetime is like a flash of lightning in the sky." Each is brief, unique, and powerful. Choose aliveness and "Put *life* in your life!" Each of us possesses the inner strength to make that choice.

WRIGHT

Thank you, Lin. This conversation has pointed out seven sparks that women can incorporate into their lives to discover their inner strength and aliveness. It has been a very inspiring insight into how to claim a more powerful and full life—for women and men.

ABOUT THE AUTHOR

LIN SCHEIB IS THE OWNER of Lightning Life, LLC, where she specializes in coaching and consulting with executives and professionals. She is a speaker, facilitator, and trainer, helping groups achieve their full potential. Ms. Scheib's multi-faceted corporate career and coaching credentials give her unique insight into the challenges and opportunities faced by professional men and women.

Lin is a personal and professional coach, certified by the Coaches Training Institute and accredited by the International Coach Federation, and is a member of the Austin e-Women Network Leadership Team. She spends volunteer hours mentoring at Dress for Success, an international non-profit organization dedicated to promoting the economic independence of disadvantaged women. Lin holds a BBA and is a graduate of the University of the Texas Graduate School of Business Executive Education Program. She has studied extensively with renowned leaders, including Deepak Chopra, Stephen Covey, and Peter M. Senge.

Lin leads, mentors, and coaches men and women internationally on topics such as work-life balance, career progression, stronger relationships, alignment of work with personal values and increased sense of control. Her coaching clients include professionals at IBM, Dell, 3M, IntegReview LLP, ViaSat Corporation, Coldwell Bankers Residential Brokerage, and GlaxcoSmithKline.

Lin believes in the capability of people to have the lives that fulfill and enrich them and the power of coaching to help them realize their true potential.

LIN SCHEIB
Lightning Life, LLC
6607 Lakewood Point Cove
Austin, TX 78750
512.343.LIFE (5433)
lin@lightninglifecoaching.com
www.lightninglifecoaching.com

Chapter 6

AN INTERVIEW WITH...

LISA BERG

BUILDING BRIDGES

A Cross-Cultural Approach to Transformation and Wholeness

DAVID WRIGHT (WRIGHT)

Today we are talking with Lisa Berg, President of One Global Bridge, a cross-cultural and human potential consulting firm. Lisa is a transformational speaker whose topics include "The Nature of Leadership for Transformational Times" and "Ancient Wisdom for Modern Times: Co-Creating Our Future." She is an inspirational singer and global networker. Lisa co-creates innovative, multi-disciplinary events for leaders who are ready to engage in evolutionary practices for our time. Lisa has lived and now works internationally. She has a master's degree in Transpersonal Psychology. She founded International Friends, a vibrant organization that facilitates transition for international women.

Lisa, welcome to *Discover Your Inner Strength.*

LISA BERG (BERG)

Thank you so much David.

WRIGHT

How do you recognize inner strength?

BERG

When I am with someone living from a place of inner strength, I see and feel their radiance and confidence. They are really comfortable in their skin. They know who they truly are. That kind of person is a true leader, in my opinion. Whomever they touch is uplifted.

In speaking to many people over the years who exude that kind of confidence, I can tell they have faced their fears and have found a way to make peace with them. They express what I call their Expanded Self, fully engaged in life and able to tap into their highest potential in linear and non-linear ways. Their lightness and trust in life is infectious!

We all have the ability to express our magnificence in this way but with the trials and tribulations we face growing up and living in a stressful world, many of us have forgotten.

WRIGHT

I agree. Many of us have forgotten. That is why we felt the need to write this book. Will you share your story with us?

BERG

I would be happy to. I grew up in the suburbs of New Jersey. My mother was afraid of the outside. She wasn't fond of dirt, bugs, or animals like squirrels and dogs, so I didn't really go out much.

Then, in my mid forties, around the time my children went off to college, I began to delve deeper into the spiritual side of life. I entered a master's program in Transpersonal Psychology, a field of psychology that builds upon traditional psychology and incorporates consciousness theory and the wisdom of many traditions into the healing of the whole person.

At that time, like many women, I knew parts of me were missing. Despite years of having my own business, living internationally, volunteering, being a good wife and mother, I really didn't know who "I" was. I felt trapped, even though I truly wasn't. My life on the outside was and still is amazing by anyone's standards, yet I knew I had to make a change and I was afraid.

What I discovered was a wild woman who was trying to emerge but didn't know how!

One of our first assignments was to go outside for at least three hours without a plan. We were to follow our feet and see what happens. I was so scared! I sprayed myself with bug spray, gathered my courage, and walked out my front door. I was taken aback by the beauty of the boulders and trees on my front lawn. I had seen them every day with my eyes, but now I was feeling my connection in a new way. I realized that there is a natural rhythm in Nature that we can tap into. I saw so clearly that we are all part of the same energy, and feeling this again woke something up deep inside me. I began to weep as I remembered a part of myself—my "Nature Girl" whom I had forgotten.

I didn't realize how much I was missing by being separate from Nature. I feel very clear and grounded, able to make decisions from my deep inner core, after something as simple as taking a short walk or sitting on the ground and letting my mind clear. I now spend time outdoors, connecting deeply with Nature as my main strategy for staying strong.

After completing the master's program and still not feeling complete, I continued to try many things looking to find something to "fix" me. That process created a lot of hardship in my family because I kept changing and they didn't know how to deal with me. It took a lot of strength for me to keep going, but I did, with as much joy, awe, and love as I could muster for myself and everyone else. I kept looking forward, believing that the destination of really knowing myself and being able to fully contribute my unique strengths to the world would be worth the wait. I am happy to report it was.

I know there are a lot of men and women doing this profound transformational work of looking deeply at their lives. It takes a lot of courage to even recognize the need for this kind of growth, not to mention the strength it takes to shift from old concepts of ourselves to a more expanded version. I applaud anyone who is on this path, whatever step he or she is on.

One thing I have learned is that there are many ways to approach this important work. Finding the right combination of techniques or strategies for ourselves is key. I know transformation isn't easy, but I believe it doesn't have to be so hard!

My repertoire of growth strategies includes ancient practices such as creative expression, guidance from ancient wisdom, and remembering my sacred relationship to the Earth, which helps me lighten up a bit. And I need that.

WRIGHT

What other ancient practices, in addition to connecting to Nature, have you found helpful in reclaiming your own sense of inner strength? What are some of the benefits you see for the world?

BERG

There are many ancient teachings as well as lessons from organizational development and human potential experts that I find particularly useful. For me personally, a teaching about opening to our innate creativity and personal story was and continues to be a powerful reminder.

Angeles Arrien, a leading cross-cultural anthropologist and one of my mentors, says that indigenous people ask, "When did you stop singing? When did you stop dancing? When did you stop being delighted with the story of your life?" That is the time, they say, when we experience "soul loss" or a loss of power.

I know that is true for me. As a little girl, I begged my parents to send me to art camp. They sent me to a sports camp instead. Boy, I hated that. The only things I liked in camp that summer when I was twelve years old, were rowing in a canoe—handling the back paddle—the arts and crafts cabin, and the theater. We put on *West Side Story* that year. I wanted to play Maria, but the counselor said I was too fat. She made me stand behind a curtain during that performance. I sang the songs and Maria, who was thinner and prettier but couldn't sing as beautifully as I could, mouthed the words.

I carried that shame for many years. I believe a part of me left that day. I never felt the same about singing or being seen. I believed I was not good enough to fully express my creative self. I graduated college with a degree in music, got married, and didn't sing for decades except for the occasional wedding or bar mitzvah.

A big part of the work on our transformational journeys is letting go of those kinds of beliefs and finding the courage to think new thoughts and try new things. When I began singing again, first in the car and then belting it out with a Bette Midler CD, I felt my power coming back.

I sing as part of my work now and I encourage people to sing along. I know it is scary for many people to tap into their creativity, whether it is cooking or singing, dancing or writing. It is one of the places where many of us are wounded. I do hope we can remember what the ancient people said, however, and reclaim that part of ourselves more often. It helps many of us move out of our heads and into our hearts to feel more balanced and empowered.

Another lesson from that teaching is to share our story. Life is so busy these days. Many of us don't make time for meaningful conversations. This is an art that has been lost in the days of television, movies, and the internet, where we are entertained but rarely listened to.

I recently visited the Achuar people of the Ecuador rainforest. The Achuar only opened themselves to the modern world fourteen years ago because they were guided to in their dreams. I learned a lot about the importance of dreams and sharing song and stories in community. The impact the Achuar have made on the world because of these practices is very impressive.

The elderly shaman (medicine man) invited me and my fellow travelers into his home, which is a gathering place for the community. He said to us through interpretation, "We don't have much. Sometimes we have to travel six days for food, but we are happy. People in the modern world have a lot, but they are not always happy."

He asked us to share our talents with the villagers. They then performed for us a wonderful greeting ritual that went beyond words and built trust between us. We sang and danced for each other. Everyone was happy.

One reason I believe the Achuar people are happy is that they are interested in each other's stories. Each morning at 4:30 the people of this tribe meet in community to share their dreams from the night before. A powerful result of this daily practice is that, years ago, their dreams showed them that something was coming that would disrupt their way of life and the rainforest they lived in.

Trusting this "sign" from their collective dreams, they wanted to prepare—not in the old warrior way of using weapons, but by reaching out to the modern world to build positive, working relationships. In doing so they have been able to keep oil companies out of their land and preserve their lifestyle and the two million acres of rainforest they steward so we can all breathe easier.

This is very exciting to me because I know we all have access to what the Achuar and indigenous people have—the ability to sense and know from a place beyond the thinking mind. Wouldn't it be wonderful if we could harness those abilities? Who knows? We might even begin to create success stories with the same impact as saving expanses of the rainforest.

WRIGHT

How does your work at One Global Bridge foster that kind of creativity and collaboration?

BERG

The underlying premise of all my work has been global unity. I have spent years creating a global network of practitioners who are on the cutting edge of consciousness and peace-building. There is a give-and-take and a generosity of spirit in this group. In the United States, my colleagues include people from The Institute of Noetic Sciences, The Pachamama Alliance, The Peace Alliance, and Jean Houston's Social Artistry program. In Brazil, I am closely associated with Unipaz (The University of Peace) and Globalnet, both associated with UNESCO. And last year I spent eight months living in Brussels, Belgium, building relationships with people in the Art of Hosting community, The Center for Human Emergence in the Netherlands, and the Hub Network of social entrepreneurs. These colleagues are doing great work in the fields of health care, the European Commission, as well as community and business ventures worldwide. Together we create unique events that combine our various talents in the arts, psychology, ancient wisdom, and deep collaborative communication practices.

The setting for this kind of work needs to be welcoming and safe because it requires becoming vulnerable and sharing from the heart, often sitting across from people who have differing viewpoints than our own. Sometimes there are long, uncomfortable silences or power struggles. This is just part of the process.

The way we do this is by creating a welcoming atmosphere filled with music, beautiful images, time spent in Nature and in concrete practices that allow people to go deep and wide to recognize their own expansive human capacities and inner resources. We provide plenty of time for integration and co-creation with the community of participants who gather.

At the Celebrate the Earth Conference I put on in Sedona, Arizona, participants came from Europe and all corners of the United States. We opened at an art gallery with musicians and food, of course. The weekend continued with music, art, and presentations that balanced offering various ways of accessing knowledge and time for deep conversation. A bond formed among the participants that was palpable. One international businessman said, "There is a real sense of community and love in this room!"

Everyone's favorite experience was being in Nature with two Native American elders who led us in prayers, ritual, story, and dance amid the magical red rocks of Sedona. Through ceremony they taught us to remember our interconnectedness with "all our relations." This is an important part of my teaching. I believe that once we remember our interconnectedness, everything else will fall into place. It is difficult to harm another person or the Earth when you remember you are closely related.

From this broadened perspective of our place in the world, we examined the truth of what is happening to our environment and talked about how we, individually and collectively, could make a difference. There were a lot of passionate conversations and action plans hatched that day and a lot of good friendships formed.

Wright

You say you're a cross-culturist. That's an intriguing title, what does it mean?

Berg

My own definition is someone who honors all cultures and knows the value of creating synergy among differing views. For years I defined culture as national identity, like the French or Brazilian culture. Then, after a transformational trip to Bali, Indonesia, I added the various spiritual and traditional values that make up the human experience to my definition. Later, my studies confirmed that my new definition had a basis in the findings of transpersonal psychology, the Human Potential Movement, and quantum physics.

It all started for me when my family and I moved to Tokyo in 1993. One day my husband came home and said, "How would you like to move to Japan?" I was unsure. I really wanted to live overseas. That had always been a dream. But now

I was in a master's program, we had two little boys, ages five and seven, a nice house and car, and friends in New Jersey. Why would I want to leave?

My husband's company sent the four of us to a five-day program in Boulder, Colorado, to help us make up our minds. We learned all about Japanese life, what culture shock is, and how to adjust to a new country with its unique customs, smells, lifestyle, and way of doing business. We even learned where we could shop and where the children could go to school. I was hooked. I loved the idea of moving to Japan after that and even more, I was determined to be a cross-cultural trainer myself.

I sought out opportunities in Tokyo to work in that field. I studied all the theories underlying the practice of cross-cultural communication, which was started by Peace Corps volunteers who wanted to really understand the values and beliefs of the people they lived with.

I designed and delivered programs to executives at Sony, NEC, Ricoh, and other Japanese companies sending employees overseas. When I returned to the United States I ran my own cross-cultural consulting firm in the Metro New York area and started International Friends, a women's organization that is still actively supporting women twelve years later. My colleagues and I delivered hundreds of programs on cross-cultural issues to international executives and their families in transition.

But before leaving Tokyo, after a five-year stay, I spent two weeks on the island of Bali, Indonesia, a trip that changed my whole view of what it means to be a cross-culturalist forever.

One day, my group was invited to a ceremony—a daily part of life in Bali. This was an auspicious ceremony to rid Adé, a little three-year-old, of his "naughtiness." As I sat in this beautiful home compound, with separate buildings set around a courtyard, I took in the smells of incense, the fragrance of the flower offerings, and the beauty of the young female dancers who performed for us with their glittering red and gold headdresses and sarongs.

Adé, it was said, was the reincarnation of his grandpa, who was a "dirty old man." Grandpa used to lift up women's skirts and Adé was already repeating this! The shamans came down from the mountains with water from nine rivers. They chanted and performed ceremonies while we all watched. The whole thing was becoming more and more surreal for me. I said to my friend Jean, "Oh come on, Jean. You can't be serious!"

And then it hit me. I looked around and thought to myself, "The people here are very happy. I really feel the peacefulness in the air here. Maybe there is something to this. Who says that Western science has all the answers?" "Why not? Who knows?" became an important "mantra" for me as a way to approach life.

Although I don't know what ultimately happened to Adé and if he is still lifting up women's skirts, I did realize it was imperative to include the spiritual dimension of life in my search to reach my highest potential so I too could live a peaceful and self-actualized life.

WRIGHT

What are some of the ideas you share with your international clients moving overseas that are valuable to those of us who find ourselves in the midst of transition?

BERG

There are many important ideas that we shared with our clients moving overseas. Right now, it is my perception that our human family and the Earth are going through a transition from one kind of world to another. Many of us are experiencing rapid changes in our lives. Our environments, relationships, religious and political organizations, finances, and businesses are changing. I know these changes are disconcerting for many people. I feel we are being given an opportunity to welcome new ways of being in the world and that the lessons I learned while living internationally certainly apply.

Here is the advice I gave to my international clients moving from one world to another:

- There is no right and wrong, only difference. Learn to appreciate people who are from other cultures and enjoy your time together.
- Find the synergy between divergent world views. In that case it was one culture to another. Now we can broaden the definition to mean finding synergy between logical and non-linear, feminine and masculine, right and left brain activities, ancient and modern wisdom. The list goes on.
- Look beneath the surface—like at the bottom of an iceberg—to really understand why someone is doing what he or she is doing. Then you can

more easily release judgment of "what" people are doing and approach them with a sense of understanding and compassion—maybe even admiration.

- Know that you will expand your sense of who you are, not diminish it in any way, by going out of your comfort zone and being adventurous. Try it—you might like it!
- There are ups and downs to transition. Like a hero's journey, expect to experience excitement, ambiguity, challenge, fear, and intrigue. Stay with it and get out and explore. Know you will get to the other side of the chaos. Be gentle with yourself at these times. The key is to find ways of taking care of yourself and those around you.

Wright

In your talks I know you suggest that people "be the bridge." Would you tell our readers more about that?

Berg

Albert Einstein suggested we widen our circle of compassion to embrace all living creatures and the whole of Nature in its beauty in order to move past our feelings of separateness and to experience our rightful place in the universe. This speaks to the ultimate bridge—the interconnection of all things. That invisible connection is the One Global Bridge I thought about when naming my company.

There is a prophecy that comes from the Indians of the Andes in South America that I believe speaks beautifully to building bridges between differing points of view. It's called the Eagle and the Condor prophecy.

The prophecy says that every five-hundred-year period is called a *pachacutic*. It was predicted that around the year 1500, the people from the Eagle world—the modern, logical, technological, mind-based world—would dominate the Condor people who represent the more spiritual, land-based, non-linear, heart-based world. As we know, in 1492 Christopher Columbus came to what is now the United States. Around the same time, the South American civilizations experienced domination by outside forces.

Now, during this new *pachacutic*, around the year 2000, the Eagle and Condor people have the opportunity to "remember" that they are each other and rejoin in a way that creates synergy between their two worlds. After developing excellence in their different domains of head and heart, they can come back and nourish each other and the world into a new possible future that works for all.

We are all a part of this prophecy. We can start by building bridges between the many aspects of ourselves. Integrating all our various parts on our path to wholeness is one of the most important ideas in psychology. Here are some of the many possibilities. You may or may not agree with all this but in any case, it is clear that we are very complicated beings. We have our personality, sub-personalities, archetypes, egos, past lives, our various roles of son, mother, grandpa, etc. We have our masculine and feminine nature, our logical and intuitive capacities. The mystics and ancient traditions would add that our guides, angels, and ancestors are part of us. We have our Higher Self and our little "self." We have our soul. We have our shadow and our light.

I know it's a lot, but remember, it doesn't have to be so hard. I choose to approach all this with a little bit of skepticism, light heartedness, and lots of humor. Why not? Who knows? You might as well have fun with it!

The journey of self-realization and integration is ongoing. It is surely a more difficult journey for me than moving to Tokyo. I believe, though, that it is the greatest gift we can give ourselves. So that is what keeps me going for the prize—a sense of feeling comfortable in my skin.

Wright

What else do you think people need today to be more successful in their personal and professional lives?

Berg

I think slowing down and learning to trust our intuitive voice that comes from a deeper level of understanding and true experience is of number one importance. I know it's not easy to step off the treadmill, much less listen to our bodies in new ways, but we really have to in order to save our health, the quality of our work, and our relationships.

Luckily, this is happening in many areas of the world. One organization I have worked with that is opening to the idea of "slowing down to speed up" is a global organization of young leaders called AIESEC. While still in college, these young people run an international global organization that arranges hundreds of cultural exchanges and conferences around the world. To say these young people are working hard is an understatement.

My colleagues and I from the Art of Hosting community were called in recently to some of the conferences to help shift the perception that going 24/7 is the most productive way of getting things done. We helped the participants—800 young people and alumni from 106 countries—self-organize parts of the conference. The room was abuzz with possibilities and commitments to create sustainable projects. Many participants told me they felt empowered and appreciated the opportunity to slow down and have real conversations. People are hungry for this, and it is actually so simple.

Wright

How do you find the courage to sustain yourself through your own challenges?

Berg

I feel the most courageous when I am really centered. There is a central point in my body where I feel calm and at peace. It's from that place I get a strong sense of knowing what to do in everyday situations or when the going gets tough. Some people use dance, yoga, tai chi, or other methods that help them cultivate that energy in themselves. I like using a chi gong exercise where I sweep energy up along my body, from above and below, send it out to others, centering in my belly and heart region. I was influenced by a practice I learned in Bali.

In the fields of Bali there is a shrine, a little temple that the farmers give offerings to throughout the day. It reminds them of their connection Man to Man, Man to Earth and Man to Spirit. I call these the "Three Points of Connection"—Earth, Humanity, and Universal Wisdom. This belief of being interconnected permeates the Balinese psyche. You can see it in the way they walk—barefoot on the earth, toes spread and gripping the ground, the women often balancing several baskets of fruits and sweets on their heads as they go to celebrations in the temples. They are connected. It is this invisible connection I find myself calling upon automatically in my most difficult situations.

On February 15, 2006, I received a phone call. My mother had committed suicide.

I gathered my senses and then my family. We drove from Washington, D.C., up to New Jersey to my mother's home. One of my sons joined us from Boston, and my sister and her fiancé from Philadelphia. My parents had lived in a beautiful home filled with luxurious things—a collection of antiques, and decorative items that were treasures. We had already heard from people, "Sorting this out is going to take time. Maybe two years. Don't rush." "Isn't this terrible! How could she do this?"

As my family stood together in the entry hall of my mother's home, I felt a surge of energy shoot down through my body and ground me into the earth. I said, with so much love in my heart, "We can do this in two months. I'm going to stay here. I'm going to commit myself to handling this." I chose to see past the conventional viewpoint or solutions people offered. I said, "I know she did this with as much love as possible. We will be okay."

It was at that moment when I realized a part of me was speaking that was coming from an inner strength, not from my head, but from my heart.

When I look back, I realize I was able to take that stand because of my practice of connecting to the "Three Points of Connection"—Earth, Humanity, and Universal Wisdom. In those difficult months, I went outside to ground myself with the Earth and trees when things got tough. I continually reached out to people for support. I kept expressing my gratitude for the many synchronicities and apparent miracles that occurred to help me accomplish what might have been an impossible task.

The house sold and the contents found their new owners within months. My sister and I are closer than ever and my sense of standing grounded in the middle of a storm now has a touchstone that I can turn to as more of life's inevitable challenges arise.

Wright

Will you give us an example of how you use that in your professional life?

Berg

Yes. It was the early days of owning my cross-cultural consulting firm. I always paid my consultants up front. I didn't wait for the payment to come three months later from the corporations. One day, after I had taken $10,000 out of my husband's and my joint savings he said, "We just can't keep going like this!" His option was that I would likely have to stop operations.

I was reading books like, *How Would Confucius Ask for a Raise?* and listening to my Deepak Chopra tapes at the time. Deepak told a story of the Maharishi putting on a peace conference. Someone asked, "Maharishi, where will all the money come from?" To which the Maharishi answered, "From wherever it is at the moment."

You know how sometimes you just "know" something is right? You totally trust a situation without any real knowledge of how things will turn out. Well, that is how I felt about this. I checked into that central core in my body. I felt strong. I trusted the money would come—just as the Maharishi did—because I was following my life purpose by bringing people together across cultures to help create a more harmonious world. And, as a bonus, my clients made more money because they were being culturally aware and making better business decisions. Of course, there was always a plan B in case money didn't show up, but I didn't have to go there.

I said to Michael, my husband, "Don't worry. I know the money will come." And three days later, honestly, I got a call from Lucent Technologies: "Lisa, we want you to put on ten programs. At $4,000 each, that is $40,000. And, we have to pay you up front because it is the end of the year and we have to spend this budgeted money in this current fiscal year."

Wright

That's pretty amazing. What role did passion play in discovering your life's purpose and how do you keep on track?

Berg

I believe our most difficult moments can be our best teachers. When I was a little girl, I was called "*broigus*," which means sullen in Yiddish. I was not happy, it's true. I just knew there was something wrong with the way I was being treated. Because I felt so unseen, I remember thinking to myself, "When I grow up I'm going to help people be the best they can be." The passion I felt to help people be happy so they didn't have to suffer as I did was a strong motivator.

When I think about why I do what I do, I see that the little phrase, "When I grow up I'm going to help people be the best they can be," drove me to spend years studying psychology and the many ways we can reach our human potential. There was a force asking me to transform my suffering into a worthy vocation. It was the future calling me forward in some way. I didn't always know where the future was leading but I trusted it would be okay.

I often felt as though I was going in and out of a chrysalis, transforming myself again and again to get this right. I knew I had to let go of the deep sorrow and grief associated with childhood wounds in order to have the energy to step into my life's purpose. Those heavy emotions were getting in the way. It also felt as though I was carrying the pain of the whole Jewish race on me at one point. Who knows? I might have been! Eckhart Tolle calls that the pain body—part of the energetic field.

There came a time when I knew I had to release all that. It wasn't mine to carry; it was making me sick and it was interfering in my relationships. I really wanted to live life fully and enjoy each moment. I did a lot of work forgiving myself and others and learning to be gentle. I can be my own worst critic! So now I am able to be much more engaged on my path of helping others because even when sad emotions come up (and they do, of course) I am better able to handle them and move on to enjoy life.

Wright

What are key points you would like to share with our readers to help them discover their inner strength?

Berg

I think it is important to note that we all have the ability to reach our potential to experience a higher state of consciousness and self-awareness. Clearly, many of us have been through experiences that have hampered us in the past. But we do have a choice now. We can choose joy or sorrow, confusion or clarity, fear or love, courage or resignation. Being courageous doesn't always mean it is easy. It means we are alive and willing to engage in life in a way that many are not ready to assume.

The Hopi Indians of North America have a prophecy that gives us important guidelines for finding our strength and keeping a broad perspective in difficult times. You can find the whole prophecy on my Web site, www.OneGlobalBridge.com. The key points from the Hopi prophecy that I would like to leave you with are:

> ". . . this is the 11th hour. . . .
> There are those who will be afraid.
> (but) this can be a good time!
>
> It is time to speak your Truth.
> Create your community.
> Be good to each other.
> And do not look outside of yourself for the leader. . . .
>
> The time of the lone wolf is over.
> Gather yourselves!
> Banish the word struggle from your attitude and your vocabulary. . . .
> All that we do must now be done in a sacred manner and in celebration.
> We are the ones we've been waiting for."

I know we can do this. When we see life from the broad perspective of an open heart and a future that is calling us forward, anything is possible.

And remember, "Why not? Who knows?" can be a valuable motto.

WRIGHT

As difficult as it might be for some people, the attitude of having a broad perspective and believing the future is calling us forward in times of stress sounds liberating to me.

BERG

Yes, it is, David

WRIGHT

Well, what great conversation, Lisa. I really appreciate all the time you've spent with me this afternoon answering these questions. You've given me a lot to think about and I'm sure our readers will have a lot to think about too.

BERG

Thank you so much, David. I enjoyed speaking with you.

ABOUT THE AUTHOR

LISA BERG IS PRESIDENT of One Global Bridge, a cross-cultural and human potential consulting firm. Lisa is a transformational speaker whose topics include "The Nature of Leadership for Transformational Times" and "Ancient Wisdom for Modern Times: Co-Creating Our Future." She is an inspirational singer and global networker. Lisa co-creates innovative, multi-disciplinary events for leaders who are ready to engage in evolutionary practices for our time. Lisa has lived and now works internationally. She has a master's degree in Transpersonal Psychology. She founded International Friends, a vibrant organization that facilitates transition for international women.

LISA BERG

501 Rio Grande Avenue, Suite #J6
Santa Fe, NM 87501
505.603.7366
Lisa@OneGlobalBridge.com
www.OneGlobalBridge.com

AN INTERVIEW WITH...

DR. STEPHEN COVEY

A VALUES-BASED APPROACH

DAVID WRIGHT (WRIGHT)

We're talking today with Dr. Stephen R. Covey, cofounder and vice-chairman of Franklin Covey Company, the largest management company and leadership development organization in the world. Dr. Covey is perhaps best known as author of *The 7 Habits of Highly Effective People,* which is ranked as a number one best-seller by the *New York Times*, having sold more than fourteen million copies in thirty-eight languages throughout the world. Dr. Covey is an internationally respected leadership authority, family expert, teacher, and organizational consultant. He has made teaching principle-centered living and principle-centered leadership his life's work. Dr. Covey is the recipient of the Thomas More College Medallion for Continuing Service to Humanity and has been awarded four honorary doctorate degrees. Other awards given Dr. Covey include the Sikh's 1989 International Man of Peace award, the 1994 International

Entrepreneur of the Year award, *Inc.* magazine's Services Entrepreneur of the Year award, and in 1996 the National Entrepreneur of the Year Lifetime Achievement award for Entrepreneurial leadership. He has also been recognized as one of *Time* magazine's twenty-five most influential Americans and one of *Sales and Marketing Management's* top twenty-five power brokers. As the father of nine and grandfather of forty-four, Dr. Covey received the 2003 National Fatherhood Award, which he says is the most meaningful award he has ever received. Dr. Covey earned his undergraduate degree from the University of Utah, his MBA from Harvard, and completed his doctorate at Brigham Young University. While at Brigham Young he served as assistant to the President and was also a professor of Business Management and Organizational Behavior.

Dr. Covey, welcome to *Discover Your Inner Strength.*

DR. STEPHEN COVEY (COVEY)

Thank you.

WRIGHT

Dr. Covey, most companies make decisions and filter them down through their organization. You, however, state that no company can succeed until individuals within it succeed. Are the goals of the company the result of the combined goals of the individuals?

COVEY

Absolutely—if people aren't on the same page, they're going to be pulling in different directions. To teach this concept, I frequently ask large audiences to close their eyes and point north, and then to keep pointing and open their eyes. They find themselves pointing all over the place. I say to them, "Tomorrow morning if you want a similar experience, ask the first ten people you meet in your organization what the purpose of your organization is and you'll find it's a very similar experience. They'll point all over the place." When people have a different sense of purpose and values, every decision that is made from then on is governed by those. There's no question that this is one of the fundamental causes of misalignment, low trust, interpersonal conflict, interdepartmental rivalry, people operating on personal agendas, and so forth.

WRIGHT

Is that primarily a result of an inability to communicate from the top?

COVEY

That's one aspect, but I think it's more fundamental. There's an inability to involve people—an unwillingness. Leaders may communicate what their mission and their strategy is, but that doesn't mean there's any emotional connection to it. Mission statements that are rushed and then announced are soon forgotten. They become nothing more than just a bunch of platitudes on the wall that mean essentially nothing and even create a source of cynicism and a sense of hypocrisy inside the culture of an organization.

WRIGHT

How do companies ensure survival and prosperity in these tumultuous times of technological advances, mergers, downsizing, and change?

COVEY

I think that it takes a lot of high trust in a culture that has something that doesn't change—principles—at its core. There are principles that people agree upon that are valued. It gives a sense of stability. Then you have the power to adapt and be flexible when you experience these kinds of disruptive new economic models or technologies that come in and sideswipe you. You don't know how to handle them unless you have something you can depend upon.

If people have not agreed to a common set of principles that guide them and a common purpose, then they get their security from the outside and they tend to freeze the structure, systems, and processes inside and they cease becoming adaptable. They don't change with the changing realities of the new marketplace out there and gradually they become obsolete.

WRIGHT

I was interested in one portion of your book, *The 7 Habits of Highly Effective People,* where you talk about behaviors. How does an individual go about the process of replacing ineffective behaviors with effective ones?

COVEY

I think that for most people it usually requires a crisis that humbles them to become aware of their ineffective behaviors. If there's not a crisis the tendency is to perpetuate those behaviors and not change.

You don't have to wait until the marketplace creates the crisis for you. Have everyone accountable on a 360-degree basis to everyone else they interact with—with feedback either formal or informal—where they are getting data as to what's happening. They will then start to realize that the consequences of their ineffective behavior require them to be humble enough to look at that behavior and to adopt new, more effective ways of doing things.

Sometimes people can be stirred up to this if you just appeal to their conscience—to their inward sense of what is right and wrong. A lot of people sometimes know inwardly they're doing wrong, but the culture doesn't necessarily discourage them from continuing that. They either need feedback from people or they need feedback from the marketplace or they need feedback from their conscience. Then they can begin to develop a step-by-step process of replacing old habits with new, better habits.

WRIGHT

It's almost like saying, "Let's make all the mistakes in the laboratory before we put this thing in the air."

COVEY

Right; and I also think what is necessary is a paradigm shift, which is analogous to having a correct map, say of a city or of a country. If people have an inaccurate paradigm of life, of other people, and of themselves it really doesn't make much difference what their behavior or habits or attitudes are. What they need is a correct paradigm—a correct map—that describes what's going on.

For instance, in the Middle Ages they used to heal people through bloodletting. It wasn't until Samuel Weiss and Pasteur and other empirical scientists discovered the germ theory that they realized for the first time they weren't dealing with the real issue. They realized why women preferred to use midwives who washed rather than doctors who didn't wash. They gradually got a new paradigm. Once you've got a new paradigm then your behavior and your attitude flow directly from it. If you have a bad paradigm or a bad map, let's say of a city, there's no way, no matter what your behavior or your habits or your attitudes are—how positive they are—you'll never be able to find the location you're looking for. This is why I believe that to change paradigms is far more fundamental than to work on attitude and behavior.

WRIGHT

One of your seven habits of highly effective people is to "begin with the end in mind." If circumstances change and hardships or miscalculations occur, how does one view the end with clarity?

COVEY

Many people think to begin with the end in mind means that you have some fixed definition of a goal that's accomplished and if changes come about you're not going to adapt to them. Instead, the "end in mind" you begin with is that you are going to create a flexible culture of high trust so that no matter what comes along you are going to do whatever it takes to accommodate that new change or that new reality and maintain a culture of high performance and high trust. You're talking more in terms of values and overall purposes that don't change, rather than specific strategies or programs that will have to change to accommodate the changing realities in the marketplace.

WRIGHT

In this time of mistrust among people, corporations, and nations, for that matter, how do we create high levels of trust?

COVEY

That's a great question and it's complicated because there are so many elements that go into the creating of a culture of trust. Obviously the most fundamental one is just to have trustworthy people. But that is not sufficient because what if the organization itself is misaligned?

For instance, what if you say you value cooperation but you really reward people for internal competition? Then you have a systemic or a structure problem that creates low trust inside the culture even though the people themselves are trustworthy. This is one of the insights of Edward Demming and the work he did. That's why he said that most problems are not personal—

they're systemic. They're common caused. That's why you have to work on structure, systems, and processes to make sure that they institutionalize principle-centered values. Otherwise you could have good people with bad systems and you'll get bad results.

When it comes to developing interpersonal trust between people, it is made up of many, many elements such as taking the time to listen to other people, to understand them, and to see what is important to them. What we think is important to another may only be important to us, not to another. It takes empathy. You have to make and keep promises to them. You have to treat people with kindness and courtesy. You have to be completely honest and open. You have to live up to your commitments. You can't betray people behind their back. You can't badmouth them behind their back and sweet-talk them to their face. That will send out vibes of hypocrisy and it will be detected.

You have to learn to apologize when you make mistakes, to admit mistakes, and to also get feedback going in every direction as much as possible. It doesn't necessarily require formal forums—it requires trust between people who will be open with each other and give each other feedback.

WRIGHT

My mother told me to do a lot of what you're saying now, but it seems that when I got in business I simply forgot.

COVEY

Sometimes we forget, but sometimes culture doesn't nurture it. That's why I say unless you work with the institutionalizing—that means formalizing into structure, systems, and processing the values—you will not have a nurturing culture. You have to constantly work on that.

This is one of the big mistakes organizations make. They think trust is simply a function of being honest. That's only one small aspect. It's an important aspect, obviously, but there are so many other elements that go into the creation of a high-trust culture.

WRIGHT

"Seek first to understand then to be understood" is another of your seven habits. Do you find that people try to communicate without really understanding what other people want?

COVEY

Absolutely. The tendency is to project out of our own autobiography—our own life, our own value system—onto other people, thinking we know what they want. So we don't really listen to them. We pretend to listen, but we really don't listen from within their frame of reference. We listen from within our own frame of reference and we're really preparing our reply rather than seeking to understand. This is a very common thing. In fact, very few people have had any training in seriously listening. They're trained in how to read, write, and speak, but not to listen.

Reading, writing, speaking, and listening are the four modes of communication and they represent about two-thirds to three-fourths of our waking hours. About half of that time is spent listening, but it's the one skill people have not been trained in. People have had all this training in the other forms of communication. In a large audience of 1,000 people you wouldn't have more than twenty people who have had more than two weeks of training in listening. Listening is more than a skill or technique; you must listen within another's frame of reference. It takes tremendous courage to listen because you're at risk when you listen. You don't know what's going to happen; you're vulnerable.

WRIGHT

Sales gurus always tell me that the number one skill in selling is listening.

COVEY

Yes—listening from within the customer's frame of reference. That is so true. You can see that it takes some security to do that because you don't know what's going to happen.

WRIGHT

With this book we're trying to encourage people to be better, to live better, and be more fulfilled by listening to the examples of our guest authors. Is there anything or anyone in your life that has made a difference for you and helped you to become a better person?

COVEY

I think the most influential people in my life have been my parents. I think that what they modeled was not to make comparisons and harbor jealousy or to seek recognition. They were humble people.

I remember one time when my mother and I were going up in an elevator and the most prominent person in the state was also in the elevator. She knew him, but she spent her time talking to the elevator operator. I was just a little kid and I was so awed by the famous person. I said to her, "Why didn't you talk to the important person?" She said, "I was. I had never met him."

My parents were really humble, modest people who were focused on service and other people rather than on themselves. I think they were very inspiring models to me.

WRIGHT

In almost every research paper I've ever read, those who write about people who have influenced their lives include three teachers in their top-five picks. My seventh-grade English teacher was the greatest teacher I ever had and she influenced me to no end.

COVEY

Would it be correct to say that she saw in you probably some qualities of greatness you didn't even see in yourself?

WRIGHT

Absolutely.

COVEY

That's been my general experience—the key aspect of a mentor or a teacher is someone who sees in you potential that you don't even see in yourself. Those teachers/mentors treat you accordingly and eventually you come to see it in yourself. That's my definition of leadership or influence—communicating people's worth and potential so clearly that they are inspired to see it in themselves.

Wright

Most of my teachers treated me as a student, but she treated me with much more respect than that. As a matter of fact, she called me Mr. Wright, and I was in the seventh grade at the time. I'd never been addressed by anything but a nickname. I stood a little taller; she just made a tremendous difference.

Do you think there are other characteristics that mentors seem to have in common?

Covey

I think they are first of all good examples in their own personal lives. Their personal lives and their family lives are not all messed up—they come from a base of good character. They also are usually very confident and they take the time to do what your teacher did to you—to treat you with uncommon respect and courtesy.

They also, I think, explicitly teach principles rather than practices so that rules don't take the place of human judgment. You gradually come to have faith in your own judgment in making decisions because of the affirmation of such a mentor. Good mentors care about you—you can feel the sincerity of their caring. It's like the expression, "I don't care how much you know until I know how much you care."

Wright

Most people are fascinated with the new television shows about being a survivor. What has been the greatest comeback that you've made from adversity in your career or your life?

Covey

When I was in grade school I experienced a disease in my legs. It caused me to use crutches for a while. I tried to get off them fast and get back. The disease wasn't corrected yet so I went back on crutches for another year. The disease went to the other leg and I went on for another year. It essentially took me out of my favorite thing—athletics—and it took me more into being a student. So that was a life-defining experience, which at the time seemed very negative, but has proven to be the basis on which I've focused my life—being more of a learner.

WRIGHT

Principle-centered learning is basically what you do that's different from anybody I've read or listened to.

COVEY

The concept is embodied in the Far Eastern expression, "Give a man a fish, you feed him for the day; teach him how to fish, you feed him for a lifetime." When you teach principles that are universal and timeless, they don't belong to just any one person's religion or to a particular culture or geography. They seem to be timeless and universal like the ones we've been talking about here: trustworthiness, honesty, caring, service, growth, and development. These are universal principles. If you focus on these things, then little by little people become independent of you and then they start to believe in themselves and their own judgment becomes better. You don't need as many rules. You don't need as much bureaucracy and as many controls and you can empower people.

The problem in most business operations today—and not just business but non-business—is that they're using the industrial model in an information age. Arnold Toynbee, the great historian, said, "You can pretty well summarize all of history in four words: nothing fails like success." The industrial model was based on the asset of the machine. The information model is based on the asset of the person—the knowledge worker. It's an altogether different model. But the machine model was the main asset of the twentieth century. It enabled productivity to increase fifty times. The new asset is intellectual and social capital—the qualities of people and the quality of the relationship they have with each other. Like Toynbee said, "Nothing fails like success." The industrial model does not work in an information age. It requires a focus on the new wealth, not capital and material things.

A good illustration that demonstrates how much we were into the industrial model, and still are, is to notice where people are on the balance sheet. They're not found there. Machines are found there. Machines become investments. People are on the profit-and-loss statement and people are expenses. Think of that—if that isn't bloodletting.

WRIGHT

It sure is.

When you consider the choices you've made down through the years, has faith played an important role in your life?

COVEY

It has played an extremely important role. I believe deeply that we should put principles at the center of our lives, but I believe that God is the source of those principles. I did not invent them. I get credit sometimes for some of the Seven Habits material and some of the other things I've done, but it's really all based on principles that have been given by God to all of His children from the beginning of time. You'll find that you can teach these same principles from the sacred texts and the wisdom literature of almost any tradition. I think the ultimate source of that is God and that is one thing you can absolutely depend upon—"in God we trust."

WRIGHT

If you could have a platform and tell our audience something you feel would help them or encourage them, what would you say?

COVEY

I think I would say to put God at the center of your life and then prioritize your family. No one on their deathbed ever wished they had spent more time at the office.

WRIGHT

That's right. We have come down to the end of our program and I know you're a busy person. I could talk with you all day, Dr. Covey.

COVEY

It's good to talk with you as well and to be a part of this program. It looks like an excellent one that you've got going on here.

WRIGHT

Thank you.

We have been talking today with Dr. Stephen R. Covey, cofounder and vice-chairman of Franklin Covey Company. He's also the author of *The 7 Habits of Highly Effective People,* which has been ranked as a number one bestseller by the *New York Times*, selling more than fourteen million copies in thirty-eight languages.

Dr. Covey, thank you so much for being with us today.

COVEY

Thank you for the honor of participating.

ABOUT THE AUTHOR

STEPHEN R. COVEY WAS RECOGNIZED IN 1996 as one of *Time* magazine's twenty-five most influential Americans and one of *Sales and Marketing Management's* top twenty-five power brokers. Dr. Covey is the author of several acclaimed books, including the international bestseller, *The 7 Habits of Highly Effective People*, named the number one Most Influential Business Book of the Twentieth Century, and other best sellers that include *First Things First*, *Principle-Centered Leadership*, (with sales exceeding one million) and *The 7 Habits of Highly Effective Families.*

Dr. Covey earned his undergraduate degree from the University of Utah, his MBA from Harvard, and completed his doctorate at Brigham Young University. While at Brigham Young University, he served as assistant to the President and was also a professor of Business Management and Organizational Behavior. He received the National Fatherhood Award in 2003, which, as the father of nine and grandfather of forty-four, he says is the most meaningful award he has ever received.

Dr. Covey currently serves on the board of directors for the Points of Light Foundation. Based in Washington, D.C., the Foundation, through its partnership with the Volunteer Center National Network, engages and mobilizes millions of volunteers from all walks of life—businesses, nonprofits, faith-based organizations, low-income communities, families, youth, and older adults—to help solve serious social problems in thousands of communities.

DR. STEPHEN R. COVEY
www.stephencovey.com

Chapter 8

An interview with...

Christina Parker & Donny Henderson

Developing A Lifestyle Of Leadership

David Wright (Wright)

Today, we're talking with Christina Parker and Donny Henderson, co-founders of The Leadership Movement. The Leadership Movement is a leadership development company dedicated to developing people of influence and integrity. Through extensive research and years of experience, Parker and Henderson have designed a program that will unleash the power and potential of any organization or individual. Combining dynamic programming and resources, along with revolutionary keynote presentations, this "Dynamic Duo" is helping shape leaders of significance.

The Leadership Movement specializes in cultivating leaders of confidence who are committed not only to leading, but to creating a movement of leadership through the conscious development of others.

Christina and Donny, welcome to *Discovering Your Inner Strength.*

Why is this idea of inner strength so important to The Leadership Movement?

CHRISTINA PARKER (PARKER)

Thanks for letting us share. For us, everything comes back to leadership. We have dedicated our lives and our careers to helping uncover the passion and power that lies within the heart of every leader.

Identifying and accessing inner strength is the crucial first step on the journey toward effective leadership.

WRIGHT

As experts in leadership, will you tell our readers where leadership intersects with discovering one's inner strength?

DONNY HENDERSON (HENDERSON)

Sure. First let's discuss "leadership" and what it means to be a leader. Let's start by asking a few questions.

So what is leadership, exactly? I mean, what are the qualities that define a leader? These are questions that have to be answered before you begin your quest for influence or success. Over the years I have heard many fairly good answers to these questions, but none that really satisfied me.

Some have said that a leader is "the boss" or someone with a title—someone who has climbed the ladder of success and has gained respect because of his or her extensive experience in a particular field. Others have said a leader is someone who is in charge—a person in a position of authority and a boss people are required to follow.

Those answers are all, at least partially, true, but I believe they are incomplete. It is true that sometimes a leader is a boss, and many leaders do have significant experience in a particular field—*but not always.* And it is true that leaders are often in charge, and many do rise to positions of authority and acclaim—*but not always.*

Let me illustrate. Have you ever watched a Little League baseball game or any youth athletic event? There is usually a bunch of young people doing their best to perform while screaming parents in the stands hope and pray that their child will score the winning run or sink the winning basket. In those environments, often one child will somehow stand out. You've seen it—this kid just seems to have a natural ability to bring the team together or to motivate them. He or she is the same age as the others so the kid doesn't necessarily have more experience than the others. He or she has no title or authority to speak of, but that child is a leader.

Likewise, many of us have had a boss with little or no experience. This person might be someone who may have had a title or was in a position of authority, but really had no business being in charge. That doesn't sound like much of a leader. It can be infuriating, right?

So, you have to ask yourself again: what are the indefinable qualities that make a leader?

Christina and I asked this question of several respected leaders from a variety of fields. They shared some amazing stories and insights about leadership. There were a couple of common threads that ran through all of their stories. The first thing we noticed was that they were all *dedicated to the development of the people around them.* Even more striking was that each of their stories had a *unique beginning*—some defining moment that seemed to fuel and fill them. They had all discovered this source of *inner strength.* Many of them called it their dream.

WRIGHT

Okay, I'm intrigued now. Tell me more about *the dream.*

HENDERSON

Well, the dream is just the starting point. See, I strongly believe that *discovering your inner strength* is the easy part. In fact, it comes quite instinctively to us.

Remember when you started out in life. When you were a child you had big dreams. Some kids wanted to be super heroes or policemen. Others wanted to be President of the United States or maybe rock stars. You had your dream and you were determined that it would come true. Nothing was impossible. You believed you were destined to change the world or maybe even save it.

So what happened? I mean, you spent all this time working and saving and fighting and pushing, only to find yourself right back where you started. Reality replaced your dreams and somehow you got lost in your life instead of living it.

Reality has a way of making you lose sight of your dreams. I don't mean that you give up on them, but maybe you just put them aside for a bit. We've all said it: "Someday I'll make time for . . ." or "someday I'll work on . . ." And the reality, my friend, is that unless we make a conscious effort to change course, that "someday" never comes.

Sounds bleak doesn't it? Well, it is, in a way, but there is good news. See, I think the answer is in the journey.

You have to view your life, your job, and your dreams in the same way you did when you were a child. Forget the skeptics and dream! Sounds tricky, right? It is actually quite simple. Here it is: focus on the dreams of the people around you. When you look for opportunities to bring out the hidden best in someone, you will see that your life is profoundly better. It is in this way of life or in this journey that you find strength and passion and joy, as you are able to inspire big dreams in someone else. Remember how good it felt as a child when a teacher or parent spoke words of affirmation to you? Remember when someone encouraged your dream? Pretty good, right?

So, what are the rewards? What are the results of living this kind of life? Well, I believe that when this happens, everyone wins. You win—your life is made richer in every way. Those countless individuals who have been touched by the investments you have made are better for it, and the world benefits from one more life lived gracefully. And all of this because you simply shifted your focus to others.

Finally (and this is my favorite one), you will leave a legacy. History will remember you.

Wright

I love it! Now put skin on it. In other words, can you share a specific instance in which these principles proved to be effective?

Parker

In our travels, Donny and I have talked to people from all walks of life who have shared stories of how lifestyle leadership has profoundly affected them. We hear success stories all the time, as I am sure you do. Let me share one that is close to my heart. It is my story.

My dream has always been to be a business owner—someone who is successful and has the respect of the people around me. I call it my "EF Hutton dream." You've probably heard the firm's advertising slogan: "When EF Hutton talks, people listen."

When I was twenty-nine I started my second business. One of my clients, Donna, owned a Bruster's Real Ice Cream franchise. One day after a consulting session she took me next door to Bruster's for some ice cream. As I walked up to the building I could smell the vanilla gently floating through the air from the waffle cones that they were making inside. I remember feeling nostalgic for the times when I used to go get ice cream with my grandparents when I was a little girl.

When I took my first bite of the ice cream, I was amazed at the richness of the flavor and the perfectly broken Oreos that were still crisp because they were so fresh. That, along with the crisp waffle cone, seemed like the closest thing to heaven that I had ever experienced. When Donna walked up to the building she could barely make it to the window because of all of the customers stopping her to talk to her as they saw her Bruster's logo on her shirt. I left that day thinking, "Wow! This is magical!"

I immediately contacted Bruce, the founder, and attended one of his contagiously energetic "Taste of Bruster's" seminars. I was approved for a franchise by Bruce and within two weeks approved for an SBA loan. Two weeks later, Donna approached me about buying their store. Within five weeks from the day that Donna introduced me to Bruster's, I was a franchisee.

I thought that I knew what I needed to know about leadership and had no reservations about the success that I was sure to enjoy. I have to admit that from a ROI perspective, I initially purchased the concept for the real estate investment. Frankly, I thought it would be like an ATM machine—I'd be able to drop in, come back in ten years, and pull out some money.

About six months into the business, my reality hit. I found a lump in my right breast. It was a small lump so I didn't really think much of it, but I went to the doctor to be on the safe side. The doctor put me in surgery the very next day.

On the day following my surgery, I found myself sitting in the doctor's office with my husband and our two small children as we listened to the doctor tell us that I had cancer and it was terminal.

So many thoughts were racing through my mind: How would my family cope without me? Would my husband be able to raise our children on his own? Would my boys even understand? What would happen to the business? Can my family survive this? My dreams were being destroyed by this terrifying reality.

I know that many people have a reality that seeks to destroy their dreams. As I said before, we hear the stories every day. For some people it is the loss of a loved one or a painful childhood or some other tragic circumstance or situation. For me it was cancer.

It was clear that I needed to begin to invest in the people close to me if my family and our business were going to make it. I had to focus my physical and emotional energy on my family and my own survival, not on the business. I was so weak I couldn't even get out of bed. It was a helpless feeling. It was time to start investing in leadership for the store, or my dream would crumble before my eyes.

In order to do this, I was going to have to learn a lot about leadership—and fast. The saying that "a company cannot grow without until its leaders grow within" is so true. Weak leaders make weak organizations and strong leaders make strong organizations. Everything really does rise and fall on leadership.

I needed my burden to be lightened and I needed someone to help carry my vision and enlarge it. Leaders who only have followers around them will be called upon to continually draw on their own resources to get things done. Without other leaders to help carry the load, a leader will become fatigued and burned-out. This is what was happening to my business and to me. This is when I learned my first real lesson about leadership. Not the kind of leadership that seeks followers, but the kind of leadership that inspires others to stand beside you so that one day you can step back as they step forward. This is what I call a movement of leaders.

In order to have this unique movement of leaders, it is not enough for the people around you to simply believe in your vision. They have to be passionate about it and make it their own. The only way that this will happen is when you take the time to consciously develop and invest in those around you, not just in the areas that the yearly review form says they must develop, but in their personal lives as well. Until people are well balanced personally, they will never operate to their full potential professionally. This is where my journey of learning started.

WRIGHT

What did you learn?

PARKER

More than I could have imagined. I had hired a young man named Oscar as a manager, thinking that he would be a great leader and that he would be able to help propel the business forward. I knew I would have to invest in Oscar if he was to be the kind of leader who could create a movement of people. That is the kind of leader I needed him to be. It became clear that it would be crucial to the survival of the business.

Oscar's development is very interesting. Oscar is smart and he's a good student when he really puts his mind to it. He had often been put in charge of activities he was involved in, and he was even the business manager of his own band. But despite his good qualities, he was not a leader—he was really more of a manager.

Managers tend to be very dogmatic. They are very much into systems. Oscar wasn't naturally drawn to people. I mean, he was a great guy and friendly, but he could easily walk through a crowd of people without stopping to connect with anyone. I quickly realized that if I did not take the time to help develop Oscar, my profits and my investment would be yet another casualty in this battle of my life.

When you have potential leaders who think like managers, your goal should be to help them develop better relational skills and to change their pattern of thinking. When you begin to take time to teach managers how to be leaders, you will often have to stop what you are doing to walk them through your thought process. You will have to try to explain why you are doing what you are doing. This can be time-consuming, tedious, and sometimes downright frustrating. It is crucial that you consistently show them the big picture until they get it for themselves. If done correctly and with the right spirit, they will get it.

This was something I had not yet done for Oscar. I had not taken the time to identify the opportunities he needed to grow into the leader that he was destined to be.

I use a simple acronym of the word "BEST" to outline the steps I needed to follow in Oscar's development. These are the same steps any potential leader needs to take. The "BEST" leaders understand that they must:

B—Believe: Be inspired to invest in others with the greatest gift of all—believing in them. When you believe in yourself and others it releases their potential to harness success.

E—Empower: Learn how to empower others to overcome obstacles in order to enhance their connection to life and increase productivity.

S—Share: Rediscover ways to share yourself with others. The human connection is the secret to lifetime triumphs. These moments of connection and compassion are the brush strokes on the canvas of life.

T—Teach: Challenge yourself to think about what your legacy will be. Taking the time to teach those around you as well as investing in yourself ensures your legacy.

In order to create the right opportunities, we must look at the potential leaders around us and ask, "What does this person need in order to grow?" If we don't fit the opportunity to the potential leader, we may find ourselves in the position of offering things that our people don't need, or worse yet, expecting results that we have not prepared our people to achieve. When you get it right, you will find that you are helping people to achieve their dreams while enhancing your own as well.

WRIGHT

Did it work?

PARKER

You bet it did. As I began to apply these principles to my own life and make efforts to develop Oscar, we began to notice some real positive changes in not only the business, but also in the lives of our employees, management, and even our customers. It didn't happen overnight, but it certainly began to happen and continues today. Our business is thriving and we are seeing substantial growth in both our bottom line and in our ability to serve our community.

The rewards of watching someone grow, learn, and develop right before your eyes can be quite valuable. Knowing that you have a hand in it is priceless.

The most fascinating thing about Oscar's story is that the principles proved to have a life of their own. This idea of Lifestyle Leadership is contagious. Oscar, now a successful business leader in our local community, is inspiring an entire generation of young leaders. He has applied these principles in his own life and we have been thrilled to see him Believing, Empowering, Sharing, and Teaching young people on the south side of Atlanta.

WRIGHT

How were you able to focus on Oscar or even think about your business during such a dark and difficult time in your life?

PARKER

Well, the truth is that Oscar became a "project" that was able to distract me from some of the pain. It was one of the many outlets that gave me something to fight for. God knew what He was doing all along.

The lessons I learned while on my back in a hospital bed and while undergoing chemotherapy are the lessons that have stayed with me and have led me to want to create a movement of leaders. These are just a few of the lessons that we try to teach through The Leadership Movement. As it turns out, cancer was the greatest gift I ever received.

WRIGHT

A "gift"?

PARKER

Absolutely. I was blessed with the opportunity to learn and understand "the meaning of life" at the tender age of thirty! Some people learn it much later in life. Some, sadly, never learn it. I was blessed to have experienced the beauty of a life lived for others at a fairly young age. Of course, I would be lying if I said that the journey was easy. The truth is—if I can be candid—it sucked. It was the hardest thing I have ever experienced. But, it was, without a doubt, a gift.

See, life and leadership are about others. I am glad I learned this lesson.

WRIGHT

What would you say to the people who have doubts about whether or not they possess the ability to make these kinds of changes in their lives?

HENDERSON

I would say, "I get it." I probably shouldn't share this, but I am not naturally compassionate. My default position has never been a sympathetic one. That is not to say that I am mean or disconnected from the world or the people around me, but I have never been one of those people who paid much attention to things outside of my little world. I wasn't fully aware of all the opportunities I was missing. I guess you could say I was a bit like Oscar in that I would probably be the guy who walked through the crowd of people before stopping to connect with someone. If I knew of an issue in someone's life, I would certainly take some time to help, but it wasn't yet a lifestyle. I can totally relate to people who feel that this idea of "living a life for others" might not come naturally to them. In fact, I don't think it comes naturally to most of us.

What I learned over time is that when I made conscious decisions to make investments in others, it began to make sense. I remember going out of my way to put myself in situations that I knew would require this kind of effort. At first it was awkward and a bit uncomfortable, but to my surprise, it became a source of strength and inspiration. Before long, I began to look for opportunities to serve or to encourage. I found that it was not only easy, but rewarding as well. So, my first recommendation to someone would be to find a way to contribute. There are plenty of opportunities in every community.

The other thing I learned is that leadership—real leadership—is not just for CEOs and Presidents. Anyone can do this. Leadership is about inspiring and encouraging others. It is pretty tough to inspire or encourage someone you know nothing about. Look for opportunities to change someone's life. Get to know the people in your circle of influence and then find ways to expand the circle. You will be surprised how quickly it becomes a way of life.

WRIGHT

Now that I understand your philosophy, would you describe the experience? Or more directly, what should someone expect from an encounter with The Leadership Movement?

PARKER

The Leadership Movement has several presentation formats available, including keynote style presentations, small group training, and one-on-one consultations. We also welcome the opportunity to create a custom presentation designed to meet the unique needs of any organization.

Participants will be challenged and renewed as they participate in a high-energy event that is designed to *establish foundational principles* that are crucial to success in today's corporate world. With the inclusion of music, humor, and state-of-the-art multimedia, The Leadership Movement event is a *virtual feast for the senses.* Participants are not only motivated, but *inspired to set and reach goals,* and to make positive changes in their lives and in their world. Our program will not only *outline and define truths* that can lead to success in every area of life, but it will also provide the *practical tools* to enhance personal leadership skills and breathe new life into any organization.

All of The Leadership Movement events feature *One Night Only,* the short film series that takes viewers on an inspirational journey through the eyes of an unlikely leader who discovers the lasting rewards of investing in others. Experience lifestyle leadership in this captivating presentation that will not only enhance your personal leadership skills, but will also breathe new life into your organization.

Wright

Where can our readers learn more about you and what The Leadership Movement has to offer?

Henderson

We encourage people to visit our Web site: www.TheLeadershipMovement.com for more information about The Leadership Movement or to obtain information about scheduling an event. Visitors to our site can view our official demo video, read testimonials, preview the short film series, *One Night Only,* or check out "The Leadership Ledger," the official blog of The Leadership Movement. We would also encourage everyone who is interested in becoming a more effective leader to sign up for our free e-mail newsletter to receive updates and insights from our team.

Wright

Do you have any final thoughts?

HENDERSON

Discovering your inner strengths is vitally important to the life of a leader, but it is not some secret treasure that is waiting at the end of a long and difficult journey. It is inside all of you. Reconnect with your dreams. And remember, in the end it is up to you. You can continue to live in mediocrity (the reality is that most people do) or you can begin to dream those big dreams again. Take a bold step on your journey and experience the rewards of a life well-lived.

I encourage you to take the step. Your journey begins now!

ABOUT THE AUTHORS

AUTHOR AND SPEAKER, CHRISTINA PARKER, is a Senior Vice President of a national company, founder and CEO of a leading professional development organization, owner of a thriving franchise business, and a breast cancer survivor. She firmly believes that the key to success in business and in life is in the conscious development of, and investment in, others. She and her husband, Greg, have two boys, Kline and Bryce.

CHRISTINA PARKER

The Leadership Movement
678.583.1063
Christina@TheLeadershipMovement.com
www.TheLeadershipMovement.com

IN ADDITION TO HIS ROLE AS CO-FOUNDER of The Leadership Movement, Donny Henderson is the CEO of a brand development and image consulting company, President and Owner of an artist management agency, and President of a music publishing company. He has dedicated his life to helping others reach their maximum potential. Donny and his wife, Carisa, live in the Atlanta area with their daughters, Julia and Jenna.

DONNY HENDERSON

The Leadership Movement
678.583.1063
Donny@TheLeadershipMovement.com
www.TheLeadershipMovement.com

AN INTERVIEW WITH...

FRANK S. ADAMO

GAIN CONFIDENCE BY TRANSCENDING YOUR FEAR

DAVID WRIGHT (WRIGHT)

Today we're talking with Frank S. Adamo. Frank is a communications coach, international trainer, instructor, speaker, and published author. He's known to his friends as "Francesco, the Godfather of Believers." He feared public speaking not for years but for decades. He's made every excuse not to speak and experienced every symptom of the fear. Because of his extensive experience, he now considers himself the foremost authority on the fear of public speaking. Frank has discovered his inner strength and now comes with his own unique perspective and understanding found nowhere else. He offers individual and group coaching sessions and a series of workshops on effective communications and presentation skills. A techie with a Master of Science degree in Analytical Chemistry, Frank specializes in working with technical professionals and simplifying technical documentations. His passion is to help others transcend their fears of speaking in front of audiences.

Frank, welcome to *Discover Your Inner Strength.*

FRANK ADAMO (ADAMO)

Thank you very much.

WRIGHT

So your passion is helping others get over their fear of speaking in public. Would you explain why it's so important?

ADAMO

I have seen a public defender looking down at the floor, dancing nervously back and forth, uttering filler words (ahs and ums) all while attempting to reduce the bail for his two clients. He may be an expert in criminal law, but because he had a fear of presenting and lacked inner strength, he didn't show conviction. Perhaps, that's why he was still a public defender, unable to move toward his full potential. Another presenter literally read his entire speech from behind the lectern while attempting to persuade his audience. But how can we persuade an audience by simply reading a speech? We really can't.

Me? I experienced many instances where I lost a job or was not promoted simply because I lacked the confidence and inner strength to communicate effectively. For example, I had applied for a supervisory position. I had the skills, knowledge, and experience to be a lab supervisor. Heck, I had been a lab consultant in Seoul, South Korea, and a lab director for a small consulting firm. But, like that public defender, I was still shy and quite fearful of speaking. As a result, I lacked effective communication skills. The company still liked my background, and so they offered me a research chemist position. Reluctantly, I accepted the position because it was my first offer after about six weeks of searching for a position. And the supervisor they did hire? Well, he was less qualified than I was, but he could communicate well.

Later, I discovered a bit of my inner strength. I left that company and started my own business. I ventured out into the world of entrepreneurship. I struggled for many years and I made several mistakes because I was still shy and feared speaking in front of groups.

I can give you more examples of presenters, including many more about myself, but I think you are beginning to get the picture. In a way, if we fear speaking in public or if we have another fear, it's as though we are tied to a ball and chain. That's how I felt for many years. It doesn't mean a lack of some success, but at the same time, we limit ourselves from reaching our full potential. For example, that public defender was able to reduce the bail for his two clients, but how many times was he unable to be victorious?

I believe many men and women limit themselves and do not achieve their full potential. Someone once stated that the greatest source of knowledge is the cemetery—all the unwritten books, all the unsung songs, all those undiscovered discoveries, and all because they never reached their full potential. And why? In my opinion, many times it was because they feared speaking out. They feared to reach out. They feared to unshackle their ball and chain to step out of their comfort zone. That's why I have the passion to help others rid themselves of their fear. I don't want others to go through life without reaching their full potential and fulfill their dreams.

WRIGHT

I understand you consider yourself the foremost expert on the fear of public speaking. Is that right?

ADAMO

Yes, because I've been there. I've been emotionally crippled by the fear of speaking to groups for many years. I understand the frustration of having the knowledge, but not the inner strength to communicate what I know. I fully understand what others are going through and so I can help them transcend their fear naturally and effectively. My approach comes from my own experiences and it is straightforward and practical. I do not encourage the use of alcohol, medicine, or hypnosis. I want no bandages or camouflage to hide the fear temporarily. You see, fear is based on the unknown. Thus I use nothing—except to teach others to understand fear and why we have it.

Let me tell you my story, I have a hereditary speech impediment, based on a very high arched palate. If you take the Grand Canyon, reduce it down to a small size and invert it, that's the inside of my mouth. This makes it difficult for me to articulate certain words and phrases. As a result, I was rather shy when I was growing up, yet I still had confidence and participated in activities such as Boy Scouts, band, and selling Christmas cards.

It was only when I was in my high school English class and I raised my hand to interpret the poem, *The Road Not Taken,* by Robert Frost, that I lost my confidence. I did a literal interpretation of that poem and said, "My parents decided to drive through the forest one Sunday afternoon and came to a fork in the road. They decided to take the less traveled path and it was so green and beautiful." It was not a philosophical answer, which was what the teacher wanted. The kids in the back of the room began to snicker at my answer, which bothered me a little; however, the teacher—an adult who should've known better—also ridiculed me for my answer.

That one incident, along with my speech impediment, crippled me not for years, but for decades. I never raised my hands or volunteered to answer questions of any sort. I even feared expressing myself in front of my friends. Even in grad school, I remember my classmates and I would meet downstairs in the basement for coffee nearly every morning. A general discussion about current events, our classes, and more would take place and everyone would have something to say—everyone but me. I never contributed to the conversations. Afraid I would be ridiculed again, I simply listened.

I've gone through all the symptoms of the fear of speaking in public—the trembling hands, the shakiness, nervousness in my stomach, and more. I've even had experiences of backing away from speaking or I froze because I was simply too afraid to express myself. As a result of my extensive experience, I fully understand and appreciate the anguish of being fearful. Further, I've been teaching classes and giving presentations on how to transcend the fear of speaking in front of audiences for more than three years. And it has been very encouraging to see others transcend their fear and discover their inner strength.

Wright

Why do you emphasize the fear of presenting in front of an audience rather than what many people consider the number one fear, the fear of public speaking?

Adamo

Most people who have to speak in public do not want to be public speakers; however, they do want to be comfortable in giving presentations and speaking in front of groups. They may have to give a sales presentation, speak at an event, or even give a toast at a friend's wedding. This is not public speaking per se, and when I teach or give workshops, almost no one in my audiences is interested in becoming a professional speaker. People who attend my workshops merely want to be comfortable and effective when giving presentations.

WRIGHT

So how do you describe fear?

ADAMO

According to the dictionary, fear is a feeling of anxiety caused by the presence of imminent danger. This is true, particularly if the fear is based on "real" fear—if we are faced with a potential death situation. For example, if we are confronted with a mountain lion, rattle snake or a bear, I'm certain many of us would be fearful and rightfully so. Though speaking in front of a group is not an actual danger—we won't die from the experience—it is a perceived fear and it is real to the ones who have it.

For me, fear is a very positive attribute of human beings. It protected our ancestors. Fear is the body's way of protecting us from danger. If our primitive ancestors hadn't had the capability of feeling fear, the human race would have been extinct eons ago.

As I mentioned earlier, fear is caused by the unknown. For example, if a solar eclipse occurred fifteen hundred years ago, everyone would have flocked together in fear because they had no idea about what was happening. Wouldn't you be frightened if suddenly the sun began to disappear in midday? Today millions flock together—not in fear—but to enjoy the experience of a rare solar eclipse.

We have the fear of speaking because most of us have not had the opportunity to speak in front of audiences. We don't have the knowledge and experience to understand how to give presentations. Thus I consider fear as a natural and positive reaction to real danger or the unknown, whether real or perceived.

WRIGHT

Are you saying that our fears are positive?

ADAMO

Very definitely. Most people use negative terms like panic attack, anxiety, or phobia to describe fear. Why? We should embrace fear because it is so very positive. As I already mentioned, without fear the human race would be extinct and we would not be here discussing this topic or publishing a book.

Additionally, fear is a very natural process in which the body physically changes to prepare us to fight or flee from danger. If we understand the purpose of fear, understand the process of how the body prepares us for danger, and realize that the symptoms of fear are very normal, then we can begin to treat fear positively. That's what I do. I teach others how to understand and then transcend their fear by treating fear positively.

WRIGHT

You mentioned that our bodies physically change. What do you mean?

ADAMO

All the symptoms we have when we are fearful are part of a natural process to prepare us to stand and fight in the face of danger or flee from it. When we feel fear, all nonessential body processes, including the digestive system, shut down. Thus, we may have butterflies in our stomach or we might feel nauseated because of undigested food and acid in our stomach. Adrenalin is released, causing the heart to beat faster because we need to supply oxygen to our muscles. Energy in the form of glucose (sugar) is also rushed to the muscles. Thus, the excess oxygen causes the shaky hands and knees, the trembling lips and voice. Cold hands are caused by the warm blood being rushed away from the hands to the muscles. And the shortness of breath is caused by the fast heartbeat. All are caused by the natural reaction to fear.

WRIGHT

Then would you suggest a few things that can be done to lessen our fear?

ADAMO

Yes. First, as I mentioned, when you are fearful, all nonessential processes in your body shut down, including the digestive system. If you are the least bit fearful, don't eat before you speak. If you are at a wedding or some type of event where a meal will be served, and, for example, you are scheduled to speak or give a toast after the meal, don't eat until after you've spoken. Since you've built up excess oxygen and energy in your muscles, dissipate the oxygen and energy by shaking your arms and legs before you speak. Run in place. Do the Hokey Pokey. Do anything to disperse that energy (but of course, not in front of the audience). Go backstage or find a nearby empty room. If you get nervous during your presentation, you might want to consider asking your audience to stand up and do a little exercise. Of course, you would want to demonstrate the exercise to help dissipate your nervousness.

Before your presentation, practice, practice, and then practice some more, and finally rehearse. The more you practice and learn your speech, the less fearful you will be. Then do a dress rehearsal. Even if you do it at home or in a hotel room, dress accordingly, set up your visual aids, and rehearse as if you were giving the actual presentation.

As often as you can, visualize yourself giving your speech and getting a standing ovation. You may not get a standing ovation, but you will lessen your fear. Many professional ballplayers visualize catching the winning touchdown or making that three-point basket at the very last second of the game. It doesn't always happen, but it will happen more often if that ballplayer visualizes it every moment he or she can. And finally, embrace your fear and make it work for you, not against you. Instead, use that energy not to fight, but to inspire and motivate your audience.

Wright

So we should embrace fear?

Adamo

We should definitely embrace fear. Take those who have been on *Dancing with the Stars.* Just like you—an expert in your own profession—they are professional magicians, ballplayers, singers, performers, actors, and the like. However, they certainly were not experts in ballroom dancing. Some have not ever danced before. Do you think they didn't feel fearful? Even though they may be well-known to the public, they danced on national television in front of millions of viewers. Some have admitted that they were fearful. But they all embraced their fears and accepted the challenge.

We need to embrace our fears to begin transcending them, and we begin by learning about and understanding the fear.

Talking about dancing, I taught a group of fifty nursing students in Tbilisi, Georgia, in 2007. Don't ask me why, but all fifty students were from India—they were not Georgians. Many, if not all of them, were quite shy and reluctant to embrace their fear. I was there to teach them about American culture and communication and interview skills.

In four days, I had them role-playing for interviews and giving presentations in front of their classmates. That fourth evening, before I was to return to the States, they gathered together to perform for me. They sang Indian songs and performed outstanding native dances.

I asked them how they could so readily perform so well, yet they had been so reluctant to communicate in front of their own classmates. Of course, the answer was that they had practiced, rehearsed, and learned to sing and dance. They were comfortable in dancing and singing because they had embraced their original fear. Now that they had learned to embrace their fear of speaking they were on their way to finding their own inner strength in speaking.

Wright

How does transcending one's fear lead to inner strength?

Adamo

As I mentioned before, fear is like being tied to a ball and chain. We can move around. We can be successful. But, it's much tougher. Thus, fear, in my opinion, can be crippling and can restrict us from reaching our full potential. Through transcending our fear, we can find our inner strength.

What I have done in the past is talk about embracing our heritage. I talk about the three little pigs. The first little piggy had a house made of straw and the big bad wolf blew down the first little piggy's house. The second little piggy had a house made of twigs and branches and the big bad wolf had more difficulty, but he eventually blew down the second little piggy's house. But the third little piggy had a house built of bricks and stone and no matter how hard he blew, the wolf was unable to blow down the third piggy's home. In real life, the wolf is like the adversities and tragedies we all have to go through in life, including having the fear of speaking in front of audiences.

We can be like the first little piggy where we are crushed every time we have to struggle in life. People like the first piggy have never discovered their inner strength. They are the ones who end up in graveyards with all those unsung songs and unwritten books.

Then there are those like the second little piggy. They can struggle through the adversities in their lives and each time they find some inner strength and can grow from it. For example, we can find enough inner strength to attend a Toastmasters club to help us transcend our fear of speaking in public.

Finally, there are those like the third little piggy who have discovered their inner strength. One incident that comes to mind is Todd Beamer and the others on Flight 73 who found the courage and inner strength to act. They were ordinary men and women who took extraordinary steps to save the lives of others while giving their lives on September 11, 2001. Each and every one of us can find our inner strength, not as traumatically as those on that flight, but at least by transcending our fear of speaking in front of audiences. And not just for ourselves, but to serve others as Todd Beamer and the others did.

Wright

Why is it so important to transcend one's fear of speaking in public?

Adamo

Simple—to give back to society. I tell my audiences that we all have a story to tell. We all have a unique life and we have all gone through our own struggles and adversities. We can help others by telling our stories about how we struggled and survived through our adversities. But we need to transcend our fear of speaking out and telling our stories. I never talked about my speech impediment and my terrible fear of speaking for more than three decades of my life. Who wants to talk about embarrassing things? However, I'm doing it now because that is part of the process of helping others through the struggles they are having.

The very first speech we give in Toastmasters is "the Icebreaker." This is where we talk about ourselves; it is a way to introduce ourselves to the other members. Oh, wow! Some of the stories are so compelling and touching. Some

Icebreakers have taken my breath away. These are the stories we have to tell to others. These are the stories that many of us take to our graves. That's why it's so very, very important to transcend our fear of speaking out and telling our stories.

Wright

Some folks I've known have mentioned Toastmasters, what do you think?

Adamo

I have been in Toastmasters since 1991. Without Toastmasters, I would not be speaking to you; I would not be teaching, and giving workshops—especially on communication skills—and I would not be doing many things that I'm doing now. Not only am I a better communicator, I'm also a much better leader because I have the confidence and inner strength to follow and fulfill my dreams.

Toastmasters is the most cost-effective and the most incredible worldwide organization to improve your communications and leadership skills. What I tell other people is that it can actually empower you to be able to fulfill your dreams, fulfill your passion, and reach your ultimate destiny of where you want to be. So I will encourage everybody, including people in my classes and people who attend my workshops to join Toastmasters because it gives you the confidence and the inner strength that you need to fulfill your destiny.

I have written a book, *31 Tips to Becoming an Effective Presenter*, which is the first in a series of thirty-one tips books. The thirty-first step in each of these books will be about joining Toastmasters.

Before leaving this topic, please let me tell you what happened to me. As I have said, I was very shy. I was actually an extreme introvert when I was growing up. When I decided to return to Springfield, Illinois, for my fortieth high school reunion—my first reunion—I told the coordinator that I was a member of Toastmasters. He then told me that the person assigned to do the invocation was reluctant to do it and he asked if I would. Of course I accepted—I was a Toastmaster. When I gave the invocation in front of nearly eighty of my high school classmates, I believe they were all in shock to see the shyest introvert in the class giving the invocation. Later, the coordinator pulled me aside and asked, "You never said more than two words in high school, did you?" This is the power of Toastmasters. It gives the power to empower.

WRIGHT

Do you have any last thoughts for our readers?

ADAMO

Definitely: join Toastmasters. Being educated as a chemist, I had classroom studies as well as hands-on sessions in a laboratory. Toastmasters is, in my opinion, the laboratory of communications and leadership. This is the place to practice, refine, and improve your communications and leadership skills. In fact, I can say that Toastmasters can be your life laboratory because it can change lives. It did for me.

In my opinion, inner strength is a process whereby we can change our mindset, gain confidence, and fulfill our passion and dreams. I urge anyone who has not only a fear of speaking in front of an audience, but any fear that is crippling themselves from your ultimate potential, to unshackle that ball and chain and discover your inner strength. Only then, in my opinion, can you capture their confidence and pursue your dreams with conviction and determination.

WRIGHT

Well, I really do appreciate all this time you've taken with me today, Frank, to answer all these questions. You've raised some really important considerations when it comes to the number one fear in this country today, and I think that what you've said here is going to help our readers tremendously.

ADAMO

I appreciate that. I appreciate having the time to be able to talk with you and I hope that people can begin to understand and transcend their fear in order to find their inner strength.

WRIGHT

Today we've been talking with Frank Adamo. He is a communications coach and an international trainer, instructor, and speaker. He feared speaking to an audience for decades; he's made every excuse not to speak and has experienced every symptom of the fear. Now he considers himself the foremost authority on the fear of public speaking, and after listening to him I'm inclined to believe he knows what he's talking about.

Frank, thank you so much for being with us today on *Discover Your Inner Strength.*

ADAMO

Thank you very much.

About the Author

Frank S. Adamo grew up on the infamous Route 66 in Springfield, Illinois, in the midst of the "Land of Lincoln." After graduating from Lanphier High School, he returned to his hometown of Tampa, Florida where he graduated with an MS degree in Analytical Chemistry from the University of South Florida. He then moved to Southern California where he began his career as a chemist. After a few years, Frank started a business in computer consulting and software applications designing.

Passionate in helping others, Frank joined the Rotary Club of Cerritos, California, as a charter member in 1985. Because of his fear of speaking in front of groups, he decided to join Toastmasters in 1991. He says that Rotary and Toastmasters have literally changed his life.

Frank is now a communications coach, international trainer, instructor, and published author. He's known to his friends as "Francesco, the Godfather of Believers." A techie, Frank specializes in working with technical professionals, and simplifying technical documentations. His passion is to help others transcend their fears of speaking in front of audiences.

Frank S. Adamo

Cypress, CA 90630

714.408.9287

frank@fsadamo.com

www.fsadamo.com

AN INTERVIEW WITH...

SUSAN BOCK

YOU HAVE THE KEYS TO UNLOCK YOUR SUCCESS

DAVID WRIGHT (WRIGHT)

Today we're talking with Susan Bock. Susan's clients call her their Business Success Expert. She works exclusively with women business owners who want to reach and sustain new levels of success. Her breakthrough work tackles the gnarly problems businesswomen encounter on their road to success. She has developed the GPS Business Coaching Model™, using the acronym GPS for Goals, Perspective, and Success. You will learn proven strategies that will identify your unique strengths and talent so you can engage in activities to propel you from where you are to where you want to be. Susan gained fifteen years of experience in corporate America prior to starting her firm. She has a PhD in Business Management, a master's degree in Organizational Management, and is a Mastered Certified Executive Coach through the College of Executive Coaching.

She is a resource for *Entrepreneur Magazine*. Additionally, her works can be found in *Coaching for the New Century*, published in 2004.

Susan, welcome to *Discover Your Inner Strength*.

SUSAN BOCK (BOCK)

Thank you, David, for inviting me to join you.

WRIGHT

The title of the book, Discover Your Inner Strength, suggests we have untapped internal resources. Would you concur and if so, what has been your experience with this discovery process?

BOCK

Absolutely—I concur! I believe we have unlimited internal strengths, resources, and talents. Our adventure as human beings can be viewed as three components: our internal world, our external world, and our actions to integrate the two.

Reflecting on events in my past, it is easy to see that the times of greatest strife, pain, anguish, or sorrow were when there was disparity between my internal world of beliefs, wants, desires, and feelings, and the external world. It would be during those times when someone might say to me, "You're never given more than you can handle." When hearing that—which was not what I wanted to hear—I seriously doubted the truthfulness of the thought. However, in time, the underlying meaning of those words emerged. I had no idea about what I was capable of handling or what internal resources were available to me. The most compelling question then became: "How could I discover this inner strength and tap into it?" Ah, the quest is born!

A perfect example of this is my career. I had little difficulty in being hired—I had great difficulty in wanting to stay employed! Although I was reliable, talented, and had all the "perfect" qualities of a great employee, I could not seem to sustain an interest or continue performing at a level that was acceptable to me or to my employer.

After several starts and stops, the opportunity came to me to work at a multinational advertising agency. Within five years, I was elected to Vice President and two years later, Senior Vice President. By the way, I was the first female senior vice president in the Western Region and this was in 1992—not exactly the olden days! Being in a male-dominated industry, this was quite the accomplishment. As a result, I found inner strength I did not know I processed. Umm, could it be as simple as that?

Alas, not so. By 1999, the business sizzle had begun to fizzle! What had been a blazing bonfire was now smoldering embers. The external environment had changed with the age of mergers and acquisitions; more importantly, I realized my internal environment had changed. I no longer wanted to engage in the fame. It was time for me to take action rather than waiting to react to whatever might occur.

Walking away from the comfort of the corner office, a high income, and all the benefits was a very scary thing to do—and that was the action required. Having no clarity about my future, the most appropriate action was to get off the bus, reflect, assess, evaluate. The compelling question of "what next?" was overwhelming. Little did I know the answer would involve starting a business that would launch me into the totally unknown realm of being an entrepreneur!

This was a perfect time for my inner strength to step into the driver's seat—because my "conscious" thinking could only take me to what I "knew." It was time for belief, faith, and those great internal resources like self-determination, self-respect, self-acceptance, self-conviction, self-esteem, and self-awareness to help guide me on this new adventure. "Courageous" is not a word I would use to describe myself—it was much more basic than that. I simply wanted the zest to return to my life. Challenges had not deterred me in the past, however, facing a future without zest scared me into action, and fear can be a great motivator!

Women in business today face what could be defined as overwhelming challenges. Having had first-hand experience, I learned early on that women in business require a fully stocked tool kit with specific skills and abilities to navigate the minefields and obstacles on their road to success.

Wright

I know there must be a lot of problems that women business owners struggle with. Would you name the ones that in your opinion are in the top three?

BOCK

Starting with a broad view, we'll look at the top three challenges facing women in business. Then we'll narrow the focus to discuss the top three challenges women business owners must confront. Interestingly, the answers are not that different.

First and foremost, education and experience being equal, women continue to earn less than men. In a Boston Globe (2007) article titled, "Gap Shrinking," staff writer, Diane Lewis, refers to a study presented at the Federal Reserve Bank of Boston. She states, "The pay gap between men and women is smaller than it's ever been, but women still face an uphill climb in the workplace."

Secondly, and perhaps a by-product of the compensation gap, many women in business are compelled to prove their value. Although it may appear the "proving" is for their male counterparts, in fact, it may be more strongly rooted in proving their worth to themselves—to their "inner" selves. To an extreme, these women are totally driven—success at any cost. Their career comes before anything else. All too often, the cost is paid by their personal and family life.

The last challenge is Wonder Woman. If you are of the age to remember the television show or young enough to have watched the animation, then you recognize the message. We bought into the belief of "having it all." We can have a successful career, be a fabulous parent and spouse, plan and participate in an active social life, run a household, keep our figures trim and fit while being a gourmet chef, entertain, read, and stay current with world events—phew! Unfortunately, that image—that belief in the "having it all" life—did not come with a how-to manual.

Let's shift our focus to the challenges facing women business owners. Whether your business is multi-national or you are a solo-prenuer, the challenges aren't that different. Isn't that interesting?

We'll start with the third challenge and work up to the number one challenge women business owners deal with on a daily basis. The third challenge is increasing competitive environments. The Internet has introduced tremendous competition. Positioning your product or service with a highly identifiable USP (Unique Selling Proposition) is crucial. In marketing parlance, it would be stated as, "What is the benefit and the benefit of the benefit of your product or service?"

The second challenge facing women business owners is limited sales and marketing resources. Considering the breadth and scope of the previous challenge, sufficient resources must be allocated for sales and marketing. A misconception of many businesses owners is that their product/service/offering is so amazing, it will sell itself! If only that were true. The consumer has become very sophisticated, informed, and knowledgeable in shopping for the best deal.

This lends import to the planning stage of a business, either in the launch of a new company or a new product or a new service. Marketing requires a methodical, well-orchestrated plan with adequate resources in talent and money.

The number one challenge for women business owners is lack of understanding of their services or products. As the business goals are not being met, the business owner learns that her marketing message is: a) lost in the plethora of other marketing messages, and/or b) a poorly executed marketing strategy that failed to create a compelling Unique Selling Proposition (USP) and/or, c) insufficient resources to sustain the message. The lifeblood of a business is market sustainability.

As a society, we have come to expect—and accept—a fifteen-second sound byte, so the marketing or sales message has to grab us in the first few seconds or we flip the channel, turn the page, go to a different station, or click to a different Web site. Attracting and retaining the attention of the consumer or client is the key.

Wright

What does this have to do with discovering your inner strength?

Bock

Let's go back to the number one challenge facing women business owners: lack of understanding of services or products. I would suggest that we, as individuals, do not have an understanding of our inner strength. Our inner strength is what sustains us, gives us encouragement, provides us with choices, and helps us look at events and circumstances from different perspectives. How can we expect to be successful in the external world if we do not know our internal world sufficiently to capitalize on our uniqueness? We each have our own USP, our own personal marketing message and our unique value—a combination of talents, knowledge, experience, and wisdom that is unlike that of anyone else in the world!

In an attempt to simplify a very complex topic, it is my belief that the single largest obstacle blocking women today from having it all, is themselves.

WRIGHT

The topic de jour in recent years has been alignment, harmony, connecting energies. Why is there such a thirst for this concept?

BOCK

What a great question. Living in a world that is ever-changing, living at a continually accelerating pace, and being offered more choices and options than ever before, it's not surprising to see people seeking a more "connected" approach to living. Having spent time considering what harmony and alignment could mean to me has allowed me to create my own definition of nirvana: when we are in harmony with all, our internal and external lives are in alignment and our actions re-energize our awareness. Doesn't that sound intriguing? Umm, maybe not!

WRIGHT

So how can we discover inner strengths?

BOCK

As previously mentioned, we have become very comfortable with a fifteen- or thirty-second sound byte. Some say the demands on our time are so significant that we only have five seconds to listen! For some aspects of our lives, that may well be the case. However, the one message we must give our undivided and long-term attention to is our internal dialog.

The most important conversation you will ever have is the one you have with yourself. The most important relationship you will ever have is with yourself. How much time do you invest in asking yourself thought-provoking questions? What effort do you expend in self-discovery? How quickly do you expect an answer? How comfortable are you to sit in the question?

Here are some questions that have the potential to stimulate your discovery:

- What is your definition of success?
- Has your definition changed in recent years? If so, how?

- What does success look like, feel like?
- What do you want from success?
- What do you expect from success?
- What are you willing to give to achieve success?
- What actions are you willing to take?
- What will keep you focused?
- What will you do when your actions are out of alignment with your success goals?
- How will you know when you have "arrived"?

Asking ourselves these questions and waiting for an answer is not a luxury we often allow ourselves. When was the last time you had a conversation with yourself? Not the dialog of critical self-talk or even job well done; but rather, an actual conversation when you asked questions—purposeful, meaningful questions—that would invite the light of day into your inner sanctum?

Our inner strength can be our lifeline and it needs, requires, and deserves, time, attention, and nourishment. By taking care of and caring for these precious gifts, we can have the honor of calling upon these strengths to help us dream our dreams, imagine our future, and take the actions to turn our vision into reality. We can act in ways that are congruent and consistent with what we desire. However, for all of this to happen, we have to engage in an internal dialog, get to know ourselves, and stay in conversation with our inner strength. Give a voice to your inner strength, your internal drive, your inner being. Don't keep it a secret!

To me that sums up what living and discovering what our inner strength is all about. Because it resides within us, it is our responsibility, on a daily basis, to open the door and shed the light on our inner strength and live in the comfort of knowing that the purpose of our strength is to help us be more than what we are. Are you choosing success or are you choosing the average and ordinary?

You can shift from ordinary to extraordinary by asking yourself, "Am I connected to and utilizing all of my strengths? If the answer is no, then you have taken the first step toward success.

Wright

What roles do insight and eyesight play in your GPS Business Coaching Model?

Bock

We build our lives, our business, and our success based on answers to questions. What I discovered with my clients is that the key to unlocking many of their inner strengths and of opening the doors to new ideas and opportunities is to ask the right questions. This became one of the foundational blocks of the GPS Business Coaching Model. Asking new and different questions will reveal surprising answers. As a business coach, I have the responsibility to ask my clients questions that will reveal their answers and their solutions which leads to their success.

This foundational block is supported by a recent shift in our societal norms. We are seeing more and more direction and energy put toward our "insight" versus the external "eyesight" that has been a real force in previous decades. We used to look at success (and at times we still do) based on the accumulation of what we can see, be it the bigger house, the better clothes, the fancier car. The "eyesight" determined our success. We are now experiencing a trend that is shifting our view from "eyesight" to "insight." Even though the smallest trinket in my younger days might have brought me great short-term joy, it was not a long-lasting satisfaction. Insight has given me the opportunity to know and understand that what resides within is what will sustain and nurture my strengths and will provide me with the ability to continue to excel.

Wright

Why are internal answers often difficult to unveil and easily discounted?

Bock

Ooh that's an easy one—it's because we've had years of practice, literally, years of practice and in some cases, decades!

Recently I was evaluating numerous approaches that I might use in an upcoming coaching session, which was a particularly gnarly situation. My husband, Dr. Marc Bock, who consistently enhances my journey on the planet, asked me three questions when I presented him with the situation. His three short questions created a substantial shift in my thinking. Here are the questions:

- What do you want from this interaction?
- What do you expect from this interaction?
- What are you willing to give?

These three questions had power and gave me pause. The more I considered each question, the more I realized that there was a broader application, both internally and externally. Once again, the power is in asking the question, waiting for the answer, and then moving into action!

Now, when I am looking at a situation and I want to find an internal answer, I use these three questions: what do I want, what do I expect, and most importantly, what am I willing to give? This requires me to engage in a decision-making process. Seeking the answers internally provides a clear plan of external action. I have to do something—take action—and it's my responsibility to be part of the solution.

Wright

Would you describe for our readers and me what actions can be taken to support and sustain our newfound discoveries?

Bock

Can every person achieve and even surpass his or her dream? Yes. Does every person achieve and surpass his or her dream? No. What makes one more likely to succeed than the other? It starts with awareness and acknowledgment that the deterrent to our success is our limited thinking. Taking action to expand beyond our thinking, to listen as though we don't have an opinion, to ask questions of ourselves, and invite the answers to be revealed, is how we can get out of our own way.

The actions we engage in on a daily basis determine our results. We have to integrate what we learn and release behaviors that are not aligned with what we want to be and where we want to go. New perspectives will be revealed. Reinforcement, encouragement, and replicating success are how we move on to the next adventure.

It's not something that we can just learn and say, "Great, now I know that, I'm done with it." Accepting a new behavior or a new discovery and integrating it into our lives often means that we have to change something we're currently doing and, as you and I know, we're always in favor of change when it involves somebody else, not necessarily when we have to change!

Do you remember the effort, determination, and perseverance required to learn how to ride a bicycle? It was painful! Likewise, learning to engage in new behaviors can be painful. We have to release what is comfortable and known in order to make room for the new.

To change something we first have to recognize that there is an end. In the book, Managing Transitions: Making the Most of Change by William Bridges, the author introduces the concept of three stages to change. The first step is acknowledging the end—we have to let go of a limiting belief, a behavior, or of an activity that is not in keeping with where we want to go, with what we want to be doing, and with how we want to be doing it.

Bridges labels the second stage as the neutral zone—the space between what was and what will be. This is when we are most susceptible to reverting to our former behavior. As quickly as possible, we need to move into the final stage—a new beginning.

Cherry Garcia ice cream is a perfect example. My goal is to maintain a healthy lifestyle. Cherry Garcia ice cream interferes with that goal when it is in my refrigerator. Using Bridges' three stages, the end would be to stop opening the refrigerator door and taking out the carton of Cherry Garcia ice cream. Alternatively, the end could be to stop buying the ice cream. The neutral zone is between my ears—do I go the refrigerator door, the ice cream store or for a walk? The beginning would be for me to open the front door, go outside, and take a walk: end, neutral, beginning.

Wright

So repeating old behaviors and replicating success; what is that all about?

Bock

If we truly want to replicate success then we need to look at our past and continue to reflect on circumstances and situations when we have been particularly successful. Take a focused looked at the behaviors around that moment, our energy, what actions we engaged in, and who was providing support and encouragement. Consider all of the elements that came into play. Our resources are not limited to the obvious external resources such as people, money, and time. Our resources are internal as well, and we have some very valuable ones called self-will, self-discipline, self-learning, and self-assurance. How much time do you spend building your "self" muscles? We have such a vast array of resources available to us if we choose to invite them into action.

Wright

You use an unusual example for explaining the difference between taking action and taking control. Would you tell our readers the distinction?

Bock

This is another foundational block for the GPS Business Coaching model. The internal dialog is manifested externally. Consider this: words become thoughts, thoughts become actions, and actions define us. The questions surrounding this are the following. What is your internal dialog? Is your mental iPod playing the downloaded "oldies" tunes? What messages are you sending to yourself? If we're using words in our communication that are not accurate (as society has become adept at doing), then we are misunderstanding ourselves and we are setting ourselves up to be misunderstood.

In the example of action versus control, we will say, "I'm taking control of this situation" or "I am in control of this situation." According to the Webster's Dictionary, that means you are "restraining or directing or dominating or commanding." Webster's defines action as the "the state of acting or of being active." When you're taking action, you are engaged in an activity very purposefully, very directly, and it is toward a particular outcome. Controlling a situation usually indicates that in fact you are attempting to circumvent or restrict what is taking place at that particular time.

Rather than becoming lax in our vocabulary, I encourage you to examine the words used in your internal and external communication—are you sending an accurate message?

WRIGHT

So, what haven't we touched on that you think would be relevant to our readers?

BOCK

I would close with this quote from Henry Ford: "Whether you believe you can, or you believe you can't, you're right."

WRIGHT

I'm afraid you're right, as I reflect on my own life.

Well, what a great conversation, Susan. I really appreciate all this time you've taken today to answer these questions. I have learned a lot. You've given me a lot to think about, and I'm sure our readers will learn a lot also.

BOCK

Thank you. It is a pleasure to help you and others.

WRIGHT

Today we've been talking with Susan Bock. She has developed the GPS Coaching Model, using the acronym GPS (Goals, Perspective, and Success). Her GPS Coaching Model accelerates the achievement of success. With her system, you will learn proven strategies that will identify your unique strengths and talent so you can engage in activities that will produce results that will propel you from where you are to where you want to be.

Susan, thank you so much for being with us today on *Discover Your Inner Strength.*

BOCK

You are most welcome. Thank you for your interest.

About the Author

SUSAN'S CLIENTS CALL HER THEIR Business Success Expert. She works exclusively with women business owners who want to reach and sustain new levels of success. Her breakthrough work tackles the gnarly problems businesswomen encounter on their road to success. She has developed the GPS Business Coaching Model™, using the acronym GPS for Goals, Perspective, and Success. You will learn proven strategies that will identify your unique strengths and talent so you can engage in activities to propel you from where you are to where you want to be. Susan gained fifteen years of experience in corporate America prior to starting her firm. She has a PhD in Business Management, a master's degree in Organizational Management, and is a Mastered Certified Executive Coach through the College of Executive Coaching. She is a resource for *Entrepreneur Magazine*. Additionally, her works can be found in *Coaching for the New Century*, published in 2004.

Susan Bock

8201 Newman Avenue, Ste. 102
Huntington Beach, CA 92647
714.847.1566
Susan@SBockSolutions.com
www.SusanBockSolutions.com

AN INTERVIEW WITH...

BRIAN TRACY

USING STRATEGY TO DISCOVER YOUR INNER STRENGTH

DAVID WRIGHT (WRIGHT)

Many years ago, Brian Tracy started off on a lifelong search for the secrets of success in life and business. He studied, researched, traveled, worked, and taught for more than thirty years. In 1981, he began to share his discoveries in talks and seminars, and eventually in books, audios and video-based courses.

The greatest secret of success he learned is this: "There are no secrets of success." There are instead timeless truths and principles that have to be rediscovered, relearned, and practiced by each person. Brian's gift is synthesis—the ability to take large numbers of ideas from many sources and combine them into highly practical, enjoyable, and immediately usable forms that people can take and apply quickly to improve their life and work. Brian has brought together the best ideas, methods, and techniques from thousands of books, hundreds of courses, and experience working with individuals and organizations of every kind in the U.S., Canada, and worldwide.

Today, I have asked Brian to discuss his latest book, *Victory!: Applying the Military Principals of Strategy for Success in Business and Personal Life.*

Brian Tracy, welcome to *Discover Your Inner Strength.*

TRACY

Thank you, David. It's a pleasure to be here.

WRIGHT

Let's talk about your new book the *Victory!: Applying* the *Military Principals* of *Strategy* for *Success* in *Business* and *Personal Life*. (By the way it is refreshing to hear someone say something good about the successes of the military.) Why do you think the military is so successful?

TRACY

Well, the military is based on very serious thought. The American military is the most respected institution in America. Unless you're a left liberal limp-wristed pinko most people in America really respect the military because it keeps America free. People who join the military give up most of their lives—twenty to thirty years—in sacrifice to be prepared to guard our freedoms. And if you ask around the world what it is that America stands for, it stands for individual freedom, liberty, democracy, freedom, and opportunity that is only secured in a challenging world—a dangerous world—by your military.

Now the other thing is that the people in our military are not perfect because there is no human institution made up of human beings that is perfect—there are no perfect people. The cost of mistakes in military terms is death; therefore, people in the military are extraordinarily serious about what they do. They are constantly looking for ways to do what they do better and better and better to reduce the likelihood of losing a single person.

We in America place extraordinary value on individual human life. That is why you will see millions of dollars spent to save a life, whether for an accident victim or Siamese twins from South America, because that's part of our culture. The military has that same culture.

I was just reading today about the RQ-1 "Predator" drone planes (Unmanned Aerial Vehicles—UAVs) that have been used in reconnaissance over the no-fly zones in Iraq. These planes fly back and forth constantly gathering information from the ground. They can also carry remote-controlled weapons. According to www.globalsecurity.org, the planes cost $4.5 million each and get shot down on a regular basis. However, the military is willing to invest hundreds of millions of dollars to develop these planes, and lose them to save the life of a pilot, because pilots are so precious—human life is precious. In the military everything is calculated right down to the tinniest detail because it's the smallest details that can cost lives. That is why the military is so successful—they are so meticulous about planning.

A salesperson can go out and make a call; if it doesn't work that's fine—he or she can make another sales call. Professional soldiers can go out on an operation and if it's not successful they're dead and maybe everybody in the squad is dead as well. There is no margin for error in the military; that's why they do it so well. This is also why the military principals of strategy that I talk about in *Victory!* are so incredibly important because a person who really understands those principals and strategies sees how to do things vastly better with far lower probability of failure than the average person.

Wright

In the promotion on *Victory!* you affirm that it is very important to set clear attainable goals and objectives. Does that theme carry out through all of your presentations and all of your books?

Tracy

Yes. Over and over again the theme reiterates that you can't hit a target you can't see—you shouldn't get into your car unless you know where you are going. More people spend more time planning a picnic than they spend planning their careers.

I'll give you an example. A very successful woman who is in her fifties now wrote down a plan when she was attending university. Her plan was for the first ten years she would work for a Fortune 500 corporation, really learn the business, and learn how to function at high levels. For the second ten years of her career she talked about getting married and having children at the same time. For that second ten years she would also work for a medium sized company helping it grow and succeed. For the third ten years (between the ages of forty and fifty), she would start her own company based on her knowledge of both businesses. She would then build that into a successful company. Her last ten years she would be chief executive officer of a major corporation and retire financially independent at the age of sixty. At age fifty-eight she would have hit every single target. People would say, "Boy, you sure are lucky." No, it wouldn't be luck. From the time she was seventeen she was absolutely crystal clear about what she was going to do with her career and what she was going to do with her life, and she hit all of her targets.

WRIGHT

In a time where companies, both large and small, take a look at their competition and basically try to copy everything they do, it was really interesting to read in *Victory!* that you suggest taking vigorous offensive action to get the best results. What do you mean by "vigorous offensive action"?

TRACY

Well, see, that's another thing. When you come back to talking about probabilities—and this is really important—you see successful people try more things. And if you wanted to just end the interview right now and ask, "What piece of advice would you give to our listeners?" I would say, "Try more things." The reason I would say that is because if you try more things, the probability is that you will hit your target

For example, here's an analogy I use. Imagine that you go into a room and there is a dartboard against the far wall. Now imagine that you are drunk and you have never played darts before. The room is not very bright and you can barely see the bull's eye. You are standing along way from the board, but you have an endless supply of darts. You pick up the darts and you just keep throwing them at the target over there on the other of the room even though you are not a good dart thrower and you're not even well coordinated. If you kept throwing darts over and over again what would you eventually hit?

WRIGHT

Pretty soon you would get a bull's eye.

TRACY

Yes, eventually you would hit a bull's eye. The odds are that as you keep throwing the darts even though you are not that well educated, even if you don't come from a wealthy family or you don't have a Harvard education, if you just keep throwing darts you will get a little better each time you throw. It's known as a "decybernetic self-correction mechanism" in the brain—each time you try something, you get a little bit smarter at it. So over time, if you kept throwing, you must eventually hit a bull's eye. In other words, you must eventually find the right way to do the things you need to do to become a millionaire. That's the secret of success. That's why people come here from a 190 countries with one idea in mind—"If I come here I can try anything I want; I can go anywhere, because there are no limitations. I have so much freedom; and if I keep doing this, then by God, I will eventually hit a bull's eye." And they do and everybody says, "Boy, you sure where lucky."

Now imagine another scenario: You are thoroughly trained at throwing darts—you have practiced, you have developed skills and expertise in your field, you are constantly upgrading your knowledge, and you practice all the time. Second you are completely prepared, you're thoroughly cold sober, fresh, fit, alert, with high energy. Third, all of the room is very bright around the dartboard. This time how long would it take you to hit the bull's eye? The obvious answer is you will hit a bull's eye far faster than if you had all those negative conditions.

What I am I saying is, you can dramatically increase the speed at which you hit your bull's eye. The first person I described—drunk, unprepared, in a darkened room, and so on—may take twenty or twenty-five years. But if you are thoroughly prepared, constantly upgrading your skills; if you are very clear about your targets; if you have everything you need at hand and your target is clear, your chances of hitting a bull's eye you could hit a bull's eye is five years rather than twenty. That's the difference in success in life.

WRIGHT

In reading your books and watching your presentations on video, one of the common threads seen through your presentations is creativity. I was glad that in the promotional material of *Victory!* you state that you need to apply innovative solutions to overcome obstacles. The word "innovative" grabbed me. I guess you are really concerned with *how* people solve problems rather than just solving problems.

TRACY

Vigorous action means you will cover more ground. What I say to people, especially in business, is the more things you do the more experience you get. The more experience you get the smarter you get. The smarter you get the better results you get the better results you get. The better results you get the less time it takes you to get the same results. And it's such a simple thing. In my books *Create Your Own Future* and *Victory!* you will find there is one characteristic of all successful people—they are action oriented. They move fast, they move quickly, and they don't waste time. They're moving ahead, trying more things, but they are always in motion. The faster you move the more energy you have. The faster you move the more in control you feel and the faster you are the more positive and the more motivated you are. We are talking about a direct relationship between vigorous action and success.

WRIGHT

Well, the military certainly is a team "sport" and you talk about building peak performance teams for maximum results. My question is how do individuals in corporations build peak performance teams in this culture?

TRACY

One of the things we teach is the importance of selecting people carefully. Really successful companies spend an enormous amount of time at the front end on selection they look for people who are really, really good in terms of what they are looking for. They interview very carefully; they interview several people and they interview them several times. They do careful background checks. They are as careful in selecting people as a person might be in getting married. Again, in the military, before a person is promoted they go through a rigorous process. In large corporations, before a person is promoted his or her performance is very, very carefully evaluated to be sure they are the right people to be promoted at that time.

Wright

My favorite point in *Victory!* is when you say, "Amaze your competitors with surprise and speed." I have done that several times in business and it does work like a charm.

Tracy

Yes, it does. Again one of the things we teach over and over again that there is a direct relationship between speed and perceived value. When you do things fast for people they consider you to be better. They consider your products to be better and they consider your service to be better—they actually consider them to be of higher value. Therefore, if you do things really, really fast then you overcome an enormous amount of resistance. People wonder, "Is this a good decision? Is it worth the money? Am I going the right direction?" When you do things fast, you blast that out of their minds.

Wright

You talk about moving quickly to seize opportunities. I have found that to be difficult. When I ask people about opportunities, it's difficult to find out what they think an opportunity is. Many think opportunities are high-risk, although I've never found it that way myself. What do you mean by moving quickly to cease opportunity?

Tracy

There are many cases were a person has an idea and they think that's a good idea. They think they should do something about it. They think, "I am going to do something about that but I really can't do it this week, so I will wait until after the month ends," and so on. By the time they do move on the opportunity it's to late—somebody's already seized it.

One of the military examples I use is the battle of Gettysburg. Now the battle of Gettysburg was considered the high-water mark of the Confederacy after the battle of Gettysburg the Confederacy won additional battles at Chattanooga and other places but they eventually lost the war. The high-water mark of Gettysburg was a little hill at one end of the battlefield called Little Round Top. As the battle began Little Round Top was empty. Colonel Joshua Chamberlain of the Union Army saw that this could be the pivotal point of the battlefield. He went up there and looked at it and he immediately rushed troops to fortify the hill. Meanwhile, the Confederates also saw that Little Round Top could be key to the battle as well, so they too immediately rushed the hill. An enormous battle took place. It was really the essence of the battle of Gettysburg. The victor who took that height controlled the battlefield. Eventually the union troops, who were almost lost, controlled Little Round Top and won the battle. The Civil War was over in about a year and a half, but that was the turning point.

So what would have happened if Chamberlain had said, "Wait until after lunch and then I'll move some men up to Little Round Top"? The Confederate troops would have seized Little Round Top, controlled the battlefield, and would have won the battle of Gettysburg. It was just a matter of moving very, very fast. Forty years later it was determined that there were three days at the battle of Gettysburg that cost the battle for the Confederates. The general in charge of the troops on the Confederate right flank was General James Longstreet. Lee told him to move his army forward as quickly as possible the next day, but to use his own judgment. Longstreet didn't agree with Lee's plan so he kept his troop sitting there most of the next day. It is said that it was Longstreet's failure to move forward on the second day and seize Little Round Top that cost the Confederacy the battle and eventually the war. It was just this failure to move forward and forty years later, when Longstreet appeared at a reunion of Confederate veterans in 1901 or 1904, he was booed. The veterans felt his failure to move forward that fateful day cost them the war. If you read every single account of the battle of Gettysburg, Longstreet's failure to move forward and quickly seize the opportunity is always included.

Wright

In your book you tell your readers to get the ideas and information needed to succeed. Where can individuals get these ideas?

Tracy

Well we are living in an ocean of ideas. It's so easy. The very first thing you do is you pick a subject you want to major in and you go to someone who is good at it. You ask what you should read in this field and you go down to the bookstore and you look at the books. Any book that is published in paperback obviously sold well in hardcover. Read the table of contents. Make sure the writer has experience in the area you in which you want to learn about. Buy the book and read it. People ask, "How can I be sure it is the right book?" You can't be sure; stop trying to be sure.

When I go to the bookstore I buy three or four books and bring them home and read them. I may only find one chapter of a book that's helpful, but that chapter may save me a year of hard work.

The fact is that your life is precious. A book costs twenty of thirty dollars. How much is your life worth? How much do you earn per hour? A person who earns fifty thousand dollars a year earns twenty-five dollars an hour. A person who wants to earn a hundred thousand dollars a year earns fifty dollars an hour. Now, if a book cost you ten or twenty dollars but it can save you a year of hard work, then that's the cheapest thing you have bought in your whole life. And what if you bought fifty books and you paid twenty dollars apiece for them—a thousand dollars worth of books—and out of that you only got one idea that saved you a year of hard work? You've got a fifty times payoff. So the rule is you cannot prepare too thoroughly.

Wright

In the last several months I have recommended your book, *Get Paid More and Promoted Faster* to more people. I have had a lot of friends in their fifties and sixties who have lost their jobs to layoffs all kinds of transfers of ownership. When I talked with you last, the current economy had a 65 percent jump in layoffs. In the last few months before I talked with you, every one of them reported that the book really did help them. They saw some things a little bit clearer; it was a great book.

How do you turn setbacks and difficulties to your advantage? I know what it means, but what's the process?

Tracy

You look into it you look into every setback and problem and find the seed of an equal or greater advantage or benefit. It's a basic rule. You find that all successful people look into their problems for lessons they can learn and for things they can turn to their advantage. In fact, one of the best attitudes you can possibly have is to say that you know every problem that is sent to you is sent to help you. So your job is just simply look into to it and ask, "What can help me in this situation?" And surprise, surprise! You will find something that can help you. You will find lessons you can learn; you will find something you can do more of, or less of; you can find something that will give you an insight that will set you in a different direction, and so on.

WRIGHT

I am curious. I know you have written a lot in the past and you are a terrific writer. Your cassette programs are wonderful. What do you have planned for the next few years?

TRACY

Aside from speaking and consulting with non-profits, my goal is to produce four books a year on four different subjects, all of which have practical application to help people become more successful.

WRIGHT

Well, I really want to thank you for your time here today on *Mission Possible!* It's always fascinating to hear what you have to say. I know I have been a Brian Tracy fan for many, many years. I really appreciate your being with us today.

TRACY

Thank you. You have a wonderful day and I hope our listeners and readers will go out and get *Focal Point* and/or *Victory!* They are available at any bookstore or at Amazon.com. They are fabulous books, filled with good ideas that will save you years of hard work.

WRIGHT

I have already figured out that those last two books are a better buy with Amazon.com, so you should go to your computer and buy these books as soon as possible.

We have been talking today with Brian Tracy, whose life and career truly makes one of the best rags-to-riches stories. Brian didn't graduate from high school and his first job was washing dishes. He lost job after job—washing cars, pumping gas, stacking lumber, you name it. He was homeless and living in his car. Finally, he got into sales, then sales management. Later, he sold investments, developed real estate, imported and distributed Japanese automobiles, and got a master's degree in business administration. Ultimately, he became the COO of a $265 million dollar development company.

Brian, you are quite a person. Thank you so much for being with us today.

TRACY

You are very welcome, David. You have a great day!

ABOUT THE AUTHOR

ONE OF THE WORLD'S TOP SUCCESS motivational speakers, Brian Tracy is the author of many books and audio tape seminars, including *The Psychology of Achievement, The Luck Factor, Breaking the Success Barrier, Thinking Big* and *Success Is a Journey.*

BRIAN TRACY
www.BrianTracy.com

AN INTERVIEW WITH...

JIM BANDROWSKI

DISCOVER YOUR INNER LEADER

DAVID WRIGHT (WRIGHT)

Discovering your inner leader is the topic I will be focusing on with Jim Bandrowski, president of Strategic Action Associates, a global training and consulting firm that helps organizations achieve breakaway results. His highly requested speech and training topics include "Breakaway Leader," "Strategic Innovation," "Breakthrough Lean Six Sigma," and "Execution Excellence." Jim is author of *Corporate Imagination—Plus: Five Steps to Translating Innovative Strategies into Action* published by Simon & Schuster. It was the first book on how to put creative thinking into strategic planning.

For the last fifteen years, Jim has been speaking, training, consulting, and researching around the world with the mission of finding the *one thing* that distinguishes great leaders from good ones. Ten years ago he found it and has since presented it to over ten thousand CEOs, executives, managers, and professionals around the globe, and asked for their ruthless feedback, which is part of his model. Jim reports he has received a surprising 99.9 percent confirmation from audiences and interviewees that this one thing is the real deal. It will be the focus of my interview with him on how to discover the remarkable leader within you.

BANDROWSKI

Thank you, David. It's wonderful to be here.

WRIGHT

Let's get right to the big question. For thousands of years, scholars, researchers, and gurus have been seeking the singular trait that differentiates great leaders from good ones, and you say you have discovered it? Please, tell me what you believe it is.

BANDROWSKI

David, in a single word, it is *Amplitude*. Great leaders unleash their intellectual amplitude and modulate their emotional amplitude.

My definition of leadership is simple. It is guiding people to a new and better place. Management is improving that place when you get there. Leaders *unquo the status*. Managers improve the status. Both roles are a part of every person's job. Everyone is leading someone, if only themselves. But the higher you are in an organization, the more your job should be focused on unquoing.

Breakaway Leaders achieve remarkable results in all walks of life by being imaginative, inspirational implementers. And by creating an innovative culture, they motivate the people around them to do the same. Their leadership style inspires their organizations to conceive and put into action inventive strategies and processes that amplify value while reducing costs. Customer *elation* is the goal, not merely delight.

WRIGHT

Jim, please first explain what you mean by unleashing intellectual amplitude and what it does for one's leadership capacity.

BANDROWSKI

Jack Welch declared: "You can't be a moderate, balanced, thoughtful, careful articulator of policy. You've got to be out there on the *lunatic fringe.*" The core competency of remarkable leaders in all walks of life is they continually visit two *intellectual* fringes. One extreme is being 100 percent *passionately positive*, to drive innovation. They set super high stretch goals, pursue a powerful purpose, dream a vivid vision, conceive ideal strategies, are irrepressibly optimistic, continuously sell the benefits of change, and lavish positive reinforcement on employees who are aligned and executing. This focus on the *light side* provides purpose, and energizes and motivates the entire organization.

But great leaders also visit the opposite extreme or fringe, which is 100 percent *constructively negative,* to assault imperfection. Yes, negative thinking—the *dark side*. But the key word is "constructively." World improvers identify and passionately pursue the vital few things that are immensely imperfect today or potentially so in the future on any one of five levels in: 1) society, to change the world, 2) commerce, to rock their industry, 3) market, to identify unmet needs, 4) organization, to improve its processes and people, and 5) themselves, for self-improvement. In each they are leveraging the power of negative thinking—done constructively. Al Gore exhibited this capacity when he spotlighted global warming in his film *An Inconvenient Truth.* He rang the alarm for the world.

Great leaders, successful inventors, and world changers are excellent problem-solvers. But they are even better problem *finders*—seeing huge problems the rest of us don't see or don't believe are possible to solve, so we think, "Why bother?" Once remarkable leaders have identified the problems and confirmed the value of solving them, they motivate their entire organizations to leap to the positive extreme to seek solutions, select the best ones, and implement them. Breakaway Leaders believe the impossible isn't.

WRIGHT

Jim, explain to me exactly how great leaders employ big intellectual amplitude.

BANDROWSKI

David, I want you to visualize the full cycle of a sine wave that starts at the mid-point, goes downward into constructive negativity, turns upward to passionate positivity, and then comes back down to the mid-point again. I call this the *Breakthrough Wave.*

Find what is broken and fix it. Exceptional leaders motivate their organizations to discover what is most imperfect in the world, industry, and company. Then they encourage and embrace any and all ideas at the positive extreme, even if they appear to be too expensive, unfeasible, or counter to company policy.

Scott Cook, CEO of Intuit, the company that sells Quicken and other software, stated in 2007, "To me, success is changing customers' lives for the better, and solving their important problems. That's what keeps our company young. That means we're constantly trying new things, things that have not been 'what we do here.' " Innovative leaders know that these wild things may work or can fuel the conception of an attractive, feasible strategy. They are constantly constructive, not destructive, throughout the Breakthrough Wave.

Ineffective leaders may have high intellectual amplitude, but they defeat innovation through destructive intelligence. For example, at the negative extreme they know every reason why new ideas won't work, and on the positive extreme they fall in love with unworthy ideas, particularly their own, or they falsely apply their organization's strengths. In the 1990s, Motorola did this by continuing to push its advantage in analog cell phone technology while Nokia leapfrogged over them with digital.

Wright

What happens when a leader and his or her organization has a low intellectual amplitude or none at all?

Bandrowski

Entrepreneurial companies by definition start out with a big amplitude to create and implement a new innovation—their growth engine. But as companies grow, either the founders or the hired professional managers can get conservative, thinking they are reducing risk. The amplitude of the company's Breakthrough Wave then dampens until it is zero. Electronic engineers call this "signal attenuation." I have had clients in just about every industry, including many in health care. What happens when a patient's EKG dampens to zero?

WRIGHT

Flatline!

BANDROWSKI

Exactly. Zero amplitude in terms of leadership and innovation will eventually result in what I call "corporate flatlining"—not recommended for management, employees, or stockholders. Amplitude is how great companies, leaders, inventors, and innovators in all walks of life achieve remarkable results, and then sustain them.

Just think what would happen if the entire world's amplitude dampened to zero. In 3000, for example, products and services would be the same as they are today. The world on its journey to a better place—abundant energy, world peace, a cure for every disease, a meal and education for every child, a vocation or avocation for every person—would never be attained.

Now most leaders aren't flatlined, but many have low intellectual amplitude. On the constructively negative side, for example, you hear statements such as "customers in our industry complain about all us suppliers" (my breakthrough antenna goes up) or "let's not discuss uncomfortable, unsolvable issues."

On the positive side it is "don't propose any ideas unless they are feasible, safe, and assured a good return on investment" or "let's not aim too high because we are sure to miss." The expression to "think out of the box" is a sixty-year-old cliché and comes from the nine-dot creativity exercise. David, I give you the box—it *is* low amplitude. The box is real, not a metaphor. And a person, organization, or country can graph theirs and how much they stay in it or go beyond it. In today's incredibly fast-moving and competitive world, you either lead out of the box or your company gets buried in one. If you reduce your amplitude to zero, the box becomes a coffin.

Amplitude has physical significance in that it is the generator of intensity and strength. For example, it determines the loudness of sound and the brightness of light. And amplitude is an expression X-Game judges use to express the height of jumps in snowboarding, freestyle skiing, skateboarding, BMX biking, and other extreme sports. Call my model *High Amplitude Leadership.* Generation X and Y want meaning. Employees want to work for a leader and company that have huge amplitude aimed at a high purpose.

WRIGHT

Let's switch to the emotional amplitude you mentioned earlier. You said that great leaders modulate theirs. How does this fit into their core competency—their one thing?

BANDROWSKI

As with intellectual amplitude, there is a constructive and destructive way to employ emotion.

Leaders with constructively high emotional amplitude on the positive extreme demonstrate great passion for the mission and vision for their businesses. They are emotionally involved and connected with their companies and this sparks passion in the rest of their organization.

On the constructively negative extreme, they feel deep empathy and compassion for their employees, customers, and the world. This leads to recognizing latent customer needs—the fuel of innovation.

But the danger is that high emotional amplitude can easily slip into being destructive. Destructive positive emotion taken to the extreme is called mania, with feelings of omnipotence, omniscience, inflated self-esteem, grandiosity, and the pursuit of excessively risky activities or investments. On the negative extreme it manifests itself in anger, yelling, despair, paranoia, delusions, fatigue, and deep depression. Combine the two extremes and you have a manic-depressive (i.e., bipolar), generally not a quality that boards of directors are seeking in a CEO or CEOs in executives.

Interestingly, many remarkable leaders could be described as having a mild form of mania called "hypomania." They brim with infectious energy and have irrational confidence in their really big ideas, as in entrepreneurs who gamble second mortgages and their children's college education funds on their new ventures. Examples of notable hypomanic leaders includes Jim Clark, cofounder of Netscape, Craig Venter, genetic pioneer and maverick, Christopher Columbus, Alexander Hamilton, Andrew Carnegie, and many more. They were provocative, unconventional, impatient, and their unstoppable zeal enabled them to change the course of history.

Steve Jobs is another example. He likes to make his own rules and has changed the game in entire industries. He sets amazingly high goals for his product developers and the rest of the organization, and is ruthless in dealing with schedule slips. He views himself as an artist, Apple's creator-in-chief, and has listed himself as "co-inventor" on over one hundred Apple patents. And he judges the world in binary terms. Reportedly, products in his view are either "insanely great" or the other extreme. He has called subordinates either geniuses or "bozos," indispensable or no longer relevant. David, do you see a touch of polarized thinking and emotion? Products at Apple are hatched in conversations something like this: "What do we hate? Cell phones. What do we have to make? A cell phone with a Mac inside." The rest is history. This works for Steve Jobs, but he is unique, so I don't recommend leaders emulate him. At 53, I've been told that Steve Jobs has mellowed a bit with age. But he still intends to change the universe.

We all have in our minds a mix of constructive and potentially destructive intellectual and emotional amplitudes. Harnessing the constructive elements and dampening the destructive ones are the keys to remarkable leadership, as well as a life of fulfillment. Eliminating all emotion in the form of zero amplitude doesn't work because it will lead to a listless, lifeless, and boring organizational atmosphere.

The key is to let your constructive emotional amplitude out of the box, and keep your unconstructive emotional amplitude *in* the box. While I would never claim to be perfect at this, many people do the opposite—they harness their constructive emotions and easily unleash their deconstructive ones. They should try what I call *emotional rebounding*: when success is starting to go to their head, rebound off an imaginary roof of the box—humility. Conversely, at the immediate onset of anger, disappointment, etc., rebound off an imaginary floor of the box—resilience. Emotional rebounding produces poise under pressure.

Wright

Will you give some examples of great executives who consciously or instinctively employ High Amplitude Leadership?

Bandrowski

The goal at Microsoft when entering any new market or product space is world domination. It doesn't get any higher than that. Yet Bill Gates has often told his employees in his annual state of the company address, "We are two years from going out of business." Microsoft for years has maintained well over $30 billion in cash, so why such a dark side remark? In its industry, products are released and cannibalized every two years, and Microsoft has many competitors who would love to crack its market stronghold. It's not that Microsoft would be out of business if it didn't release a new version of software every two years, but it could lose its dominant lead and trigger the tipping point into a downward spiral. Bill Gates knows complacency kills corporations.

Andy Grove, former CEO of Intel, is another leader who exemplifies the use of constructive intellectual and emotional amplitudes. On the dark side, he wrote the book *Only the Paranoid Survive*. Its central point was that leaders need to constantly be vigilant for what he called an industry inflection point—when a technology or market abruptly leaps to a new and better solution. Productive paranoia is good, clinical paranoia is not. Your company had better be doing the inflecting or here comes that burial box again.

Three other High Amplitude Leaders I can think of include Jack Welch, John Chambers, CEO of Cisco, and A. G. Lafley, CEO of Proctor & Gamble.

WRIGHT

Why not first go upward in the Wave to passionately positive. Can this path also be successfully taken?

BANDROWSKI

Yes it can, David, but with caution. In the Breakthrough Wave, one finds what is broken and then invents a solution. I call the path you just mentioned the *Creation Wave*, which is to create a new vision, strategy, or invention first, as in Appreciative Inquiry. But then one must go to the dark side to confirm if there is a real need for it.

The problem is that many people, teams, and entire organizations fall in passionate love with their ideas and don't want to vet them in the spotlight of harsh reality.

Look what happened to Webvan. Its CEO, George Shaheen, was the former CEO of Arthur Anderson. The company bet a billion dollars of raised capital on building massive, automated grocery warehouses around the country on the premise that a huge market existed for consumers who would order groceries and pay a premium to have them delivered to their homes. Which competitors already had "warehouses" of groceries? Existing supermarket chains that waited for Webvan to go belly up and then they jumped in and served the niche market.

Both the light and dark side are needed, regardless if you begin your *Innovation Wave* positively or negatively.

WRIGHT

Jim, are you saying that remarkable leaders never moderate their intellectual amplitude? Are they ever balanced between the two extremes of passionately positive and constructively negative?

BANDROWSKI

Very perceptive, David. Yes, they spend quite a bit of time balanced in their intellectual wave—scientists call this a state of equilibrium. This may be counterintuitive, but that's exactly where savvy leaders make decisions—in the box. You don't want to judge the potential of a strategy or new venture in either the passionately positive or constructively negative states of mind. One's amplitude that precedes decision-making creates the menu of potential innovative strategies. It is now time to be balanced in one's thinking and select the best ones.

Intellectually balanced is the state in which corporate, divisional, marketing, operations, and other plans should be written. It is also where one prepares a budget, provides a forecast to one's banker or Wall Street, or makes a commitment. These should not be stretch goals (I will discuss this later), but promises with a 95 percent confidence level that you can deliver on them.

WRIGHT

Besides in their leadership style, what are the other primary ways leaders apply amplitude?

BANDROWSKI

The great ones apply their core competency of leading out of the box to ten crucial competencies: 1) strategic leadership, 2) marketing leadership, 3) financial leadership, 4) technology leadership, 5) process leadership, 6) change leadership, 7) organizational leadership, 8) facilitative leadership, 9) self leadership, and 10) global leadership.

As strategic leaders, they help their organizations crystallize its direction, and develop a compelling vision and innovative strategy for achieving it. This is the central responsibility of all leaders, whether they are CEOs of large publicly-held companies, entrepreneurs with a new venture, presidents or prime ministers of nations, chairmen of non-profit organizations, directors of social institutions, heads of religious movements, or team leaders. For starters, world changers don't set reasonable goals as taught in management courses through the acronym "SMART" (Specific, Measurable, Achievable, and Relevant with Timing). They motivate their organizations to go after what I call *SMIT* goals (as in smitten with love), which stands for Specific, Measurable, *Impossible* with Timing. By the way, I used to describe these goals as specific, measurable, *unreasonable*, with timing, until a CEO informed me the acronym didn't work.

Strategic leaders then work with their teams to drill deep into the dark side to discover unmet market needs, hidden profit veins in the industry, emerging trends, organizational wastes, and other breakthrough opportunities. After prioritizing the biggest targets, they cycle back to the positive extreme to focus their organization's creativity in conceiving breakthrough and disruptive innovations. Knowing that most wild ideas are not feasible, they very open-mindedly float wild ideas gently down to earth, trying to build on them before "box reentry." A great technique is to give every wild idea at least one minute of striving to make it work, rather than immediately killing it. Borrowing a term from Ken Blanchard, I call this the *One-Minute Open-minded Manager.* In fact, if every executive, manager, and supervisor did this with every idea proposed to them by colleagues and subordinates, it could transform the culture of an organization to be much more open and innovative overnight. It's the fastest way to satisfy a CEO who says, "I need a new corporate culture by Wednesday."

From here, strategic leaders enter the box to work with their teams to select the best strategies, write a clear plan containing a compelling mission, vivid vision, strategic values, stretch goal, strategic scorecard, brand positioning, overall strategy, major strategies, strategic action plans, and a financial forecast.

Then the best leaders say to their organizations, "Come with me to the dark side," and have everyone brainstorm everything that can go wrong with the plan, and then build in preventatives for each. Eighty percent or more of the risks can be identified and minimized through this bullet-proofing approach, and it dramatically increases buy-in.

From here, *Breakthrough Leaders* cycle the organization back up to the light side where it sells the strategy to all stakeholders—employees, customers, the board, alliance partners, suppliers—everyone.

Leaders at all levels need to spend more time thinking strategically—working on the business rather than in it. As Stephen Covey says, they need to sharpen the saw. If they spend more time sharpening the saw of strategy, and do it with amplitude, they will be able to saw right through their competitors on their way to elating customers.

Wright

Please explain the other nine "crucial leadership competencies," as you call them, and how do leaders employ amplitude in them?

Bandrowski

As marketing leaders, they deeply understand the needs of external and internal customers, and how to compellingly communicate to them. As financial leaders, they identify hidden profit veins in their companies and industries, and develop strategies to capitalize on them. As technology leaders, they see the inflection points coming and guide the organization in determining which technologies to embrace in product, service, and IT development. As process leaders, they encourage the organization to identify variation and waste, then apply my *Breakthrough Lean Six Sigma (BLSS)* approach to bring *bliss* to customers, employees, management, and stockholders.

As change leaders, they make things happen using my nine-step *Execution Excellence* methodology, which combines the benefits of changing with the consequences of not changing, and they then lavish positive reinforcement on those who act in alignment with the strategy. As organizational leaders, they identify, develop, and retain Breakaway Leaders at all levels of the company. As facilitative leaders, they guide everyone around them through the Breakthrough and Creation Waves to identify issues and opportunities, and develop solutions and strategies for them. As self leaders they are constantly identifying their personal strengths to leverage (light side) and weaknesses to improve (dark side), and take action on them.

Last, as global leaders, they articulate a compelling vision, mission, and strategy with a multi-country, multi-environment perspective that connects employees, customers, and suppliers on a global scale. In each of the ten crucial competencies, amplitude can yield remarkable results.

WRIGHT

From my perspective, your tenth crucial competency of global leadership is vital for everyone today. Do you agree?

BANDROWSKI

Yes, David. A global view is imperative to the success of all types of organizations. Virtually every business, including the local coffee shop, has global competition, suppliers, or market potential—usually all three. There is a desperate need for leaders at all levels and in all regions of the world to become globally literate and sensitive from a cultural and business perspective.

Action learning with an emphasis on global innovation is one solution. For example, one of the organizations I deliver workshops through is ALC Education in Tokyo, a division of ALC Press Group, the largest publisher of English language learning materials in Japan. With some of the largest companies in Japan as its clients, ALC's Global Management Program transforms today's managers into tomorrow's innovative global leaders.

WRIGHT

Jim, when and how did you conceive your High Amplitude Leadership model?

BANDROWSKI

In the late 1970s, I began doing research on creative thinking and specifically how innovative leaders, scientists, and others solved impossible problems and achieved breakthroughs. I wrote two monographs for the American Management Association in the mid-1980s, and then the book, *Corporate Imagination—Plus,* published by the Free Press division of Simon & Schuster in 1990. This book explained in depth my strategic leadership process that I summarized earlier. At the 1985 international conference of the Planning Forum, I presented my model in a speech entitled "Putting Creativity into Planning." The conference brochure the following year stated that I was "rated the most interesting of the twenty-five distinguished speakers at the previous year's conference," which surprised me given that back then I had not yet developed into a professional speaker.

Before I could leave the podium, two strategic planning officers from Merck (the company that became *Fortune* magazine's most admired company in

America for seven straight years) hired me on the spot. They insisted I cancel my flight home to San Francisco, fly first class with them to Merck's corporate headquarters in New Jersey that night, and present the same speech to Merck's top management the next day. I consulted to Merck for many years, helping management redesign their corporate and international planning systems, among other projects.

Then in 1995, as I was doing extensive speaking, training, and consulting to *Fortune* 1000 companies around the world, I noticed that innovative leaders applied the same amplitude in their leadership style. The model was born, and I have been presenting and vetting it with audiences ever since. This interview and chapter is the first time I have allowed it to be published. I will describe High Amplitude Leadership in detail in my forthcoming book, *Rock Your Industry: Employ the Core Competency of Remarkable Leaders—High Amplitude Leadership.* It unifies the leadership models of the gurus of the past and present, and intensifies them to a new level of performance.

Wright

At Merck, for example, did increasing its amplitude directly impact its financial results?

Bandrowski

David, at Strategic Action Associates, financial impact is the primary way we measure our clients' ROC—Return On Consulting. For example, in 1989 while helping Merck with its global strategy, my research uncovered Medco, the first mail order distributor of pharmaceuticals. I thought the company was a disruptive innovation in the drug industry. It had enormous growth potential because it cut the cost of prescription drugs to the consumer by 30 percent, when the health care industry was clamoring for lower drug costs.

I recommended Merck acquire the company when it was $500 million in revenue (a speck in the $700 billion worldwide drug industry) and described Medco in my book *Corporate Imagination—Plus*, published in 1990. It took Merck's top management four years to finally acquire Medco in 1993, paying $6.6 billion for this now $2.2 billion in sales company.

Ten years later, in 2003, Merck spun off the division for a huge profit because Medco's $26 billion in revenue began to overshadow Merck's pharmaceutical business. In 2007, Medco's revenues were $44.5 billion, 90 times larger than when I found the company. And in 2008 it captured the number one position in the Health Care: Pharmacy and Other Services sector on *Fortune's* America's Most Admired Companies list. Of all companies surveyed, Medco was ranked number one in "People Management," ranked number two as "Most Admired: Long-Term Investment" (second only to Berkshire Hathaway), and ranked number three in the United States, based on "Innovation" (trailing only Apple and Nike).

WRIGHT

Can the correct amplitude be learned and applied to everything a person does, or is it a God-given trait wired into one's leadership DNA?

BANDROWSKI

Yes, it can be learned, as proven in our workshops, and can elevate a leader's thinking, actions, and performance. But a total transformation of an individual to one who applies it well in all ten crucial competencies would be over-promising. In fact, the perfect High Amplitude Leader may not even exist. Tony Jimenez, Chevron Leadership Forum Program Manager at Chevron Corporation, who has acted as my sounding board on the development of my model for twenty years, recently told me, "Jim, you are describing a mythical leader that we would all like to become." In the 1990s I trained Chevron's top two thousand executives and managers. It took one hundred and seventy-two sessions.

WRIGHT

How do great leaders use amplitude to develop themselves and others?

BANDROWSKI

As Brian Tracy says, "Many people spend more time planning a picnic than they spend planning their careers." Develop a strategic plan for You-Inc., including a mission, vision, values, goals, strategies, strategic action plans, scorecard, and a contingency plan. Then implement, regularly monitor your progress, and coach everyone around you to do the same.

With regard to self-development, follow the advice of Marcus Buckingham of the Gallup Organization who has written excellent books advocating that people should discover and focus on their strengths, and bosses should do the same for them.

I recommend intensifying this through the amplitude of the Creation Wave. First, leap to the light side and brainstorm your unique strengths, defined by Buckingham as specific activities you do well. Supplement this list by asking other people for their opinions about you, and perhaps take one or more assessments. Next, prioritize your strengths in terms of how they apply to your current and potential future positions. Then blend your highest strengths into your personal brand. But before going to market, go to the dark side and brainstorm as many things as possible that could wrong with this brand positioning—how it could be misunderstood, how it could generate less income than you desire, how you may be employing an old strength to a new situation where it no longer applies, such as doing rather than managing. Then build in preventatives for them, or if necessary, reprioritize your strengths. When your strengths-brand survives this gauntlet, find projects, functions, or a company that will enable you to excel by adding your unique value. Alternatively, consider redesigning your current job or proposing a new job to your company that maximizes your brand's contribution. And don't forget to always keep learning new skills to strengthen your strength.

Buckingham emphasizes leveraging your strengths so much that many people think he prescribes ignoring your weaknesses. Quite the contrary. He describes in his books excellent ways to deal with one's weaknesses such as getting a little better at them, designing a support system, using one of your strongest themes to overwhelm your weakness, finding a partner with a strength in your weakness, and/or just stop doing it.

Again, I recommend powering this up with amplitude, but this time using the Breakthrough Wave. Go to the dark side to identify your weaknesses for your current and potential future jobs by brainstorming them yourself, asking others for their ruthlessly honest opinions, and taking assessments such as a 360 diagnostic. Prioritize your weaknesses in terms of which ones need to be improved the most, and then drill for the root causes of the weaknesses. Now, leap to the light side and conceive ideal solutions to the root causes. Then float them down to reality, select the best ones, develop a short- and long-range action plan, take consistent action, measure your progress, and continuously improve.

We all know how tough it is to change ourselves, and even recognize when we are doing something wrong, for example cutting people off in mid-sentence when excited. I recommend creating a support group of companions who will signal you the moment you do it. You will need thick skin when receiving caring but cold-blooded feedback in real time, but if you accept and act on it, the speed and trajectory of your improvement can be huge. At the least you will mitigate your weakness, and you may even be able to turn it into a new strength.

Strengths are important, but dealing with one's weaknesses is equally important. A leader must have a competency and style profile that is outstanding in one or a few areas, and good in the rest. One glaring weakness can crash a career.

When I was in college, both male and female students used to rate each other on attractiveness. Remember the 1979 movie, *10?* Well, in a profile of a person's physical and personality characteristics, a single one or two score in any important criteria negates all of the nine and ten scores of the person's other features. I recall one woman telling me she dumped a strikingly handsome, rich, fun, sexy guy because he'd lose his temper too often—a destructive emotional amplitude. So to capitalize on our strengths, we need to increase our important weaknesses to at least an acceptable level of five or six. Oh, and she also told me, dating three threes doesn't add up to a nine.

So find ways to regularly seek candid, constructive feedback from everyone around you. Consider feedback a gift—accept and act on it, throw it away, or re-gift it.

WRIGHT

What are you working on now, in addition to traveling the world giving keynote speeches, delivering training programs, and doing consulting projects for clients?

BANDROWSKI

I am putting the finishing touches on my next book, *Rock Your Industry: Employ the Core Competency of Remarkable Leaders—High Amplitude Leadership.* It greatly expands on what I have covered with you today and delves deeply into how leaders at all levels can unleash the constructive amplitudes of their entire organizations. Packed with hundreds of examples, it will provide actionable, practical advice on ways to reinvent their industries, take their businesses to the next level, and achieve extraordinary financial results. Chapters will cover leading with amplitude, fostering disruptive innovation, inventing *Breakaway*

Strategy, reinventing processes, executing change, facilitating breakthroughs, advancing oneself, and most important, developing everyone around you.

WRIGHT

Jim, thank you for sharing your thoughts on leadership. They are truly seminal.

BANDROWSKI

David, it is an honor to be part of this book. May breakthrough be with you.

About the Author

Jim Bandrowski is a global speaker, trainer, and consultant who helps organizations achieve breakaway results. President of Strategic Action Associates in Danville, California, he is author of *Corporate Imagination—Plus: Five Steps to Translating Innovative Strategies into Action* (The Free Press division of Simon & Schuster). *Entrepreneur Magazine* said: "This book is for those wanting new momentum in their industries." *Industry Week* stated: "James Bandrowski's system emphasizes action that helps companies beat their competition."

Jim's specialties are Breakaway Leadership Development, Strategic Innovation and Planning, Breakthrough Lean Six Sigma, and Execution Excellence. His firm's clients include GE, Disney, Merck, AT&T, Hewlett-Packard, Boeing, Kodak, TRW, Electronic Arts, Chevron, Exxon, Saudi Aramco, Abu Dhabi Ports Department, McKesson Corporation, Safeway, Century 21, C. Itohshu, Mazda, Andersen Windows, American President Lines, Kaiser Permanente, United Health Care, HealthNet, U.S. Navy, Chateau St. Michelle, Columbia Crest, and Cakebread wineries, and a variety of government agencies, cities, and non-profit organizations.

For the last fifteen years Jim has been speaking, training, consulting, and researching all over the world with the mission of finding the *one thing* that distinguishes great leaders from good ones. Ten years ago he found it and has since presented it to over ten thousand CEOs, executives, managers, and professionals, as well as shared it with hundreds of great leaders while interviewing them. Jim has received a remarkable 99.9 percent confirmation from these audiences and interviewees that his one thing is the real deal. This one thing was the focus of this chapter, and Jim would love to receive your candid feedback on it, suggestions on how to improve it, and hear about how you have applied it.

Jim Bandrowski

President, *Strategic Action Associates*
696 San Ramon Valley Blvd., Suite 367
Danville, CA 94526
(925) 820-8838
www.StrategicAction.com
JimBandrowski@StrategicAction.com

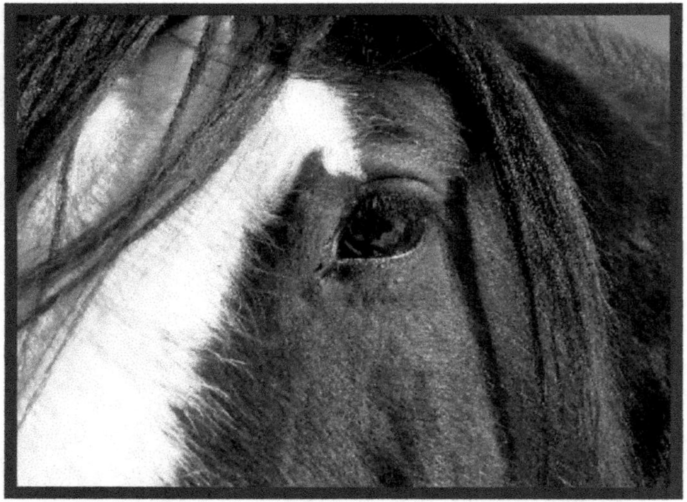

Be Wisdom

BE - Lead Mare

Spirit of Leadership

Pebble Ledge Ranch, Novelty OH

Be...

* Grounded
* Centered
* Focused
* Clear
* Aware
* Open
* Yourself
* Authentic
* Truthful
* Forgiving
* Gentle
* Still

May the Horse Be With You!

AN INTERVIEW WITH...

CHRISTINA PITTS

THE PHOENIX CHALLENGE: RISING TO FULFILLMENT

DAVID WRIGHT (WRIGHT)

Today we're talking with Christina Pitts of Pitts-Aldrich Associates. Her wealth of experience as an educator, executive, lawyer, public speaker, and as an athlete, author, organ donor, and more, creates a colorful mosaic of wisdom and expertise that enables her to help clients achieve enduring success. She works from front line to boardroom, in profit and non-profit sectors, offering a range of valuable consulting and coaching skills to businesses and individuals. She volunteers her services and talents to non-profits as a board member, instructor-lecturer, fundraiser, mentor and advisor. Christina recently published her first novel, a chronicle of middle years told in stories, letters, and poems. Nature soothes her soul.

Christina, welcome to *Discover Your Inner Strength.*

Christina Pitts (Pitts)

David, I'm honored to participate. Thank you for the opportunity to share my insights for this valuable anthology.

Wright

Please tell our readers what inspires you.

Pitts

I'm inspired and motivated by my vision—*A Legacy of Exceptional Contribution*—and by my mission, *Inspire the Power of One to Greatness.* Since identifying these guiding principles nearly twenty years ago, they remain intact, channeling my growth and contributions, professionally and personally. I'm inspired by them in everything I do, to help individuals, teams, businesses, communities--and myself--continue to seek and find greatness.

Specifically, for this anthology, what inspires me is the hope that even one insight I offer will be a catalyst for readers to rediscover, or redefine, or begin to find their power and their inner strength to fulfill themselves as human beings.

Many times each day I recognize my own challenges, and marvel at opportunities to grow into my larger self at every moment: at work, at home, at play, in nature. I continue to learn that when we *embrace* challenges and *intentionally and thoughtfully make choices*, we gain new understanding, new wisdom, and new vigor to generate desirable outcomes.

I'm inspired by our human potential for fulfillment-wholeness-greatness. And I hope to inspire our readers to know that each of them can thrive, especially in adversity. Sharing The Phoenix Challenge enables me to "pay it forward" to our readers, helping them to discover their inner strength.

Wright

Who is your audience?

Pitts

Everyone who's derailed by any change or crisis *and who is willing to engage in self-discovery, study, and skills-building* to attain the life they desire for themselves.

All of us achieve personal and professional success, and celebrating those successes comes easily. All of us endure personal and professional losses, and most of us struggle mightily trying to endure and overcome. With The Phoenix Challenge I hope to reframe the notion of "struggle," shifting to a paradigm of "easy acceptance with grace."

What I suggest isn't new thinking. It's a restatement of teachings that come to us from mythology, philosophy, and religion; from art, music, poetry; and from daily living and interaction.

I'm offering a synthesis of what I've learned from my own and others' experiences, encountered throughout my professional and personal life.

Those who are self-aware will immediately understand The Phoenix Challenge. For these readers I'm affirming what they already know either directly or intuitively, and this chapter is a refresher. It's a re-charge, with perhaps a slightly different image as they tweak the kaleidoscope.

For those who are not so self-aware, or those who reject the importance of self-awareness, the value proposition in reading on is this: if you commit to read with an open mind, I'm certain I can ignite a spark of realization (1) that the shoe fits: there is no challenge you've experienced that is unique to you; and (2) if you're willing to sincerely accept The Phoenix Challenge, you will enrich your life experience and move closer to your sense of achievement, accomplishment, and fulfillment: closer to self-actualization.

Wright

So what exactly is The Phoenix Challenge?

Pitts

Simply this: willingly *allow* ourselves to "crash and burn" so that we can "rise again" in better, stronger form.

The Phoenix Challenge is about hunkering down in times of struggle and going through rather than avoiding the pain. It's about accepting what is, seeking to understand the opportunities that lie within, around, and as a result. It's about enduring chaos to understand what ultimately will bring enrichment. The Phoenix Challenge is about letting go in order to renew and transform.

When I agreed to this interview about discovering inner strength, the image that immediately came to mind was that of a stunning bird rising from ashes. I recalled a scene from the World War II film, *Flight of the Phoenix.* I pictured Yosemite's flames; recollected clients' circumstances. Without hesitation I connected *Discover Your Inner Strength* with the mythological phoenix, and knew that this would be an essential topic to explore with our readers.

In various mythologies, the phoenix is a sacred bird that at the end of life descends to build a nest of twigs that it ignites. Flames consume the phoenix, and in the throes of death the bird transforms into new life, a more powerful and more beautiful magnificence. In Chinese mythology the phoenix represents virtue, power, and prosperity. And in some myths, the firebird's tears heal all wounds. "Universally, fire is regarded as a spiritual symbol of awakening....a purifying force that can be constructive or destructive, depending on how we use it."—Angeles Arrien, *The Second Half of Life*

The Phoenix Challenge invites us (individuals, teams, organizations) to be that mythological bird which uses the flames as a constructive force for transformation. At times of challenge, we must consciously and intentionally allow ourselves to descend to the depths, enduring the chaos, in order to ascend as someone stronger. The learning, while we're descending to our inner selves, yields enlightenment, and that enlightenment produces our enrichment.

The myth plays out in all aspects of life. Siddhartha becomes the Buddha; Christ rises on the third day. In their symphonic music, *Death and Transfiguration* and *Concerto Elegaic*, Strauss and Rachmaninoff delicately render the descent and ascent. The Japanese poet, Masahide, declares: "The barn has burned to the ground. Now I can see the moon."

We see the myth in all of Nature. As with the fires of Yosemite, lightning ignites flames on African plains, scorching thousands of acres of earth, and the extreme heat germinates within hours new plant life. The emperor moth evolves over *years*, until in its final stage it dissolves completely, then flies from the cocoon as a creature of stunning beauty. In another context, Katrina offers lessons that we hope, someday, will save lives and cities. These represent immutable laws in nature that we can embrace and learn from, exemplifying the essence of The Phoenix Challenge.

Jane Hamilton's *A Map of the World* can easily be your story or my story of mistake that leads to tragedy; guilt that begets depression and threatens loyalties; perseverance that generates ramrod strength and newfound marvels of relationship.

In my career and life experience; in conversations with family, friends and colleagues over the years; in my research, and my study, I know this to be true: meeting challenge head on, determining to accept with grace, *and* to understand and learn will yield great wisdom and a renewed sense of achievement and accomplishment—a new kind of pride in personal competence.

> *Deep in the wintry parts of our minds we are hardy stock and know there is no such thing as work-free transformation. We know that we will have to burnto the ground in one way or another, and then sit right in the ashes of who we once thought we were and go on from there.*
>
> —Clarissa Pinkola Estes, *Women Who Run with the Wolves*

WRIGHT

Please give us some examples of what The Phoenix Challenge looks like for us.

PITTS

Here's a simple example. I erroneously erased from my computer an application for an important scholarship for a year-long self-development program. The document represented days of thinking, and was arguably my best writing in recent months.

I was alone in the parlor of an old B & B on the coast of Maine, gazing at a sparkling ocean as I crafted, over six slow hours, answers to challenging questions. In a rush to depart for a run along the river before meeting friends for dinner, I saved the wrong version, and instantly knew I'd made a horrible mistake. First came disbelief, then denial, then utterly painful reality. My frustration ranged from hot tears, to self-recriminations, to hopeful cheers—all stifled so as not to make a spectacle of myself. Over the next several hours I acknowledged that I had a mini-Phoenix Challenge. Back in my hotel room...

- I recognized my descent into an emotional freefall, a fireball of anxiety-energy.

- After telephoning my computer geeks, I accepted with considerable regret that the document was irretrievably lost, and that nothing would change that loss.
- I stared out the window at a heavy rain, and examined my mistake to understand it and what led to it, and determine how to prevent it ever happening again.
- Out on my run, as I absorbed the beauty of the lush riverside, I sought the lessons about the application process itself, and declared that the next iteration would be the right one!
- Finally, I let it go. I put it out of mind to enjoy the evening and following days with dear friends.

When I returned home, people came to the rescue as sounding-boards and editors, helping me to re-capture the essence of what was lost, and craft more cogent responses. The team rescue effort was exhilarating! Completing the final document, I smiled with a silent *'Atta Girl.* I'd done my best. I had faith that the right person would receive the scholarship and comfortably accepted that the "right person" might not be me. If someone else was selected, then unseen other opportunities would come to me as a result of engaging in the process. And those benefits continue to flow to this day.

Here are other examples that represent more significant Phoenix Challenges:

Job

Jim was fired from the job from which he hoped to retire. In the span of forty months the Shining Star imploded to *Persona non Grata.*

He'd been recruited from his previous position because of his distinctly different talents that would complement those of other executives. Jim welcomed the opportunity to orchestrate a turnaround for his business unit.

The first few years appeared to go well. People who sought challenge and professional development thrived under Jim's leadership, and the organization he led was producing tangible results it hadn't seen in some time. Jim's performance reviews were very favorable.

Then the tide turned. Suddenly (it seemed), his relationships with his bosses soured. Within six months he was out of a job, his life spinning out of control.

Throughout the months of his downfall, Jim guessed that he was losing favor. He sought coaching and counseling to check his perceptions (his bosses said everything was fine), and to find ways to weather the storm of what he was certain was impending termination. Through the turmoil and sadness, his health suffered.

During this tumultuous period that lasted nearly a year, Jim continued with coaching, working hard to understand objectively what led to his downfall. He strengthened bonds with those who sincerely supported him and offered respectful candor; he severed ties with people he could not trust. He was able to find a job where his skills would be valued. Though he sold his home at a significant loss, he's relocated and now settled in a house "more beautiful than the last," in a peaceful, rural area.

Jim's practicing new skills that will help him better recognize warning signs, and is focusing on describing what "Life Two" means to him: defining smart steps to realize the dream, while recognizing that the real joy is not the dream itself, but *building* on situations as they arise. Jim's beginning to believe that the fun is in the going, that nothing will ever be "always perfect," and that he can "let go" anytime because something more fulfilling awaits.

Test

I went to law school on a dare. Attended at night because I couldn't afford to quit teaching and become a day student. The measure of my full-time-job-and-law-student angst is that back in the '70s law school demanded rigorous study for five or more years for night students, while only three years for day students. I was so compelled to finish that I covered the *night school* curriculum in *three years*.

I was driven, obsessed with getting it over with because I was in thrall with illusion and foolishly trying to hold together what I knew in my heart was an unhealthy relationship. When it ended, I was a wreck and in tears, it seemed, every waking moment. I couldn't concentrate while studying for the bar exam, and, of course, failed—just barely, but not worth appealing.

That failure taught me two things: 1) others are not in control of or responsible or accountable for my happiness and, 2) I must move on from my grief because the next place must be better than the place of misery I'd created for myself. So I focused, studied, and despite the considerable odds against those taking the exam a second time, passed with flying colors. I found a job that thrilled and challenged me. I met people thirty years ago who continue today to nurture my spirit.

Team

The Accounting Department was floundering under tired leadership and internal competition that created many silos. The CFO determined that transformation was essential and asked the department to engage in a lengthy initiative to "bring the department into the 21st Century."

A few months into the initiative, all of the directors left and the department was in horrendous turmoil. Of the remaining staff members, only half committed to the transformation. The department was without a leader, attempting to reorganize, retool, and create for itself a vision, strategy, and model of teamwork that would set a new standard of excellence in the company. All this, and with their regular jobs, too.

Running aground was not an option for the "Staunch Six," as they called themselves. They rallied to the enormous challenge of transforming with no designated leader at the helm and disengaged others standing aside. Long-term relationships teetered, loyalties waivered, demands mounted. Yet faith in their commitment to personal and professional growth carried them through the turbulence.

A year later, at a company-wide celebration, the department officially launched a revitalized accounting service dedicated to exceeding customer expectations. At eighteen months a new department leader joined the ranks, others signed on, and enhanced processes and systems promised great and enduring success.

Now, nine years later, different leadership at the company has reverted to "the old ways," and unfortunately the Staunch Six no longer have the support for change and growth they once had. Four remain in the department, continuing to practice lessons learned in the often painful yet inspirational process of transformation. Two left, taking their skills and learning elsewhere.

Despite the significantly changed circumstances, including separation, the Staunch Six continue to counsel, guide, and mentor each other so that on an individual level they continue their upward spiral of self-fulfillment. Whenever appropriate, they share with business colleagues their Best Practices in meeting their own Phoenix Challenge.

Tragedy

Several years ago, within the span of four months, my brother died, I lost my job and my apartment, an important relationship soured, and a parent grew seriously ill. All this on the heels of launching my solo consulting practice. The saving grace was my deep belief that these losses would somehow enhance my life in years to come. I pulled out all the stops: forged ahead building the business, kept friends and family close, studied, found mentors, and nurtured my need for R & R and play. *And it wasn't easy.*

Often I look back on that period and see the blessings. Allowing myself to grapple with the chaos and confusion enabled me to understand how the impending loss of my brother, though terrible, gave me an opportunity to deeply enrich our relationship before he died. Losing my job validated my values and ethics, positioned me to produce new and exhilarating work, and enabled me to realize the extensive, valuable network I'd created in former positions. I found a home where the surroundings promoted dazzling creativity. I discovered new faith and strength and power in myself.

The Phoenix Challenges of that time prepared me well when my father died. Over nine days of his coma before death, I would not leave my father alone, except for a few hours to "touch home" and refresh myself, and only when another remained at his side. In the many hours when others weren't with him, I sat with him and talked to him; held his hand, touched his cheek; slept at his side through all the dark nights. My behavior confused many, and I held fast against their entreaties to "leave and take care of yourself," knowing in my heart that caring for myself meant remaining with my father, thanking him in words and touch and silence for our life together.

When my mother died years later, my brothers and I became orphans. The tragedy of never going home again to parents' unconditional love and guidance, of no longer being anyone's child, proved a mighty struggle for me. There were moments when I felt that without my mother I could not go on. And yet I did.

Again I understood that I must not avoid the grief, but head directly into it. So I cried. I remembered. I questioned. I studied. I sought advice. I surrounded myself with people who could listen. I sought moments, hours, days of solitude. I continued to try to grow from within.

A new lesson for me is that grief can so skew other realities that one risks making serious mistakes of judgment. I nearly ended enriching friendships of over forty years. Thankfully, with those lifelong friends and others, and in self-reflection, I patiently and deliberately questioned thoughts and actions to gain deeper self-understanding, and together we salved the wounds.

Betrayal

As CEO of a well-known non-profit, Alexis worked hard to enhance programs and services, increase membership, grow volunteer ranks, and develop staff and board to their full potential. Though the hours were long, she loved the work because the organization's mission so inspired her.

Five years into the job, a few board members decided to set a new course for the nonprofit, which undermined much of the work of prior years. Alexis was asked to step down, a decision which appeared to many to be personally-motivated rather than a sound business strategy. She felt betrayed in particular by those who worked so hard to recruit her.

Like Jim, the process of suddenly losing a job threw Alexis into a tailspin. Among other challenges, she had some serious health issues and depleted all her savings. Most distressing to her was to see the organization that she'd worked so hard to build heading toward almost certain collapse. After nearly twenty months searching for another job, she found an interim executive position.

Throughout her ordeal, Alexis held on, certain that something better awaited her. Yes, she was angry. At times paralyzed. Often disappointed. Yet faith in herself kept her moving forward: job-seeking, soul-searching; discovering, challenging—growing.

Recently, the board contacted her. They admitted a serious mistake in letting her go, feeling "terrible about the circumstances" and their role. The board asked her whether she would be willing to consult with them to help revive the organization.

After only a few seconds' pause, Alexis answered, "Of course. I love the organization and I'd be honored to help."

There are common threads in each of these stories:

- change/crisis
- creating important challenges to the status quo
- suggesting shifts in attitude/thought/action

- forcing a choice: face the challenge head-on, stand still, or (attempt to) avoid it.

What others and I have learned in our Phoenix Challenge experiences is that these difficulties open doors to opportunities for fulfillment. The turmoil of change or crisis (challenge to the status quo) is part of the natural ebb and flow in all circumstances of life, and we can choose either to follow the current or spin endlessly in the eddy's vortex or thrash about in the ripples of the undertow. In choosing to "surf the waves of change" (as a client so aptly puts it), we elect to rise above, setting aside fear to embrace learning and growth.It's essential to recognize that *we have a choice*. Viktor Frankl, in *Man's Search for Meaning*, teaches us that

> *Man is ultimately self-determining. What he becomes he has made out of himself. In the concentration camps...we watched and witnessed some...behave like swine while others behaved like saints. Man has both potentialities within himself; which one is actualized depends on decisions, but not on conditions.*

And Kierkegaard reminds us that *not* to decide is in itself a decision.

WRIGHT

Is there a process I can use that will help me succeed in a Phoenix Challenge?

PITTS

I've crystallized and condensed The Phoenix Challenge into a seven-step process, creating a simple framework that I hope will resonate.

The process seems easy, the work is not. It requires strength and courage and mental skills to help us act with intention and awareness while navigating the journey to wisdom and self-fulfillment.

The 7 Steps of The Phoenix Challenge are grounded in many stories over many years: my own, as well as those of clients, colleagues, friends—all of us grappling with significant challenges professionally or personally, or both. In the end, it comes to this: embrace the tough times—the challenges and chaos—sometimes with a wry smile, sometimes with gritted teeth, as opportunities to initiate and experience something more desirable. Ultimately, we're able to look around us in the face of these challenges appreciating *prosperity*—sensing beauty, tranquility, joy, comfort, peace, and experiencing well-being in the moment.

The Foundation

Step 1 – Become Self-Aware. Embrace every opportunity to develop self-understanding and *to seek and practice skills!* Consider your self: Who Am I? What gives my life meaning? Consider your work: What skills do I need to hone? To Learn? How can I be a better team member? A better leader? Who are my trusted advisors, mentors, coaches, allies? Consider your network: Who are trusted others outside the workplace who can help me to expand my knowledge and wisdom?

Step 2 – Practice Reflection. Give yourself the gift of extended quiet moments alone to reflect, to meditate, in order to learn from each experience. Explore the full range of your living: successes and tragedies, missteps and marvels, adventures and mishaps. Tap inner reserves; we all have them, and we have more strength than we're aware of. And do not dwell on the past or pin hopes on the future!

Step 3 – See the Signals. Pay attention and observe. Very few changes or crises come suddenly, without warning. There are flags flying in the wind if we'll only pay heed. Before a tsunami, the animals become silent. In the workplace there are mutterings, new groups forming, or unaccustomed calm. Ask questions and deeply explore them, because it is with the questions that real learning takes place. Confirm with trusted others your impressions, then with wisdom confront rather than deny.

Step 4 – Prepare Yourself. As Covey suggests, *be proactive* to overcome the natural resistance to or tendency to flee from that which we fear. Recall and re-center yourself around your personal direction (Step 1). Find a teacher who will offer new insights; find a mentor, a thought partner to guide; find a playmate to help you laugh, especially when the going gets tough. Practice skills and behaviors that already stand you in good stead; and adopt and practice new skills and behaviors.

The Challenge

Step 5 – Acknowledge It. When change or crisis or any challenge to your status quo comes knocking, open the door and acknowledge it. Know it—intellectually, emotionally, and perhaps most important sense-ibly. Use your five senses to grasp the reality, and your sixth sense—intuition—to see the ambiguities and patterns. Give the turmoil a name. Welcome it and the opportunity for growth, enrichment, and enlightenment. Acknowledge your anxiety, your pain, your frustration. And hold gently that wonderful self you've identified at Step 1 and expanded through Step 4.

Step 6 – Let It Be. Know that the storm will pass and that the sun will rise again. Use your coping skills to *be* with the tumult. As many of you know from change dynamics models, the time of greatest chaos is the time when creativity and inspiration crystallize. The "Aha!" comes in this time of confusion and leads you out of the wilderness and into the Promised Land. Rediscover laughter and believe that "this, too, shall pass, and I shall be better for it."

What we run from in Phoenix Challenge situations is the fear of destruction. The phoenix, after all, is consumed in a fire. We fear the pain of the fire and the "end" that is destruction. Yet the lesson of the phoenix is that it is the very pain that brings forth new life, and the tears salve and heal the wounds. As a client declared to me recently, "Short-term pain for long-term gain."

So seek the lessons. Integrate them into your being. Gandhi suggests, "*Be the change you want to see.*" Let go of the need to control: recall Covey's Habit 1 about being proactive and Spencer Johnson's parable of the mice and the cheese—we can only control ourselves.

Step 7 – Let It Go. Believe in the moment. Go *with* the flow, and embrace the current's momentum. Free yourself so that you're fully aware, prepared, and energized for the next Phoenix Challenge moment, which will come. Eliminate or minimize "inappropriate attachments" to people, position, places, problems—they bog us down, acting as a burden.

Eleanor Roosevelt offers, "Yesterday is history; tomorrow a mystery. Today is a gift." We are reminded that "One door closes, another opens;" and "Every cloud has a silver lining." Poets encourage our faith that the fire will *not* destroy us:

And he said, "Come to the edge."
And I said, "I cannot. I am afraid."
And he said, "Come to the edge."
And I said, "I cannot. I will fall."
And he said, "Come to the edge."
And I did.
And he pushed me.
And I flew . . ."
—Guillaume Apollinaire

Finally, as meaningful as others' words are, our own words have even greater power to influence and encourage us. Find language (as words, as feelings) that resonates with you, and use your language to capture what you sense in the moment to propel you forward, to buoy your spirit. Speak the change you want to see; attract the state you desire.

Wright

Is there any way to shortcut the pain of the descent and fire?

Pitts

No. There is no shortcut to transformation. The Phoenix Challenge is not a "magic pill" or any external "save" or "fix." It's about the hard work of self-actualization—embracing change and finding a way to make it gracefully through each minute of the night to find wisdom with the dawn.

If we attempt to shortcut the process, we'll continue to make the same or similar mistakes, which in the long run will set us back instead of moving forward in our lives. As a colleague recently shared, "When we skip any steps, they keep showing up!"

Elisabeth Kubler-Ross researched and identified five stages of grief in her pivotal work *On Death and Dying*. She emphasizes that in order to deal effectively with the grief that accompanies knowledge of death, we *must fully* go through each of five stages in sequence: Denial, Anger, Bargaining, Depression, and Acceptance.

In one myth, the phoenix must live *five hundred years* before it builds its funeral pyre, to be engulfed in its flames, then become the ashes that engender new life. No shortcuts for the phoenix, no shortcuts for us in The Phoenix Challenge.

Think about how people develop a skill in sports or music. No one walks onto a ball diamond for the first time and throws as an expert shortstop; no one picks up a violin for the first time to play like Itzhak Perlman. Each of us in learning a new skill takes one step forward, two steps back or three steps forward and one step back. Another step forward, and perhaps two steps back . . . and that next movement forward is an exponential leap to stellar performance! All of a sudden, it seems, everything clicks and magic happens. The reality is that all along we have been in a process of progress and regress, selecting building-blocks of learning to become competent—even stellar.

Another comparison: climbing a canyon wall. We continually look for handholds and footholds—track up and sideways and sometimes backward—and we never let go to move until we feel solidly safe to take the next step. The same with shortcuts—there are no shortcuts on that canyon wall.

Wright

What is the single most valuable skill we can apply in our daily living?

Pitts

Be present in the moment. Be fully aware because *now* is the only certainty. *Today is the gift.*

Out for a jog last summer, I practiced being in the moment. Tried not to think about this chapter, not to rehearse a client conversation, not to wonder about dinner, just to be in the moment of running—breathing the fragrance of summer flowers, hearing the buzz of lawn mowers, feeling the strength of my sinews and bones, glimpsing sailboats in a race, tasting the lakeside air. Well into the home stretch of a five-miler, I stepped, with the right of way, into an intersection. A mail truck ran the light. In an instant I shoved myself away from the truck and stumbled back to the curb. Knowing I could have been seriously injured or killed, I shuddered at my close call, and immediately understood the wonder of being in the moment, because my last sensations were immersed in *everything* that existed around me. The present (in its entirety) was the gift. And, I realize now, that it was being in the moment that saved me from serious harm.

How does this connect to The Phoenix Challenge? If we're present in the moment, then we're certain to succeed with The Phoenix Challenge. Why? Because we're *acting* by being with the present circumstances. We're not seeking to substitute the present with a memory or a wish.

Be present. In order to "be" we activate ourselves and our senses to deeply perceive the moment. We do not stand still: the phoenix, after all, builds its own funeral pyre.

Presence in the moment is a difficult concept to articulate. I encourage readers to find other sources to clarify this "way of being." A friend recently sent a copy of the cover story in *Psychology Today*'s November-December 2008 issue which offers "How to Live in the Moment...Savoring the Now!" This is an easy read attempting to simplify what is so difficult to achieve. Or plumb the depths with Eckhardt Tolle's *The Power of Now* and *A New Earth.* Or drift calmly toward presence in your life with Mark Nepo's *The Book of Awakening.*

WRIGHT

As I listen to your words, I envision the Yin-Yang symbol. Is this related to The Phoenix Challenge?

PITTS

I believe it is. Yin-Yang embodies many concepts. Among these is the belief that reality is neither black nor white, but is both black and white, the wholeness that surrounds and encompasses what appear to be opposites. The circle of Yin-Yang is about all that lies within and between and around the black and white, as well as the black and white. In the context of Yin-Yang, the duckling is *both* ugly *and* beautiful, and in the end, it's a unique duck. Similarly, the moment is neither good nor bad, it simply is what it is. The moment is all that we have, and we must make choices about how we will experience each moment.

In the context of The Phoenix Challenge, achieving our greatness (fulfillment) *requires* the experience of Yin-Yang:

Through the gateway
of feeling your weakness lies your strength...
of feeling your pain lies your pleasure and joy...

of feeling your fear lies your security and safety...
of feeling your loneliness lies...fulfillment, love and companionship...
of feeling your hopelessness lies true and justified hope...
of accepting the lacks in your childhood lies your fulfillment now.
—Eva Pierrakos, *The Pathwork of Self-Transformation*

The circle of Yin-Yang represents our journey in life with its gifts and its challenges: the black and white *balance* each other. There will be chaos and turmoil; there will be clarity and peace. The question for each of us is whether we will allow ourselves to experience fully the Yin and Yang of each moment in our lives. If we lay a solid foundation for ourselves (Steps 1-4 of The Phoenix Challenge and the wisdom in other chapters in this book), knowing what is our personal Yin-Yang (not what others define it to be), then we can embrace the conflict, chaos and change to find the unexpected gift of "the moment" (Steps 5-7 of The Phoenix Challenge).

Wright

Does The Phoenix Challenge ever end?

Pitts

No. Phoenix Challenges exist for us everywhere, because everything around us is constantly changing, evolving. Nothing in existence is static.

Change is inevitable; how we choose to deal with change will, in the long run, either enhance us, or diminish, paralyze or destroy us. Every day we are tested in large and small ways to meet a challenge head-on, to crash and burn. Accepting The Phoenix Challenge puts us on a marvelous and continuous spiral upward, toward greater and greater wisdom, which I believe brings greater and greater fulfillment.

I know this through the experiences of my clients who represent all sorts of people in all sorts of industries. I see this with friends and family every day. I live this continuously in my own life circumstances.

In closing, we each have unique gifts to bring to the world. When we understand our gifts and limitations, we're better equipped to travel the paths of our life journey. We more easily recognize and accept the journey's obstacles, and learn from them.

The Phoenix Challenge is about embracing the magical learning from the unexpected. As we practice The Phoenix Challenge, we won't avoid the descent, we will embrace it; we won't fear pain and destruction, we will know the beauty of *potential* and *ascend* from the ashes.

WRIGHT

What a great conversation. I've learned a lot here today, Christina, and there's a great deal to take in and to ponder.

As you've suggested, in a Phoenix Challenge it's essential to stop and take stock. To see around us to understand. Then, to choose very deliberately how we will move forward.

I appreciate the dialogue to help us understand the power of The Phoenix Challenge.

PITTS

We teach what we most want to learn, David, so I'm on this journey alongside each of our readers. I hope The Phoenix Challenge becomes another helpful tool to discover and leverage inner strength.

WRIGHT

We've been talking with Christina Pitts, from Pitts-Aldrich Associates. She has a depth and breadth of experience that offers valuable perspectives, as we have learned here today.

Christina, thank you so much for being with us for *Discover Your Inner Strength.*

About the Author

A wealth of experience—as educator, executive, lawyer, public speaker; as athlete, author, organ donor, and more-- creates a colorful mosaic of wisdom and expertise that enables Christina to help clients achieve enduring success. She works Front Line to Board Room, in Profit & Nonprofit sectors, offering a range of valuable consulting and coaching skills to businesses and individuals. She volunteers her services and talents to varied nonprofits: as board member, university instructor & guest lecturer, charity fundraiser, advisor. Christina recently published her first novel, a chronicle in stories, letters and poems. Nature soothes her soul.

Christina Pitts
PITTS-ALDRICH ASSOCIATES
1501 Oxford Road
Grosse Pointe Woods, MI 48236
313.881.3433
www.pittsaldrichassociates.com

AN INTERVIEW WITH...

PAULA LARUE

DISCOVERING STRENGTH THROUGH ADVERSITY

DAVID WRIGHT (WRIGHT)

Today we're talking with Paula LaRue. Paula is an accomplished criminal justice professional. She is the author of *Stalking: Surviving the Hidden Terror,* and she produced the documentary, *Stalking, Terrorized, Threatened, and Harassed.* A recognized expert on stalking, safety, and criminal justice, Paula is frequently featured in television and radio interviews. She is currently the Dean at a Michigan college. She has taught criminal justice at several colleges, has conducted security training for various corporations, and taught at the Detroit Police Academy and the Center for Excellence in Police Management Studies. Paula has a master's degree in Security Administration from the University of Detroit and a bachelor's degree in Criminal Justice from Eastern Michigan University.

Paula, welcome to *Discover Your Inner Strength.*

PAULA LARUE (LARUE)

Thank you David, it's nice to be here.

WRIGHT

So what is a crime prevention specialist?

LARUE

A crime prevention specialist is someone who has expertise in providing information to help prevent people from becoming crime victims. It's someone who has expertise on what to look for so you don't experience a crime situation. A crime prevention specialist is also an expert who is concerned about helping the family and friends of crime victims understand what victims go through and how to help them.

WRIGHT

So what does that have to do with discovering your inner strength?

LARUE

We all have inner strength. I have talked with crime victims who have suffered great tragedies but who have found the strength to move on with their lives.

My inner strength comes from the desire to assist others so that they won't have to go through similar experiences. For example, an ex-boyfriend was stalking one victim. One day he broke into her house and shot her. He then shot himself in the head in front of their two-year-old daughter. This victim was able to pull herself through this horrible tragedy and go on successfully with her life.

The victims I've talked with have demonstrated the strength of the human spirit, which indicates that this kind of inner strength is within all of us.

WRIGHT

So what has driven your own personal success?

LaRue

My personal success has been driven by witnessing the strength of others. I've seen and interviewed many crime victims who have gone on to lead successful and prosperous lives after going through horrendous experiences. They give us hope and inspiration. I've also been driven with the desire to help others know that if you keep moving forward you will succeed.

Wright

Someone told me years ago that if I were walking down the road and I saw a turtle sitting on a fencepost that I could bet he didn't get up there by himself. So who were your mentors in your personal success?

LaRue

My mentors were my parents. They immigrated to the United States from Italy. They worked hard and became successful. They showed me, through their actions and words, that if you have goals, work hard, and treat people the way that you want to be treated, that success would be yours—and they were right. It's something I always keep in the back of my mind.

Wright

So how do you define inner strength?

LaRue

Inner strength is the higher force that gives purpose to our lives and that can motivate a person to keep going when faced with adversity. But it can vary from person to person. With some people, it's their children or their religion or faith. I've also found that it can be an internal stubbornness, meaning that people will not allow outside factors to defeat them. It's important for people to know what their higher force or motivating factor is so that they can draw upon it as needed.

WRIGHT

You say it varies from person to person, so where do you get your inner strength?

LARUE

I get my inner strength from witnessing what others have done when faced with tragedy. I've seen what they've accomplished and how inspirational they are.

For example, one of the victims I spoke with had married a guy who was very persistent in his obsession to marry her. Over time his behavior changed toward her. He became abusive. He would cut up her clothes so she couldn't leave the house. He would take the phone out of the house so she couldn't make calls. He would physically assault her. When she took steps to leave him he kidnapped her at gunpoint as she was going to work. He took her to a friend's house and sexually assaulted her. She managed to call for help. He spent four years in prison for the kidnapping. She has since gone on with her life. She remarried and looks forward to a better future.

WRIGHT

How did you become interested in crime prevention?

LARUE

I was always interested in why people commit crimes. I didn't understand why a person would rob, steal, or murder someone. I started to research into the causes of crimes and met and spoke with many crime victims. Helping people to protect themselves from crimes seemed the next natural step to take in my career. I've always been very interested in helping people so that they don't get hurt.

WRIGHT

What drives you to help others?

LARUE

I know that people can conquer their fears and move on to live successful lives; but some victims don't feel that way. I'm driven with the desire to let victims of crime know that they're not alone and that they can accomplish what they want to do. I'm also driven because I can provide information that may help prevent people from becoming crime victims.

WRIGHT

You said that you had learned from some of your victims when you were thinking about going into crime prevention. In your experience in dealing with these crime victims, what have you learned from them?

LARUE

I've learned many things. I've learned that the human spirit is very strong. I've learned that people can go through horrendous experiences and still continue successfully with their lives. Regardless of adversity, people are always hopeful for a brighter future. No matter what happens to people, if they think that tomorrow will bring something better, and if they continue to pursue that, it will.

For example, I interviewed a stalking victim who worked in a beauty salon. Her ex-boyfriend kept showing up at the beauty salon and it was frightening the customers and staff. She ended up losing her job. At first she felt hopeless, but then she became determined that her ex-boyfriend would not control her life. Today she owns her own beauty salon.

WRIGHT

When you're a victim of a crime, particularly a violent crime, how can you find the strength to continue with your life?

LARUE

Continuing on with your life helps to identify with your higher power or purpose and focus on who or what will benefit if you move forward with your life. Crime victims have said to me, "I go on because of my children; I want my children to live a happy, normal life." They've also said, "I go on because I'm angry that this happened and I won't let it stop me from accomplishing what I want to do." While others have said, "I go on because I want my life back." The list goes on and on, but the bottom line is that people want control of their lives. They may not realize it at the time, but they will do whatever it takes to get them where they want to be.

WRIGHT

What advice would you give to friends and family of a victim of a serious crime?

LARUE

I try to help family and friends of victims to understand that victims could be blaming themselves. Family members and friends need to help victims understand that the crime was not their fault. The criminals perpetrated the illegal act(s) on the victims. I also try to explain to family and friends that they should try to help victims find their higher purpose or power. They should also help victims focus on what is important to them so that they see their way through the situation.

WRIGHT

Have you found that victim support groups help?

LARUE

Yes, support groups can be very helpful to crime victims. Support groups can help with the recovery process. They help victims understand that they can go on with their lives, they can still be successful, and that they can still achieve their life goals. The process of recovery is not a linear process—there are good and bad days. Support groups can help victims get through the bad days and help them keep the proper perspective.

WRIGHT

I saw a movie where the whole premise was that a lady was raped and her husband, without even knowing it, blamed her. He thought that maybe she had done something to cause it. Is that something that happens a lot?

LARUE

It does happen a lot. In many cases we don't understand the dynamics of the crime situation, so we may put some of the blame on the victim. We might think that if the victim had been more careful, then the crime wouldn't have happened. If we place any blame on the victim we put the responsibility of the crime on the victim, which is wrong.

One reason we might subconsciously place some blame on the victim is because it makes us feel safer. We believe we would be more careful; so we would be less likely to be a victim ourselves. However, crime situations don't work that way. The bottom line is that the fault lies with the criminal, not the victim.

WRIGHT

Are there similarities between victims of other tragedies and victims of crime?

LARUE

Yes, there are many similarities between victims of other tragedies and victims of crime. In both areas for example, victims can't believe the situation occurred, or they may have trouble sleeping or eating. They may be fearful of leaving their homes. Sometimes victims don't feel safe—they constantly feel that something bad is going to happen. Unchecked, it can affect them for the rest of their lives. Reactions and recovery times will differ from victim to victim.

WRIGHT

So why do some people have a difficult time moving forward with their lives?

LaRue

Well, it depends on the person. Some people may focus on things they can't control or they may become obsessed with trying to understand why it happened to them. Others are simply afraid to move on or they just don't know how to handle the situation. Some people have support from family and friends to help them overcome adversity. That seems to be a big help. However, there are those people who have a more negative outlook on life, so it takes them a little bit longer to move forward with their lives. It all depends on the individual, his or her mindset, and strength of purpose.

Wright

So who can benefit from your research?

LaRue

Really, anyone can benefit from my research. People who are crime victims or have suffered any adversity can benefit from knowing how others have been able to move on and succeed. Family and friends of crime victims who would like to know how to help them can benefit from my research. In addition, people who want to take preventive measures regarding their safety can benefit. It really can help anyone.

Wright

So what advice do you have for people struggling to find their inner strength?

LaRue

My advice is to look within yourself; you have the power to overcome any adversity in your life. Focus on those who depend on you and who can benefit if you advance with your life. Always remember that you have the power within yourself to do whatever you want to do. If you're struggling and don't feel that you can handle what has happened to you, seek the help of others. Whether they are family members, friends, or others who have had similar experiences, remember that you are not alone and there are many resources and avenues available to you. You need to find the strength to take the first steps to recovery. In the recovery process, the first step is the hardest.

Wright

Tell me, why do some people whose life is difficult seem to be stronger than others who seem to have easier lives?

LaRue

That's a good question; it depends on the mindset of the individual. Some people can have what others see as a difficult life; however, the person experiencing it may not see his or her life as difficult. So it depends on the person's outlook, purpose, or drive. Some can find their purpose or drive easier than others can.

Some people, who seem to have a very easy life, may see their life as very difficult. Regardless of the situation, it's how we proceed to go on with our lives that is important.

Wright

What is the message that you want our readers to know so that they can benefit from your research?

LaRue

My message is that regardless of the circumstance you find yourself in, focus on what you can do. Take small steps every day to accomplish your goals. Remember that there are people who have, against all odds, refused to give up control of their lives. You can go on successfully, even though you have much adversity in your life. Never give up. You can and have the strength within yourself to do what you want to do in life. Always remember that you're not alone, there is help out there for you. Don't be afraid to reach out and ask for it.

Wright

Well, what an interesting conversation, Paula. I haven't talked with you in a long time and it's great catching up. You have really given us some great information here. You've given me a lot to think about and I'm sure our readers are going to learn a lot from this chapter in the book.

LaRue

I hope so David. This book will be an inspiration to everybody because of all the information that you're providing to them.

Wright

Today we've been talking with Paula LaRue. Paula is an accomplished criminal justice professional. She is a recognized expert on stalking, safety, and criminal justice. Paula is currently the Dean at a Michigan college.

Paula, thank you so much for being with us today on *Discover Your Inner Strength.*

LaRue

Thank you, David. It's always a pleasure.

About the Author

PAULA LARUE IS AN ACCOMPLISHED criminal justice professional. She is the author of *Stalking: Surviving the Hidden Terror,* and she produced the documentary, *Stalking, Terrorized, Threatened, and Harassed.* A recognized expert on stalking, safety, and criminal justice, Paula is frequently featured in television and radio interviews. She is currently the Dean at a Michigan college. She has taught criminal justice at several colleges, has conducted security training for various corporations, and taught at the Detroit Police Academy and the Center for Excellence in Police Management Studies. Paula has a master's degree in Security Administration from the University of Detroit and a bachelor's degree in Criminal Justice from Eastern Michigan University.

PAULA LARUE
plarue@comcast.net

Chapter 15

An interview with...

Betty LaMarr

The Head-Heart Connection

Discovering a Path to Business and Life Success Without Compromise

David Wright (Wright)

Today we're talking with Betty LaMarr, international speaker and author. She is president of Nadisa Associates, an executive coaching and consulting business. Betty's many years in business are distinguished by significant accomplishments in a wide range of senior positions. She has served as the senior vice president of sales and marketing for a South African telecommunications company, executive vice president of an Orange County IT consulting firm, global alliance executive for a Boston-based technology integration firm, and director of business development for a worldwide diversity consulting firm.

She received her MBA from Pepperdine University after earning a BS in marketing from California State University in Los Angeles. Betty is certified as a coach by the International Coach Federation and serves as a board member of the Professional Coaches and Mentors Association. She is also an advisory board member for National Association of Women MBAs.

Betty, welcome to *Discover Your Inner Strength.*

BETTY LAMARR (LAMARR)

Thank you, David. I'm happy to be here.

WRIGHT

What is it about *your* life that is a demonstration of how values create a basis for business and personal decisions?

LAMARR

After more than two decades in high technology, I realized there were a few things I could have done differently to have a better career and a more satisfying life:

1. Recognize that it's okay to use both my head and my *heart* in business. One doesn't necessarily compromise the other.

2. Understand that personal values create the *foundation* for business and life decisions that contribute to success or distress.

3. Appreciate that life is a *journey* and not a destination, allowing the opportunity to live a conscious and satisfying life at home and at work.

I'd like to share a personal experience about how my values came into play in my professional life. I've had a few careers in corporate America. But after being in the computer industry for more than twenty years, I left the corporate life and moved to Africa. I left a job I'd had for thirteen years where I had upward mobility and where things were going really well for me professionally.

In fact, I was the first member of my family to work in a major corporation and the first female in my region to become a sales manager and then a district sales manager in charge of $100 million in revenue. After being a trailblazer for many years in high technology, I was positioned to become the first African-American female vice president in the company. That represented a great deal of pride for the women working there. Clearly, I had job success and security. But I did *not* have a high level of personal satisfaction. That caused me to do some reflecting.

I was over forty and looking at my life. I asked myself: *What do I want my life to be? What kind of legacy do I want to leave?* I had come to a crossroads. I was questioning whether my life would be about climbing the corporate ladder or about making a contribution bigger than just having a job. As I walked through this dilemma, I realized I didn't want to just make more money and buy more expensive clothes. I truly wanted to make a contribution to the world community.

I decided to ask my company for an international assignment. The company offered me a choice of France or Switzerland. I turned them down. I wanted a position I knew would make a difference in people's lives. When the opportunity came to work with a telecommunications company in South Africa, I chose that instead. I could use my skills and talents to benefit people who had been denied the opportunity for growth for many years and at the same time give greater meaning to my life. I would no longer be defined by the corporate definition of success. I would measure the meaning of my life based on the impact I had on other people.

Many people I spoke to about my decision described me as "courageous," "adventuresome," and a "risk-taker." Of course, that's not how I saw myself. I just wanted to make a difference in the lives of those whose voices were not being heard, and I wanted my legacy to be about more than corporate achievements.

At the time, I didn't realize that this decision was about my values, that my desire for independence from the traditional definition of success was taking precedence over my need to make money. I just knew that there was an "incongruence" in me. I finally got comfortable with my decision after asking myself: *What's the worst that could happen?* My answer was in knowing that if all else failed, I would have an experience that I had never had and I could return home without embarrassment to the life I had before.

That decision was a turning point for me. I didn't realize it at the time, but my values were speaking loudly. The experience allowed me to get in touch with what values really mean and how they change over time. What was important to me at thirty was different than at forty. In hindsight, I realize that the values of independence, making a contribution, and spirituality were much more important to me than the values of money, prestige, and power.

WRIGHT

What is a situation you encountered that you think might be a lesson for our readers?

LAMARR

The most important is what I call my "Head and my Heart" lesson. You see, most of us are trained to live from the neck up. Our culture values knowledge, quick thinking, and a solid education. We get a lot of acknowledgement for our degrees and our accomplishments. The more difficult the science, the more we appreciate it. The intuitive professions aren't valued as much.

As I grew professionally in high tech, I was trained to think logically and rationally. When making a decision, I learned to look at historical results and outcomes, and to keep emotions out of the equation. What that meant over years of managing people and revenues was that when I came to work I left 50 percent of me at the door. I had a low level of confidence in my intuition and feelings because I was taught they didn't matter in a business environment.

I focused on results and tasks rather than on people. Business conversations were more about "doing" rather than "being," about sales and the challenges of getting the results we wanted. I steered clear of the touchy feely stuff. I feared people would see me as soft or weak or ultimately take advantage of me. Is that amazing, or what? I didn't know I could exercise my personal power in a way that served both me *and* the company.

That was in the seventies and eighties when women were trying on the male model of "command and control" management. We didn't have female role models being celebrated for using their gifts—as women who just happened to be in power. I'm thankful I eventually reached a level of self-awareness that allowed me to move from "high tech" to "high touch." Doing so put me in touch with *all* of the power I possess, both intellectual and intuitive.

What I discovered in the process is that living in your head keeps you disconnected from how you feel. And knowing how you feel is the key to honoring your values. When you're out of touch with your feelings, several things can happen:

- You make decisions that may not be in your best interests.
- You increase your threshold for stress and anxiety, often lowering resistance to diseases and illness.
- You become disconnected from your heart, and miss out on the richness that your feeling state provides. Living in your head impacts your ability to be deeply touched by experiences.

You know you're out of touch with your feelings when you find yourself feeling detached in situations when others are emotional. You feel numb. As a corporate manager, people sometimes told me, "Betty, you seem a bit aloof." People felt I wasn't in touch with their hearts, with their sense of being. I eventually learned that the connection between your head and your heart is essential to living well and feeling good about showing up every day. That's being authentic. In order to be authentic, you have to know who you are. And without authenticity, you'll end up sleepwalking through life.

Wright

You spent more than two decades in major corporations in the high-technology industry; what is one lesson you learned that you believe others might still use today to increase their job satisfaction?

LaMarr

If I think of it as an opportunity to give people just one tool out of my bag that will put them on the path to discovering all the *other* things they'll need along the way, it would be: *remember that you're better than you think you are.* When you have an opportunity to take on an assignment that stretches you, put your fears aside. When you say "yes" to a big idea, the universe conspires to support you. Living with that attitude increases your self-confidence and provides rich experiences that average people won't have in their lifetimes. *And* you'll gain much satisfaction for living an extraordinary life and pursuing an extraordinary career.

Sometimes people fail to make a decision because they don't feel assured of success. They forget there are many lessons just in the experience.

WRIGHT

Values are often considered positive. Do you think there are times that values can have a negative impact on your life? If so, do you have a personal example?

LAMARR

In my coaching practice I help people connect with their values. I teach that your values can be conscious as well as unconscious. There are times when you *react* to your values and times you *respond* to your values.

Let's look at the value of integrity or honesty. I had a client who told me her boss asked her to make copies of a book after the copy room had denied the project due to copyright law. She felt she was compromising her values by being asked to do something illegal. So those feelings you experience, the tensions you feel, and the upset that comes up in your body when you're facing those kinds of decisions are a clear indication that you're out of alignment. Remember: there's greater commitment to what you're doing when you're in alignment with your values.

Are there times that values can have a negative impact? Yes. Does being in touch with your values always give you a positive outcome? No. But being in touch with the feelings behind your values is likely to give you a more positive outcome than not being in touch with them.

I've seen many situations when people's values—the things they hold dear—have caused suffering.

One of my clients placed strong value on belonging and affiliation. This person loved to join organizations and had a high need for acceptance, which in turn caused her to tolerate behavior from others that made her feel unappreciated. She felt she was always competing for attention from other members of the group. She was like a rat in a maze, running from one side to the other.

When a person looks for approval from the outside, it becomes difficult to feel complete or satisfied because different people want different things. If you're not confident, if you don't have your own sense of self, you'll continually pursue acceptance. Instead, I encourage people to maintain an understanding of their values, look at how they feel, and then honor those feelings.

Even in my own life my values have not always served me best. At one point in my pursuit of excellence, I defined "excellent" as "not making mistakes." To accomplish a task, I looked at how things had been done in the past, thinking that would ensure success. I got things done, but without creativity or innovation. I also missed the opportunity to learn from my mistakes. If I had seized the opportunity to excel without self-judgment, I would have built more confidence in my own ability instead of just doing what others had done before.

WRIGHT

How do you think our readers could be more conscious of their values and stay in a place where they're not compromised?

LAMARR

You have to know what's important to you at this point in time. People often will merely outline the values they heard in their family for years. But people have different values at age twenty than at thirty or forty. That's why it becomes important to take an assessment to get in tune with your most cherished values. People say they know their values, but after taking a formal values assessment they realize they really *didn't know* what their values are. There's often a gap between what they think their values are and what the assessment points out to them.

The point is—the more you understand yourself and your important values, as well as your non-negotiable boundaries, the less you'll be compromised. That's not to say you'll never make compromises. Every day people are faced with values that clash with theirs. A conflict could come from your spouse, your employer, or your friends. It's important to recognize someone else's values, especially when they infringe upon or affect your life. But it's *more* important to recognize your own core values. I encourage everyone to take the values assessment I provide here. It will help you begin to walk the talk. It will help you close the gap between *knowing who you are* and *doing who you are*. Take the values assessment below to learn what your most important values are.

Values Assessment

Rate each value using the scale below. Consider what the words mean to you; don't worry about formal definitions. Think about whether each value feels important to you. Make your decisions quickly, and be discriminating in your choice of what is "very important."

Rating Scale

1 = Very important; 2 = Somewhat important; 3 = Importance varies; 4 = Little or no importance:

- Achievement
- Advancement
- Adventure
- Affluence
- Authority
- Autonomy
- Balance
- Beauty
- Belonging/affiliation
- Clarity
- Challenge
- Change
- Collaboration
- Community
- Competence
- Competition
- Contribution
- Courage

- Creativity
- Fun
- Financial security
- Fame
- Family
- Friendship
- Happiness
- Health
- Humor
- Intelligence
- Inner Harmony
- Influence
- Intimacy/love
- Integrity/honesty
- Justice/fairness
- Knowledge
- Loyalty
- Orderliness

- Perseverance
- Personal growth
- Physical fitness
- Power
- Privacy/solitude
- Recognition
- Relationship
- Respect
- Responsibility
- Risk
- Sensuality
- Security
- Stability
- Spirituality
- Status
- Vitality
- Wealth
- Wisdom

Of the values that you rated as "very important," choose the ten that are most important to you. Write them down, and then jot down a few words or phrases that explain what the words mean to you. Then rank each value from one to ten (with one being the highest). The rankings will provide you with a list of your important personal values.

WRIGHT

There's a lot of change around me right now and I'm in a transition, so I feel the need to take what comes along. How can I still honor my values under these conditions?

LAMARR

When faced with change, we tend to be fearful of the unknown. We want to stay in that familiar place of yesterday. But there's nothing like change to emphasize what your values really are. Have you ever heard someone express a point of view about culture or politics and had a strong reaction? That kind of visceral reaction is how it feels when you're asked to do something against what you believe is right for you. I want you to get in touch with that feeling.

You'll always be better served by being in touch with what's really important to you. If you compromise your values, you'll find that over the long run you won't be happy; you'll have more stress in your life. Let's say you take a job just to take it, but your feelings tell you it isn't the right fit. As soon as you show up on the new job everybody else will also know it's not a fit. Suddenly you're facing yet another failure and a potential setback to your self-esteem. Instead of compromising, get in touch with who you are and respect what you need. There are certain things that are non-negotiable, so take your time.

WRIGHT

How is it that by our own core values we measure our success and happiness? Is it our values that tell us what's important in our lives?

LAMARR

Without values or beliefs, we would be mechanical—driven here and there by the unexpected changes of life. Without values, we would be creature-like, compelled to action solely by our urges and passions. Clearly, we're all motivated to move our lives in certain directions—and because we're *not* mindless creatures, that motivation is determined by core values.

Personal values are the things we believe are important, that motivate us, and to which we give priority. Your values are an expression of what you perceive to be important truths about life. But if I asked you what your personal values are, chances are you'd struggle to find the answer. Most of us are not fully aware of our personal values, which range from the commonplace, such as the belief in hard work and punctuality, to the psychological, such as self-reliance, concern for others, and harmony of purpose.

As you evaluate your core values, keep in mind that people relate to personal values in a number of ways. For example:

- Those who value *thoughtfulness* continually think about the things they cherish and believe in.
- Those who value *individuality* place value on responsibility; they are self-reliant and act with self-respect.
- Those who value *truthfulness* cannot bring themselves to tell a lie.
- Those who value *family* or *friendship* will sacrifice personal interest for the good of others.
- Those who value *goodness* cannot bring themselves to do something they know is wrong.
- Those who value *power* are driven to implement their values. The most successful people constantly evaluate their values and are continually driven to turn them into reality. For those individuals, values are an inexhaustible source of inner power that energizes them, driving them to the heights of success, while at the same time bringing deep fulfillment.

Your values determine your decisions and guide your life, which means that getting in touch with your ideals is an important step toward success and happiness. Those core values are reinforced by your emotions, which in turn become a vision that you hope to realize for your life. Whether you actually make the effort to implement that vision is another matter.

WRIGHT

Today, I hear so much about a "purpose-driven life." How do I live my purpose and my values?

LAMARR

There is much conversation today about the purpose-driven life, and I absolutely support that. But we're not here on this earth for just *one* purpose.

We're here for small purposes, for big purposes, and for purposes that we won't even understand until they've long become a memory. If you spend your time looking for that one true purpose in life, you're wasting your energy. You could wake up one day to find that life has passed you by. In the same way, we worry about "sunk costs" or "sunk time." In other words, we worry that a particular experience or choice we've made has been a waste of time and effort. But there are no sunk costs. Most life experiences are transferable. In everything you do, there's a lesson you can take to the next life opportunity.

I've been reminded over the years that good experiences are good, and bad experiences are good. They all prepare us for what comes next. Life is not so much about living right as about living well. And the definition of living well is when your daily choices are so satisfying that if because of some fluke you don't wake up tomorrow, you can look back and say: "Life was like a good movie; it was worth the price of admission."

WRIGHT

If I feel that my values are always in conflict with my work, my partner, spouse, and others, how do I hold on to those values without appearing unreasonable?

LAMARR

Friends, partners, employers—they all have values that have an effect upon your life. Consequently you could find yourself living according to the values of other people instead of following your own. At work you might focus on pursuing increased productivity, profits, and sales targets. Yet how many of those values match yours? If you spend your life meeting only the values of your employer, would that make for a happy and successful life? It might if you measure your success based solely on winning promotions and pay raises. But how many people go through life feeling that true success is much more than earning money? Increasingly, success is measured by other criteria. So for a majority, following an employer's values would not lead to a successful life. Considering that for most people success is measured by more than just financial gain, it's important that you follow your own definition of success.

In relationships with other people we stress the values of loyalty, reliability, honesty, generosity, and trust. On a down-to-earth level we might place great value on cleanliness, punctuality, and order. Therefore, when you feel uneasy or uncomfortable about how others operate in their values, your attitude, disposition, and happiness are affected. I've had clients who worked in environments lacking integrity in dealing with customers. They literally felt sick just by doing their jobs, because what they were required to do went against their values. Many of them made compromises daily. Those are the people who end up with high blood pressure and other stress-related health issues. Does stress affect your happiness? Of course it does.

Discomfort and stress about your decisions is an indication that something is out of alignment with either your values or your interpretation of those values. So being clear about your values can keep you anchored when the situation around you is falling apart. It can keep you in touch with your authentic self, with who you are, and most important of all, with the person you want to become in your continuing development as both a human being and spiritual being.

WRIGHT

What advice would you give to those looking for more satisfaction in their work and in their life?

LAMARR

You *can* have it all; you just can't do it all at the same time. You have to make choices and establish priorities. Some days your priority will be work, at other times personal relationships or family. Think about a symphony or jazz combo. When all the instruments are playing together, you hear beautiful music. If just one instrument plays alone, the music soon gets boring; you need harmonies and rhythms brought into the mix. When it comes to balance in our lives, many think that all things have to be equal, but that's not the case. There are times when you might play a solo and then come back to the combo. That doesn't mean you're out of balance; it just means you've created an opportunity to showcase a single talent.

You do this in life when you go through phases where you have a particular interest in a project or hobby, like golf. You spend a lot of time on that particular interest, but that doesn't mean you don't like work or family. It just means that you want to experience something else. So don't be hard on yourself. Most opportunities are not once-in-a-lifetime events. It's important to enjoy this journey called life and to remember it's not just about the destination!

WRIGHT

What a great conversation! I really appreciate the time you've spent with me today and answering all these questions. I've learned a lot. You've given me a lot to think about.

LAMARR

Thank you for inviting me, David. It's been a joy to share my thoughts and ideas. I hope everyone can take away something worthwhile from my message today.

WRIGHT

Today we've been talking with Betty LaMarr, international speaker and author. She is president of Nadisa Associates, an executive coaching and consulting firm. Betty is certified as a coach by the International Coach Federation and serves as a board member of the Professional Coaches and Mentors Association. She is also an advisory board member for the National Association of Women MBAs.

Betty, thank you so much for being with us today on *Discover Your Inner Strength.*

LAMARR

Thank you.

About the Author

Betty LaMarr, international speaker and author is President of Nadisa Associates an executive coaching and consulting business. She supports leaders and business owners to assess developmental opportunities in their organizations to accelerate change in people and profits. For more information please email: betty@nadisa.com and check out the website at www.nadisa.com.

Betty LaMarr

13428 Maxella Ave. Suite 749
Marina Del Rey, CA 90292
Phone: 310. 574.9181
info@nadisa.com
www.nadisa.com

Chapter 16

AN INTERVIEW WITH...

LT. COL. BOB WEINSTEIN

HOW TO GET YOUR PRIORITIES STRAIGHT

DAVID WRIGHT (WRIGHT)

Today we're talking with Lieutenant Colonel Bob Weinstein, USAR-ret. For more than thirty years he has focused on leading others, first as a military instructor with the U.S. Army Command and General Staff College and now as a professional speaker and beach boot camp instructor in the areas of leadership, performance, productivity, priorities, team-building, fitness, and weight loss. Adding to his diverse background, he is a law school graduate and was a practicing attorney for ten years. He is a member of the National Speakers Association and is certified by the American Council on Exercise. He has a book coming out this fall (2008) titled, *Change Made Easy, Your Basic Training Orders to Excellent Physical and Mental Health.* Known nationally as "the Health Colonel,"™ Bob has been featured on the History Channel, Fox Sports Net, PAX Television, NBC6 South Florida, Univision, Telemundo/NBC Universal, and in *The Miami*

Herald, Las Vegas Tribune, The Washington Times, and many others. And one more thing, he doesn't have pets because they can't do push-ups.

Bob, welcome to *Discover Your Inner Strength.*

Bob Weinstein (Weinstein)

Thank you; thank you for having me. I'm still offering a reward for anyone who presents me with a dog that can do push-ups by the numbers.

Wright

So what do people need to do to get their priorities straight?

Weinstein

The topic of priorities is actually a topic for me personally and I decided that in this process I'll just share what I've discovered with others as well.

Let's get right into it. Follow these steps:

- Audit and inventory your life up to the present.
- Fine-tune those areas that need work.
- Chart your course by either journaling and/or using the method of listing your long- and short-term goals as a way to calibrate and double-check your priorities and goals on a daily basis.
- Make adjustments along the way and stay on track.

Imagine you are now the *President of the United States of Your Life.* Your country to govern is your life. You're going to take a look at the various cabinets and action plan each of them for improvement. You're in charge, so call a meeting of your various departments so that you can assess to improve them as *Commander and Chief of your own decisions and choices.*

1. The Department of Family, Friends, and Relationships
2. The Department of Finances
3. The Department of Justice, Ethics, Values, and Character
4. The Department of Formal and Informal Education
5. The Department of Health

6. The Department of God
7. The Department of Jobs and Careers
8. The Department of Social Life
9. The Department of Others
10. The Department of Self-esteem
11. The Department of Home-life Security
12. The Department of Time

I decided that the *Department of Time* was so important that it needed to be elevated to a cabinet level position. It's one of the major reasons people do not do certain things or stay focused on others, sometimes to the detriment of any one of the other departments even if they are more important or so important that they need to be a part of an overall life action plan.

Identify what your basic universal values are—values where people are more important than rules, regulations and programs.

It is possible on a case-by-case basis or in general that a program intended to be for the benefit of people has started to be a disadvantage and even harmful to them.

Before you can know your priorities, you have to know who you are and what your purpose is in this world we live in. A great tool to help you accomplish this is the development of a vision and mission statement. The vast majority of people will not write a vision or mission statement. I am targeting these people. I want to make it easy for people to get a better grasp on their long- and short-term goals in life. "Grasp" is the operative word here, not just an intellectual exercise that is done and forgotten. My job is to make it possible for all people to envision where they want to be in life's journey and how they want to finish life's race. The great benefit is they will discover hope and immediate fulfillment while pursuing their worthy life goals.

I had an interesting experience the other day that is a great example of seeking out and pursuing your priorities. I do volunteer work with the Covenant House, a faith-based organization that helps homeless and runaway youth. Once a week at the local Covenant House in Fort Lauderdale, Florida, I take them out to the beach for a fitness workout. My main mission though is to challenge and encourage them to overcome whatever obstacles in life they have experienced and to pursue their worthy dreams.

One of the kids kept saying, "I need structure in my life." Every time we'd stop for an exercise he'd say, "I need structure in my life." I thought, "Wow, that is pretty powerful, because essentially what he was doing was putting himself in the mode to recognize what's more important for him, get himself back on track, and overcome those traumatic experiences. This boy came from a rough background and a difficult household.

What he was doing is a prime example of one of the things that we all need to do. We need to walk around every single day thinking about what our priorities are in life. It must become what I call "PT"—*Predominant Thought.*

WRIGHT

So how can one know what his or her priorities are?

WEINSTEIN

This is a scary one for a lot of people and that is why it's avoided or skimmed over. It takes a bold and courageous person to look at his or her life from the beginning up to the present. It's tough for people to let it roll like a film and "see" what impact their own decisions have had—both good and bad—as well as what impact other people and circumstances have had on them, both good and bad. It's important to conduct this review of one's life without bitterness or damnation of others or of oneself. I think one of the biggest ways to know what your priorities are is to take a look at the areas of your life. You should look at each of those *Departments* I listed first of all. Get a feel for things that need to be changed (and every one of us has that inside of us).

Let's get specific. One of the areas can be weight loss, another can be the financial arena, another could be more time for the family, for the children—it can be finding that balance between work and the private side. This process really requires getting very concrete and very specific about what you want.

I think two of the key questions to ask are these: *If I had no restrictions whatsoever—if I could have my life exactly the way I wanted it, how would I design it? What would it include?* I think those questions open up doors of opportunities just like the young man from the Covenant House walking around and saying, "I need more structure in my life." That was a catalyst to redesign his life and refocus his life and his thinking in a more positive direction.

We also need a sense of focusing on others and benefiting others with all that we do. It then becomes much easier to identify what's more important. I can hear some of you now asking, "Hey, what about me? What about taking care of my needs? Others first?" Focusing on others to take care of your needs is a paradox of life that actually works. It is the greatest life recipe for happiness and fulfillment. As Zig Ziglar says, *"You will get all you want in life, if you help enough other people get what they want."*

Some of the popular ways of thinking in our society need to be transformed into unpopular but effective new ways of thinking. General Patton put it best, "If everyone is thinking alike, someone isn't thinking." Whether or not someone is going to be able to pay his or her rent or mortgage will be a high priority item. It may only take a slight shift in thinking to make a major impact on budgeting. That person making a positive shift in thinking may say, "Hey wait a minute, I'm barely making my monthly payment; why don't I start budgeting to stay three months ahead of my rent or mortgage? Who said I have to think month to month? Why don't I start budgeting to pay for a quarter in advance, even though I'm only required to pay for the month?" That will raise the awareness of the overall budget and also make it much easier to determine what is really a necessary expenditure and what isn't. That's a part of getting your priorities straight.

WRIGHT

So what's necessary to make important priorities become a part of your life?

WEINSTEIN

What is necessary is to start practicing—start moving out and start doing. Take it one step at a time. A Chinese proverb states this clearly, *"A journey of thousand miles begins with the first step."* Action speaks louder than words. Mahatma Gandhi said that *action expresses priorities.* He did not say that good intentions are all you need and make sure your attitude is right and that's all. No! He said action expresses priorities—nothing more, nothing less. Someone may clearly say, "I know that my health on an importance scale of one to ten is a ten." As a matter of fact, I think the vast majority of people will agree with this assessment. Let's hold that thought and take a reality check with some statistics that reveal self-deception.

- Three quarters of all Americans believe they have healthy eating habits (from a 2004 poll conducted by Ipsos Insight).
- Half of those polled thought they were overweight.
- Almost all Americans know that most people are overweight,
- Only about one third of Americans think *they* are overweight, says a phone survey conducted by the Pew Research Center.
- Most American adults do not get at least thirty minutes of physical activity a day and one quarter of American adults aren't physically active at all.

Let's call this the difference between active and passive belief. Active belief pursues priorities. An example of active belief is one that is energized, a belief that is the equivalent of being put on Viagra. Something's happening. Passive belief is dead in the water and really makes any priority impotent.

So what we really believe is a priority is what we are actually doing, not what we simply think as a passing thought. How we think does, however, play a major role and here's how. To think for change, we need to take what was a simple thought of excellent health and make it the predominant thought about health. That will put us in a position to get up in the morning and begin strategizing about how to reduce portion sizes of what we eat whether at home or in a restaurant, avoiding unhealthy choices, and scheduling that exercise. This way of thinking translates into doing. It gets all that important stuff in the calendar. As the President of the United States of Your Life, this includes all the life cabinets and departments of your life administration: families, finances, friends, career, education, health, character building, helping others, and doing what God likes.

Wright

Many of us have struggles with our lives—with living out our priorities. How can we truly live the priorities we've recognized to be so important?

WEINSTEIN

"Lock and load" on your long-term priorities and goals and you will succeed. Go through, around, and/or over all obstacles and challenges. Never, ever give-up on a worthy goal or worthy priority.

Yogi Berra knew just what it meant to overcome challenges and obstacles and stay focused on what he wanted to accomplish when he said, "It ain't over 'til it's over." That is the mindset and approach for success. We are going to have struggles and there will be challenges along the way. The struggles are there to increase our awareness about who we are and where we want to go in life. It is a test of where our character stands as well as an opportunity to strengthen character.

If we truly understand our long-term goals, when those obstacles come up along the way, it's easier for us to overcome them. It still may be a difficult challenge to overcome them, but it is definitely much easier if we understand what our long-term goals are and we have them well cemented within us.

Having short-term goals is a wonderful thing and if we look at the entire marketing industry, the buzzwords are: easy, quick, won't take much effort, and that sort of thing. Those short-term goals are wonderful and it's the reason why we jump on the bandwagon so quickly for them—we know we're going to get immediate gratification, or at least that's the expectation. The long-term lifestyle related goal, however, is the one that really carries us through and helps us to finish the life race.

WRIGHT

Life is so dynamic and ever changing. Is it possible to identify our priorities and simply stick with them, or do we need to take a second look every now and then?

WEINSTEIN

We need to design our lives in such a way as to allow the opportunity to step back and take a second look—and a third, and a fourth (well, you get the point). In our society, everything is about doing, doing, doing, and we forget that there is a higher quality of doing—the opportunity to step back and think, catch our breath, reassess, and look at the situation. If we're constantly moving out, constantly thinking, "I've got to be busy," then many times that will cloud our view and keep us from seeing what our long-term goals are and whether or not we're still on track.

WRIGHT

So how can I make sure I'm on track with my priorities? How can I tell how I'm doing?

WEINSTEIN

Measuring your priorities performance is the best way to find out how you're doing. That ensures the development of goals that support your priorities. Measure it and it will improve. Measuring encourages achievement of your worthy goals and priorities. If my long-term goal is to stay healthy, then a short-term goal would be, for example, to notice when my pants are getting too tight. I will then know it's time for me to make some adjustment there. That belt suddenly becomes an easy form of measurement with which to watch my weight.

Another way would be to do what you told me you have done. Go out and buy a suit that fits your ideal weight. Never mind that's it's too small right now. That new suit becomes the constant reminder of where you want to be with your goal—to achieve and maintain your ideal weight. That's a positive challenge to look at your lifestyle overall and get concrete and specific about the changes that need to be made to get into the new suit. That would include eating smaller portions and exercising five to seven hours per week.

WRIGHT

What is the most important thing to keep in mind while pursuing my priorities?

WEINSTEIN

The most important thing is your long-term goal, whatever that may be in your life.

WRIGHT

So is that more of a vision or a mission to carry on for a lifetime?

WEINSTEIN

It would be a vision of the overall quality of all the key areas of your life that result in your happiness and fulfillment. The vision or vision statement would include the following: be financially successful, be healthy, have a good family life, do what God and others like.

WRIGHT

I had a conversation, Bob, with a friend of mine last night. He told me that his father, who is not young but not elderly either, is having some problems with his health. The place where he is staying is costing about $8,000 month, and he is there because of some lifestyle choices he had made. So when you talk about vision and long-term, it would also include things like that wouldn't it? As we get older, daily and monthly care can mean saving a whole lot of money.

WEINSTEIN

It certainly can and it will have a financial impact later on. As I mentioned, when I was in Tennessee (and I mention it to my audiences all the time), we don't want to belong to that club called *WWC (Wheelchairs, Walkers, and Canes)* if we can avoid it. Ending up like that doesn't happen by chance in most of the cases. I would say, approximately 80 percent of people in that situation are there because of a lifestyle they led. It just did not have to be—there weren't any big things they had to do to make it different in order to lead a healthy lifestyle. When some of our retirees and younger folks start spending more time with the remote of the television, that's what compounds those issues as well, and health goes downhill even more.

According to A.C. Nielsen, the marketing information company, the average American spends more than four hours a day watching television. The American Time Use Survey of 2007 conducted by the Bureau of Labor Statistics determined that Americans spend most of their free time watching television.

The President of the United States of Your Life (and that means the average American who governs his own life and lifestyle) should be declaring a state of emergency because television time is not just affecting health. It means less quality time with family and friends, less time to help others, less time to work on our character by reading non-fiction books on how to improve our life, less time for improving career skills, and less time for a spiritual life. Television mostly provides junk food for the mind and it kills the body.

Wright

Do you think there's a way to overcome those times in my life when I just don't feel like pursuing my priorities?

Weinstein

This is where we need a dose of what I call *Vitamin D* (D for *Discipline).* It's interesting that the word "discipline" has become a dirty word in our society; it's rarely mentioned. It seems that we're always trying to work around the aspect of good old discipline and instead, we seek out a quick fix. Anything worthy of achieving is never easy. When nothing else seems to work and I don't feel like it, then I also tell myself, "Get up and do it," "Turn the television off," "Get back on your most important task, even if you don't feel like it, and start moving."

It's interesting—once those first couple of steps are taken, the additional steps are much easier after that. There's a lot of *inertia* in those first steps. And until that other law of physics kicks in called *momentum* it's going to be difficult. We need to be very aware of *Newton's Law of Motion, "An object at rest tends to stay at rest and an object in motion tends to stay in motion . . ."*

Be a constant list-maker. List your tasks, list your goals, list your priorities, list your ideas, and list your reminders. Do it daily. This method is quick and challenges you to think about what you're doing and where you want to go in life. List making helps me remain aware of all of my tasks, goals, and priorities, both long- and short-term. List making helps me to further develop plans and strategies.

Let me give you a breakdown of how I prioritize things to do:

- VIP—Very Important Priority
- VI—Very Important

- I—Important
- NSI—Not so Important
- UI—Unimportant

VIP is of the highest importance and needs my time first. It is usually a task or goal that has long-term, positive impact. Let me give you an example from my list dated August 30, 2008:

1. VI—Follow-up Columbus, Ohio, speaking engagement
2. VI—Add "attorney" to bio and background
3. VIP—Book chapter on priorities
4. VI—Exercise book
5. VIP—Tri-fold marketing brochure
6. VIP—Keynote prep "Catch Your Second Wind" for September 17, 2008
7. I—Set-up a blog site
8. I—Enhance keyword search for Web site
9. VIP—Final revisions, new book, *Change Made Easy*

WRIGHT

Is there anything more important than following one's priorities?

WEINSTEIN

The best test for this is to check your priorities at any given time with this higher law called the Golden Rule, which was shared with ancient prophets and again emphasized by Jesus Christ, *"You must love the Lord with all your heart, all your soul, and all your mind. This is the first and greatest commandment. A second is equally important: 'Love your neighbor as yourself.'* " (Source: Matthew, Chapter 22, verse 37–39, *Holy Bible, New Living Translation.)* Notice that this law states that loving your neighbor is *equally* important as the first. I believe we always need to understand that there are going to be people in greater need than we are, whether they are homeless, troubled youth, troubled adults, or orphans. There are situations that will come along for me to be helpful, even if it's just helping someone whose car has broken down when I'm on the road.

I still remember the days of Boy Scouts—about doing a good deed every day. I think we also need to have our eyes open for those types of situations and not get so locked into the pursuit of our priorities that we have blinders on when it comes to helping others, especially those with an immediate need. The bottom line is that we need to make sure we are not having a "me" day. Simply stated, a "me" day is when everything and everyone revolves around me—I am the focus of all. Of course, that kind of outlook will make us blind to the needs of others and is a recipe for unhappiness.

WRIGHT

So are my priorities always more important than others'? What if someone is in need of special help or support and I'm busy focusing on my priorities?

WEINSTEIN

Here's a great story that exemplifies helping others. What truly matters in this life is helping others win, even if it means slowing down and changing our course.

Just such a situation came up at the Seattle Special Olympics in 1976. The event was a one-hundred-yard-dash involving about ten competitors, all with various disabilities. Well, they got a few paces into the race and one of them stumbled and fell. One or two of the contestants turned around, went back, and helped their fellow contestant to the finish line.

There are situations where winning in life doesn't always mean that I cross the finish line of my ongoing priorities in life's race first. I must also look at my fellow men and women and understand that any one of them—at any given moment—may suddenly become the higher priority in my life. That's practicing the *Golden Rule.*

WRIGHT

What if I'm not really sure what values are more important?

WEINSTEIN

Start with the *Golden Rule.* Reading scripture in the Bible has helped me. The Seven U.S. Army Values were a great guide for me. They are: loyalty, duty, respect, selfless service, honor, integrity, and moral courage. Be a seeker on the lookout for ways to do what is right and not just what is comfortable.

Wright

Is it important to give some thought to our mortality and its meaning?

Weinstein

Thoughts about mortality came quickly for a man named Randy Pausch who died of cancer in July 2008 at the age of forty-seven. He found out from his doctor that he only had six months to live. He had small children and a wonderful wife. He prepared the whole family for his death. He quickly relocated to where the entire family would be close to other family and friends.

Randy was a professor so he decided to hold "The Last Lecture." It was about values and life lessons. The entire lecture was videotaped and can be viewed on the Web. The lecture also became a book titled *The Last Lecture,* and is an international best-seller. The last lecture was a way for Randy to share his life lessons with his children as they grew up even though he himself would not be around.

The other thing is prayer. We need quiet time to really reflect about and figure out what is more important and what is less important. As mentioned, people are always more important than things and programs. The Golden Rule, taken to its highest level, makes the Creator and people more important than things and programs.

Wright

Is there any other way to help me strengthen my priorities?

Weinstein

Have a good solid support system. Find other people who also can support you and whom you can support. I'm sure you've heard of the twelve-step program; it is a fascinating program. I've met a lot of people who have been in that program, whether it's because of alcohol abuse or drugs or some other type of addiction. And those who are leading the programs are people who have also had issues with drugs or alcohol. It's an interesting concept—people are helping other people in a type of situation that helps them in turn to also improve their lives. The truth is that a lot of us could use a twelve-step program to get back on track of doing those things that matter most.

You can take the twelve-step program and apply it to any area of your life for the sake of improvement. It's outstanding for this purpose because it breaks old habits and ways of thinking and replaces it with the new you.

The original twelve-step program was founded in 1935 by Bill Wilson and Dr. Bob Smith. "Dr. Bob," as he was fondly called, summarized the program: "Trust God, clean house, help others," a simple formula that can certainly guide us all to get our priorities straight. The original Twelve Steps as published by Alcoholics Anonymous are:

1. We admitted we were powerless over alcohol—that our lives had become unmanageable.
2. Came to believe that a Power greater than ourselves could restore us to sanity.
3. Made a decision to turn our will and our lives over to the care of God, *as we understood Him.*
4. Made a searching and fearless moral inventory of ourselves.
5. Admitted to God, to ourselves, and to another human being the exact nature of our wrongs.
6. Were entirely ready to have God remove all these defects of character.
7. Humbly asked Him to remove our shortcomings.
8. Made a list of all persons we had harmed and became willing to make amends to them all.
9. Made direct amends to such people wherever possible, except when to do so would injure them or others.
10. Continued to take personal inventory and when we were wrong promptly admitted it.
11. Sought through prayer and meditation to improve our conscious contact with God, *as we understood Him*, praying only for knowledge of His Will for us and the power to carry that out.
12. Having had a spiritual awakening as the result of these steps, we tried to carry this message to alcoholics, and to practice these principles in all our affairs.

This is a radical expression of the Golden Rule—of doing the right thing. Replace the words about alcohol and being an alcoholic and you could insert whatever challenge you are facing to improve your life and your personal behavior where improvement is necessary but has seemed to be out of reach.

Wright

This all sounds great, so how do I get started right now?

Weinstein

Take one area of your life that needs fine-tuning, action plan the corrective steps, and then move out boldly on your way to improving the quality of your life. Put on that presidential hat and *take charge as the President of the United States of Your Life*. Cast out any fear of change or failure or any fear of confronting your own shortcomings (and we all have them). You are worth it.

Listen to that inner voice inside that says, "I need a little fine-tuning in the health department. I need a little fine-tuning in the department of eating. I need more time with my children, wife, or husband. I need a little fine-tuning in the department of finances. I need to strengthen that spiritual muscle." Go through each of those areas where you're feeling just a little bit of inner pain about improving an area of your life that somehow appears to be stalled and not moving forward. That's the starting point. Then just take it one step at a time. It does require action, it requires moving out. Every day sit down and spend a couple of minutes prioritizing. It only takes a couple of minutes to list your priorities of tasking, both short- and long-term.

In this connection, I'll add one final story that really fits. It was a workshop that was done where the presenter of a time management class brought out a big glass jar. He brought out twelve stones. He put all the twelve stones into the jar until no other stone fit, and he asked those who were in attendance at the workshop, "Is the jar full?" Their answer was, "Yes." So he then proceeded to pull out a cup full of gravel. He dumped the entire cup of gravel into the jar. He asked the class once again, "Is the jar full?" Their response became skeptical. Instead of saying yes, some said maybe. He then pulled out a cup full of sand and proceeded to pour it in the jar. Again, he asked, "Is the jar full?" Their response was no.

The presenter then asked the class what the point of the demonstration was. One of the individuals stood up and said, "I know. No matter how little time we have we always have time to squeeze something else in." The presenter quickly clarifies, "No. That's not the point. The point is that if you don't put the big rocks in first you will never get them in. The big rocks are the big priorities in life. That's why it is so important to figure how to get your priorities straight."

WRIGHT

Great example isn't it?

WEINSTEIN

Yes, it's a great example. It impressed me quite a bit.

WRIGHT

Well, Bob, I really do appreciate all this time you've taken with me this afternoon to answer these questions. You've given me a lot to think about. It's about time I was getting my priorities straight, and I'm glad you decided to participate in this particular chapter of our book. I have learned a lot and I know our readers will.

Today we've been talking with Lieutenant Colonel Bob Weinstein, USAR (ret.). For many years Bob has focused on leading others, first as a military instructor with the U.S. Army Command and General Staff College and now as a professional speaker and beach boot camp instructor, all in the areas of leadership, team-building, fitness, and healthy lifestyles. As we have found out today, I think he knows what he's talking about.

Bob, thank you so much for being with us today on *Discover Your Inner Strength.*

WEINSTEIN

You're welcome, it was my pleasure.

ABOUT THE AUTHOR

FOR MORE THAN THIRTY YEARS, Lt. Col. Bob Weinstein has focused on leading others, first as a senior military instructor with the U.S. Army Command and General Staff College, and now as a professional speaker and beach boot camp instructor in the areas of leadership, team-building, health, and fitness. Adding to his diverse background, he is a law school graduate and was a practicing attorney for ten years. He is a member of the National Speakers Association and is certified by the American Council on Exercise. Look for his new book, *Change Made Easy, Your Basic Training Orders to Excellent Physical and Mental Health*, scheduled for release in the fall of 2008. Known nationally as "The Health Colonel,"™ Bob has been featured on, among others, The History Channel, Fox Sports Net, PAX Television, *Comcast Newsmakers,* NBC6 South Florida, HDNews, Telemundo/NBC Universal, Univision, *The Miami Herald, The Sun-Sentinel, Las Vegas Tribune,* and *The Washington Times.*

LT. COL. BOB WEINSTEIN (USAR-RET.)

757 SE 17th Street, #267
Fort Lauderdale, FL 33316
954.636.5351
TheHealthColonel@BeachBootCamp.net
www.TheHealthColonel.com

Chapter 17

AN INTERVIEW WITH...

ANN RONAN

POWER YOUR PASSIONS AND PROSPER

DAVID WRIGHT (WRIGHT)

Today we're talking with Ann Ronan, founder of Authentic Life Institute, a virtual community for those who want to live a passionate and a prosperous life. She has successfully guided hundreds of professionals through career changes, providing direction, clarity, confidence, and caring, as they work through the bewildering process of transition. She is dedicated to increasing prosperity consciousness in all members of the community. Ann holds a doctorate degree in Adult Education and has completed master career coach training. She is a former staff member of Brown University in Providence, Rhode Island, and is a current adjunct faculty member of Loma Linda University in Southern California. Today Ann will talk to us about how to power your passions and prosper. From an early age she had a hunger for figuring out what it is she would enjoy doing while making money at the same time. Her journey has been filled with twists and turns and she would like to share some of the things that she's learned with us today.

Ann, welcome to *Discover Your Inner Strength.*

Ann Ronan (Ronan)

Thank you, David.

Wright

So how do you define passion?

Ronan

You know, the dictionary says it's a strong or powerful emotion or feeling. I think it has a lot to do with enthusiasm. Enthusiasm is when you have a great excitement for something. The word comes from the Greek, and in the Greek language it means to be inspired by a god or even to be possessed by a god. So when you have a passion it can just take a hold of you and you just can't help but follow it and do it.

Ralph Waldo Emerson is one of my favorite writers and he said that nothing great was ever achieved without enthusiasm. I think you can measure when you have passion for something by how much energy you have to do it.

As a small example, I love baseball; I'm a big Red Sox fan. I can be exhausted at the end of the day and say, "Oh I'm just going to stay home." If someone calls and says, "I have tickets for a baseball game," all of a sudden I'll have all kinds of passion and energy and enthusiasm, and I'll be off to that game. That's how I define passion—having the energy and enthusiasm to do something. I think it comes with some excitement.

When you find you have a passion for something, it often brings fear. I say to people, "You know what, if you've got excitement mixed with that fear, then it's a good kind of fear—it's not the kind of fear of being afraid to walk in the parking lot at night or fear for your safety. If your fear comes with some excitement, to me that's a clear signal it's something that you've got to move toward."

WRIGHT

Would you tell our readers how you have followed your passions?

RONAN

Oh my gosh, yes. When I was younger I watched my parents do work that they didn't really like. They just said, "Well, work is hard and this is how life is." When I started to work during high school I thought, "No I don't accept this. I know I have to work, I know I have to make money. I know I have to contribute to society, but why the heck can't I have fun doing it, or enjoy it?" So I have continually paid attention to the things I like doing.

For instance, I learned that I can write. I have an ability to write, I love writing, I love being by myself and writing, and a lot of people don't. In my mind I thought everybody could write and it was no big deal, but it's not—it's a challenge. I discovered that people would pay me to write!

So my advice is to follow your talents and don't just take them for granted. I have a talent for speaking and facilitating groups because I truly care about people, so I have also followed those passions and have learned to make money with them.

WRIGHT

Aside from your personal role models, will you tell us about some of the people who have served as your role models for living a life of passion and prosperity?

RONAN

There are many. Off the top of my head I think of the big ones. As you said, they're not my personal role models but they are "larger than life." One of them is Warren Buffet. Warren Buffet, as most people know, is one of the richest men in the world. He decided to give away most of his money to the Bill Gates Foundation. What I love is that, if you read his biography or hear what is said about him, you can see that the seeds of his passion were right there when he was a child. It's been said that in his senior year of high school he and a friend spent $25 to purchase a pinball machine—a used one. They put it in a barbershop and made money from it, and within months they owned three machines. So he had this entrepreneurial passion—this spirit—even in high school. It is said that when he filed his first income tax return, he deducted his bicycle as a work expense.

So here's a man who found what he liked and found mentors who did what he wanted to do in the stock market, and all those things that he does with his huge business; but he remains true to his authentic self. He is still somewhat of a Midwest, down-home guy, known for his funny quotes. He doesn't drive fancy cars or live in a fancy house, but he's one of the wealthiest men in the world. What I really admire is that he is doing such good with that prosperity.

Another role model is Oprah Winfrey, and I bring her up because I think everyone knows Oprah. She has been ranked the richest African American of the twentieth century and she's certainly a huge role model for women. According to a lot of magazine articles, she's the most influential woman in the world. That's a pretty big thing, yet she came from tough beginnings and she overcame them. Again, you can find the seeds of her passion in her childhood. Her grandmother said, "Oh I'm not surprised that she chose the media for her career—as soon as she could talk she was on the stage. She would play games interviewing her doll; she'd interview crows on the fence." So even as a child she wanted to do public speaking. She's another big role model for me. She's definitely followed her natural talents and her passions. People have been able to see by way of her television show what her different passions are. She's giving back to the world in the most beautiful way with her Oprah Angel Network and with the Oprah Winfrey Leadership Academy for girls in South Africa. She shows us that you can do what you love, you can do what you're good at, you can make lots of money, and you can do good in the world.

Wright

That sounds really great. What gets in the way of people identifying their passions?

Ronan

I think it includes a lot of things, but it probably starts with messages we hear when we're children. As I shared earlier, I heard the message from my parents that work is hard—you just do it and life is that way. All too often no one encourages children to follow their passions. We're taught to sit still in school and do what we're told. Many of our beliefs are formed in childhood.

We hear negativity in the media, or the teacher tells you that you can't do something well and it forms a very strong belief that can block your way to living your passions. You might think life is not supposed to be enjoyable, life is not supposed to be good, and this is the way it is. Those kinds of beliefs get in the way of your stopping to think about what your passions are and how you can follow them to prosper.

I think another thing that gets in the way is when people think they have to make one choice. I talk to young people who are trying to choose careers. They have big expectations and think, "I've got to pick the right career now because it's forever," and that's just not true. We can identify several different passions over a lifetime and go into several different careers. It's not unusual for people to have five to ten major career changes in their life and even more. I'm on about my eighth, and that's complete career change, not just a different job or a different organization, but complete career change. I think people get stuck with a mindset of thinking, "If I identify this one passion and follow it that's it—I can never do anything else," and that's false.

Wright

What methods can people use to identify their passions?

Ronan

I mentioned this when I talked about Warren Buffet and Oprah Winfrey. One of my favorites is to realize that the seeds of your passion are there in childhood. I really believe you were born with some natural inclinations. So I often like to ask people to take some time to do what I call the inner work. You've got to go inside and spend a little bit of time being quiet. In today's busy world, I know for a lot of people that's not something they're used to doing, but it's crucial. At that point think about what you love to do in your free time. If you had time and you could do anything you wanted, what would you do? Another question to ask is what did you like to do as a child? What was the one thing you did that you were really proud of? Even if it was selling the most candy bars in school, whatever it was, what were you most proud of?

When you start to think of those things, themes will come out of your life's stories. You can then start to really look at what it is that you like to do.

Another thing you can do, in addition to the inner work, is to ask friends and family, "What do you think I do well? Is there something I'm doing easily that you think is great?" As I mentioned earlier, I didn't know my writing was a great skill that I could make some money at and enjoy doing. I didn't know I had that gift until a teacher pointed it out to me. So ask other people, "What do you see in me that's special or that I'm good at?"

Then the last thing that I would do sounds simple, but it might not be. Ask yourself, "What do I want? And how will I know when I have it?" Once you start to honestly answer that question, you may find that it may not be just material things, it may be that you want a new car or a nice house. I suspect that you're also going to find other qualities you want in your work. I'll just give you some personal examples. I wanted flexibility in my schedule so I could travel (I love to travel) and I wanted to be able to set my own goals.

So ask yourself what you want and those passions will emerge.

WRIGHT

I don't generally like to quote statistics, you can find all kinds of differing statistics on almost everything, but I've read over and over again that some people say 90 percent of all Americans get up every morning and go to a place that they don't want to be.

RONAN

Yes, I have read that too, David, and isn't that a shame? We spend so many hours at work, why not do something you enjoy—something you are good at?

WRIGHT

So the question is, what keeps people from pursuing work that they're passionate about?

RONAN

That's a great question. I think part of it is that people don't get quiet and go inside to spend some time thinking about what they would like. They just get caught up in the drudgery of every day routine. They think, "Well, I've just got to get up and get the kids to school and get myself to work." That's easy to do and I don't blame them—it's very easy to just get caught up in life. But I think that if you take some time to really go inside and spend some time thinking about what you would really like, you'll find that you are dissatisfied or there is a seed of some discontent wanting to come out.

That's what happened to me in one of my last jobs. I had been very satisfied with a career for almost fifteen years. I worked hard to get where I was in that career and I had enjoyed most of it. All of a sudden, during the last year I was there I found myself getting angry with people, which is against my nature, I'm pretty patient and easy-going. I had to stop and think. I went inside and realized that it was really not the other people who had changed—they were all doing the same things and they expected me to do the same things. I was angry because there was a voice in me that was saying, "It's time to go and to do something new." I wanted to ignore it because I had worked so hard to get where I was. I had a nice office, worked for a prestigious institution, and had what felt like security. But once I started to listen to what I call that divine voice of discontent, I had to start making moves toward a new career. I did not make a huge leap, it took me a full year and I worked with a coach every week to get past all my fears of giving up the identity I had created in my very prestigious career.

I think what keeps people from pursuing work that they're passionate about is they need to get support from someone outside themselves. It can't be someone really close to you who depends on your income. Your spouse or your family are usually the greatest supporters you'll ever have, but when you are considering changing your job, they become afraid, which is normal. You can reassure your family or your loved ones that everything is going to be okay.

You will need to go outside your family circle and talk with people who can be objective and can listen to your fears and help you dismantle them with some reality checks. Choose someone who will truly be supportive so that you can feel confident. Then plan and go forward. But you need to be careful about who you seek support from because most people will try to squash your dreams. It's not because they're mean, it's because they fear change also. Find someone who will truly support you, listen to all your ideas, no matter how crazy they are, listen without judging you, and be very caring and supportive. I think those are the things that keep people from pursuing their dreams.

WRIGHT

How do you define prosperity?

RONAN

I define prosperity as having love, health, and all the material things—including money—that I need to enjoy life and this planet, and have plenty to enjoy what makes my heart sing, and plenty to invest and grow and plenty to share with others. That for me is true prosperity.

Eric Butterworth is someone I admire. He said, "Prosperity is not just having things, it is the consciousness that attracts the things. Prosperity is a way of living and thinking and not just having money or things. Poverty is a way of living and thinking and not just a lack of money or things." You might meet people who have very little in the way of material things but they're very, very happy people. You might meet people who are very wealthy in material things but they're not very happy. Prosperity is truly a consciousness—a way of living and thinking. To me it is a mindset, and unfortunately, in most people I meet, that mindset toward prosperity is small, they're playing too small.

When you consider the universe and the number of grains of sand on the seashore and the number of stars in the sky and the blades of grass, there is so much everywhere in the universe. That's just the nature of it—there's plenty. I believe that there is a Source we all come from—a Creator—and that Source provides. So to me that same Source who created the bountiful universe is the same Source we can draw from and it is limitless. When you really get that, you can relax, do your work of purpose, and prosper.

WRIGHT

So what gets in the way of people being able to prosper?

RONAN

Well, as I mentioned just a minute ago, mindset—the thoughts they have about money. These thoughts can be amazingly negative and very repetitious and that's normal. You turn on the news today and all you hear is a bad economy, the price of gas, and you're bombarded with negative thoughts about money all the time. So I would like to say to readers right now: make a commitment to watch how you talk about money for the next twenty-four hours. How many times do you say or think, "I can't afford it, that's too expensive," "Oh, that's not for our family, we don't live that way," or, "I wish I could travel but it doesn't fit my budget," or, "I live on a fixed income, there's no way I can have more"?

It's our thoughts that get in the way and ideas that have been planted. It is often quoted that money is the root of all evil when the true statement is "For the love of money is the root of all evil" (1 Timothy 6:10). So money itself is not evil, it's just an exchange. You exchange your energy and time for money. I mentioned Warren Buffet and Oprah Winfrey earlier. These two people can do amazing good with their money, but the mental blocks are what get in the way of most people prospering.

The other thing I think that gets in the way of prospering is that many people just don't expect to be paid to do work they love to do. So folks need to define prosperity in their own way. Most of the time, what they're going to find is that prosperity includes living in the place where they want to live, being with people they love, and doing the work they like to do. It's that simple.

Wright

So how can people overcome their blocks to accepting prosperity?

Ronan

There are several things they can do and once again, I'm going to remind readers that all change is internal change, so it has to start with the mindset. You want to practice being aware of your thoughts and changing them. At first you might have to fool yourself a little bit. When you catch yourself saying, "I can't afford it," you could change the tone of your sentence by saying instead, "Well, I choose not to buy that right now but I may in the future."

I have practiced this, so I speak from my own experience. I came up from very humble beginnings and definitely had a limited mindset about money. I thought I could only earn a certain amount. I don't know where I got the figure from but I made up an amount and never got past that in the various salaries I earned. Then I started to learn about the importance of the inner world and my own thinking and how it impacts my life—what I speak impacts my life more than anything on the outside.

Once I learned that, I started to practice. At first it felt very awkward but there have been amazing changes that have come into my life due to this practice of working with my thoughts and what I say. I am now in a very good position and I live in the most beautiful place near the ocean. I am able to share and grow and do amazing things with money. It still stuns me sometimes when I think that it was my own thinking that held me back.

I even did kooky things. Here's one. I decided that I wanted a Jaguar. Most material things are not that important to me, but that car was a beautiful car and to me it served as a symbol of having truly overcome my fear of money. I cut out pictures of Jaguars and pasted them in front of me near where I worked. When I would look out my window and see my old Chevy I would picture a Jaguar there. Visualization is very powerful and athletes use it all the time to practice their moves. It really works.

Another example is that I often told myself I could not afford to stay in fancy hotels—not that I need to every time I travel, but if I wanted to it would have been nice to feel as though I could. So I would go to the most expensive hotel near my town. It is a beautiful, older, expensive hotel. I'd sit in the lobby and pretend I was a guest and I'd try to feel what it would be like if I could actually check in and stay there. I started to get the feeling of what it might be like to have this fantasy come true.

You want to change your thinking? Start thinking in a new way and then practice feeling how it would feel to have all the prosperity that you would like.

Another important practice is gratitude. You can't feel grateful and feel lacking at the same time. The minute you begin to feel gratitude, fear drops away. So I tell people to practice being grateful for what you have right now because when you practice being grateful for what you have, even though it may seem small, you will get more.

Practice forgiveness. It's been shown that people who are holding a lot of resentment against others have a hard time breaking through and prospering. Practicing forgiveness is another key element to achieving prosperity.

The last thing is to circulate your money. This is a very, very powerful practice. I think this is the one that made a big difference for me and my beliefs shifted deeply. I was attending a spiritual center and giving a small amount of money on Sundays. One Sunday I sat there and I thought, "Oh my gosh, what would it feel like if I could add a zero to this, or another zero to this and be able to give that amount? How much more good could I do in the world?" When I had that feeling, and felt it deeply, all of a sudden I really shifted my thinking. I was able to give back in many ways to my spiritual center and to many other different organizations. The circulation of money shows that I trust that more money will come and it does—it always does.

WRIGHT

So what is the message you want people to hear so that they can learn from your experience?

RONAN

I would say give yourself that priceless gift of being more reflective; take some time to go into your inner world, and begin doing these inner practices. I'll say it one more time: your inner world creates your outer world; that's powerful stuff. Take some chances and be courageous. This lifetime is short and you might as well enjoy the ride. I think you'll feel most alive if you take risks. We are really meant to continually evolve into more than what we are today, that's just human nature—it's the nature of everything alive to keep evolving.

So stretch beyond, take small steps and know that your life matters. You are a creative human being, you are special, there is no one here in the world just like you and you have something to give to the world, so don't hide that, let it out.

WRIGHT

Good advice—very good advice. I really appreciate all this time you've taken with me today, Ann, to discuss this really important subject. You have taught me a lot here today and you've given me even more to think about.

RONAN

Great, I'm glad and delighted.

WRIGHT

Today we have been talking with Ann Ronan, founder of Authentic Life Institute. She provides direction, clarity, confidence, and caring to those working through the process of transition. From a very early age she had a hunger for figuring out what she would enjoy doing while making money at the same time. I don't know about you, but I believe she's accomplished that.

Ann, thank you so much for being with us today on *Discover Your Inner Strength.*

RONAN

Thank you, David.

About the Author

Ann Ronan, PhD, founder of Authentic Life Institute, helps others to acknowledge what they love to do and to do more of it. She has successfully guided hundreds of professionals through career changes, providing direction, clarity, confidence, and caring as clients work through the sometimes bewildering process of career transition. Her clients include professionals wanting to make a satisfying career change, solo-entrepreneurs wanting to grow their businesses, and organizations that wish to retain their most valuable resource—their employees.

She holds degrees in Adult Education and Ministry and completed Master Career Coach training through the Career Coach Institute. She formally worked with Brown University in Providence, Rhode Island, and is a current faculty member of Loma Linda University in Southern California. Ann co-authored *When Work Isn't Working: Spirituality in the Workplace 101* and *Work as a Spiritual Path. She* has been a featured speaker at hundreds of local, regional, and national conferences, as well as a guest on numerous television and radio shows.

Ann Ronan

32302 Alipaz Street, Ste. 269
San Jan Capistrano, CA 92675
909.717.1113
ann@authenticlifeinstitute.com
www.authenticlifeinstitute.com

AN INTERVIEW WITH...

DENNIS O'GRADY

THE *TALK2ME*© COMMUNICATION ROADMAP

DAVID WRIGHT (WRIGHT)

Today we're here with "Talk Doc" Dennis O'Grady, PsyD. Dennis is a Dayton clinical psychologist whose main thrust is communications. He uses his own *TALK2ME*© communication system not only in his private practice couples communication sessions, but also in training business and corporate groups. O'Grady has proven that those who are committed to learning, new tools of communication will indeed demonstrate increased enthusiasm, comradeship, and zeal, which result in steadily rising performance and increased profits at the office. Not only that, but the newly acquired tools can also be incorporated into private relationships at home.

Dennis, welcome to *Discover Your Inner Strength.*

DENNIS O'GRADY (O'GRADY)

Thank you, David. It all comes down to communication.

WRIGHT

What is the *TALK2ME* system?

O'GRADY

It's a positive and highly effective two-way communication system—or highway, as I have termed it—that sets you up for success and it's not hard to learn or quickly apply.

You are either an Empathizer-type (E-type) or an Instigator-type (I-type) communicator. You were born that way. It's like being left- or right-handed.

As an example, my middle daughter is a high school freshman. She is naturally left-handed and prefers to kick left-footed in her soccer games. However, her game has improved markedly as she developed her weak right foot and does not always depend on her strong left foot.

Communication works the same way—if you can use the natural strengths of *your* communicator type and add to them the strengths of your *opposite* communicator type, you have twice as many tools in your Communication Toolbox to get the job done. Flexibility and responsiveness, instead of knee-jerk reactions, is the name of the Communication Game, especially during stressful times.

To be an effective communicator in this fast changing, competitive world requires honesty and open, two-way communication.

During the customized communications seminars I lead, participants use the *TALK2ME Driver's Manual of Good Communication* to learn the habits of highly effective communication. By incorporating the key components of the *TALK2ME* system, you can vitalize your strengths and avoid your Achilles heel when working and talking with others.

The first rule or key to good communication: Know thy communicator type. You are either an E-type communicator or an I-type communicator.

The second rule or key to positive communication: Know the communicator type of your talk partners. (You will have less difficulty with your opposite type when you adopt his or her unique inner strengths as your own—at least while you are seated at the Communicator Table.)

The third rule or key to effective communication: Use the strengths of *both* Empathizer and Instigator communicator types to solve pesky problems.

Frankly, I never expected to make a discovery of this magnitude in my career. I have been professionally practicing psychology in the field of family and couple communication for more than thirty years, and I've been using the *TALK2ME* system for four years now. I honestly don't know how I managed to practice successfully without it.

Wright

Why do you use the metaphor of driver's education and cars to bring your training points home?

O'Grady

Although you and I were born to *be* great communicators, we weren't *born* great communicators. You weren't born with good driving skills, either. But both skills can be taught and become better with practice and application.

Empathizer communicators are represented by a car that's ocean blue in color. That's because E-types' emotions run as deep as the ocean and they put the *motion* in the word "emotion."

Instigator communicators are represented by the burnt orange color car. That's because I-types burn as bright as the sun and they love to instigate needed changes and lead the charge ahead.

One communicator type isn't better than the other. Both have particular strengths and the avoidable Achilles heel. However, until this important discovery, we had been in the dark and prone to communication crashes on the two-way communicator highway, simply because we didn't know about the differences.

I have used *TALK2ME* with my clients from all walks of life. They constantly report "the light came on" as if the headlamps of a car were switched on during nighttime driving.

It all boils down to good communication. For example, the same thing makes a manager or leader great and a husband and wife a team instead of divided and dispirited—positive and effective communication skills that work under pressure.

WRIGHT

What's so new about good communication?

Are you traveling on the two-way communication highway?

O'GRADY

What's so new about good communication? Nothing. It all begins and ends with good communication—it always has and always will. And most of us know in our heart, mind, and guts that not much good gets done without positive talk tools.

Why are communication crashes and clashes so common? Well, most of us aren't licensed to drive on the two-way Communicator Highway. We're too smart for our own good. The *TALK2ME* Communication Toolbox has everything needed to talk *with* others instead of talking *to* others.

When you don't know the talk type of your communication partners, without intending to, you can offend and hurt them. And if people don't trust you, you will drive off the road and into the ditch. Sadly, many communication accidents that cause great misery are due to ignorance, not unethical behavior.

In my case, I had a doctorate degree in psychology without much practice in two-way (E-type/I-type) communication with my new wife. I had more practice driving a car as a teenager! Now, how's that for an accident waiting to happen?

WRIGHT

In other words, the squeaky wheel gets the grease . . .

O'GRADY

It's too easy for either communicator type to focus on the dark side of the communicator coin. This creates "spinning your tires" and "staying stuck in a communicator rut" that gets nobody down the road. Here's how:

1. E-types complain that I-types don't listen to them.
2. I-types complain that E-types don't drive past their moods fast enough.
3. Many times, unspoken or unheard frustration mounts between people of opposite types. The result? Nothing much changes.

Wright

How can you tell which communicator type you are? What key traits of the two new communicator types are simply ways to tell which talk type you are? As a communications psychologist, how did you research the two types?

O'Grady

"It's my way or the highway!" is one clue that a talk crash has occurred between the two types of talkers.

Although I use ocean blue cars to represent Empathizer-type communicators and burnt orange cars to represent Instigator-type communicators, you could just as well use apples and oranges or cats and dogs.

The blue E-types and burnt orange I-types each talk a different language. Once you understand this, you will understand why you typically don't get along with your opposite type, *and* you can learn how to improve things. You can activate new strengths that you just didn't realize existed.

Wright

So, how do you know if you're an Empathizer, or E-type, communicator?

O'Grady

1. By nature, you are a sensitive person.
2. You are an empathetic leader.
3. You are a good follower and a team player.
4. You struggle with your feelings getting hurt too easily and for too long.
5. You are a great listener because you listen open-mindedly with three ears.

Likewise, here's how to know if you're an Instigator or I-type communicator:

1. By nature, you are a less sensitive person.
2. You are a strategic leader.
3. You are a good problem-solver and debater.
4. You struggle with biting your tongue or sticking your foot in your mouth, wishing you could take back your words.

5. You have guts galore and courage to lead the way ahead through the unknown.

You listen selectively with a goal in mind, and you expect people to push back and spark a conversation.

By using *TALK2ME* and the "typecasting" function of the color-coded communicator cars, you can build a bridge of trust in all of your important relationships.

WRIGHT

You're saying that true inner strength stems from using new communication tools purposefully.

O'GRADY

"But I didn't do it on purpose . . ." is negative communication, because positive communicators are "*on* purpose." So I also teach people how to: navigate the potholes on the Communicator Highway, give good feedback, use compliments wisely, motivate their people, resolve resentments, get high grades on customer satisfaction—or family interaction—surveys, *and* make big deposits in their "Interpersonal Communication Relationship Savings Account." Could it be that easy? Yes, it is.

After you have acquired the knowledge of how to interpret and deal with traffic signs on the road less traveled, instead of using the old one-way divisionary street tactic of, "It's going to be my way or no way," you will drive on the new two-way visionary thoroughfare—"It's our way *and* our two-way highway!"

WRIGHT

Does one size "talk shoe" fit all?

O'GRADY

Because we tend to assume that one *talk* type fits everyone—our own type, to be exact—I often shock workshop participants by asking them to exchange shoes with a neighbor. Changing shoes proves the point that our next-door neighbor's shoes may be not only a different color or style, but they may not fit. Does one size talk shoe fit all? No way. But by knowing your talk partner's type, you are able to walk in another's moccasins for a mile—and more.

The *TALK2ME* system also helps connect the two hemispheres of your brain: emotional and logical. This makes your life easier as you drive over the bridges that span your home, community, and work lives.

WRIGHT

I assume that there are rules to follow. What is the first communication rule?

O'GRADY

Well, David, before you can become a success at communication, you have to know your own and your talk partner's communication types. There is no reason you can't get better quality results in both your work and personal relationships. You have to know whether you are an empathetic (Empathizer-type) or a directive (Instigator-type) co-leader or partner. If you don't know what I'm talking about, it's as though you're driving down the rush-hour highway with a blindfold on. Don't bitch when you end up in a ditch.

Let's quickly find out about those in your personal world where you live, labor, and love. How would you complete these?

- My life partner is an Empathizer (prefers emotions) or Instigator (prefers logic) communicator.
- As I was growing up, my family could have been described as an Empathizer (sensitive) or an Instigator (hard driving) family.
- My oldest child would be described as an E-type kid who is tuned in or an I-type kid who can control the mood of the family.
- My brother/sister would fit the description of being a terrific listener or a loud speaker.
- My boss is a calm Empathizer communicator or an Instigator communicator who likes to stir the pot.

WRIGHT

Aren't Instigators, male or female, natural born leaders?

O'GRADY

According to my 2005 Dayton Leadership Studies, 75 percent of leaders were Instigators—they don't allow slights and rejections to keep them down or make them frown for long.

Exuding confidence, I-types seize more opportunities and take more risks.

However, it's now the era of *both* types of communicators. The point of using the *TALK2ME* Toolbox is to learn how to adopt the strengths of your opposite communicator type.

Your communicator type has nothing whatsoever to do with gender.

Half of the female population are hard-talking Instigator communicators, and half of all tough guys are heart-listening Empathizer communicators. In the movie *Rocky*, Rocky Balboa was an Empathizer communicator. And Lucy, in the Charlie Brown comic strip, is an Instigator communicator. Want to see the communicator car colors in action? Check out the Pixar movie *Cars*.

WRIGHT

Will you give me a brief case example of a leader at work who became a better communicator at home by using the *TALK2ME* system?

O'GRADY

Here's how fifty-five-year-old executive vice-president, Ted, told me he was using the *TALK2ME* Communication Toolbox with his wife, Alice, to improve their marriage:

> My wife and I deal with problems now instead of letting them get out of hand. Our talks turn out positively. We used to waste time fussing and fighting, generally miscommunicating or isolating. Now, we communicate clearly. Really, a burden has been lifted off my shoulders with the benefits of a more trusting, honest, and positive relationship. These are changes that we created. These changes didn't happen overnight, but fairly quickly. "You told me these are commonsense tools that aren't commonly used to improve your communication game, if you're game," my wife said. Boy, did we ever need to improve our game!

Now, Ted was a thick-skinned Instigator communicator while his wife, Alice, was a thin-skinned Empathizer communicator. Being opposite communicator types, Ted used to quietly fume when Alice got stuck in the rut called *the past.* But Ted was soon talking from her blue suede Empathizer shoes when he understood she wasn't to blame for her talk preferences.

Here are some of the accelerated strides Ted and Alice achieved from putting to work the Talk Tools Ted learned:

- We're laughing a lot more.
- We don't dwell on the past, but move on down the road (a big part of letting go of the past is our improving communication).
- We don't let bad moods ruin the day or rule our roost.
- We don't get stuck spinning our wheels in communication ruts.
- Small issues don't become major anymore.
- We're able to joke around instead of getting angry.
- We've teamed up to pull the wagon in the same direction versus engaging in a tug-of-war.
- My attitude about communicating has changed a lot.
- I look forward to coming home.
- Our talks turn out positively.
- It's all been very positive (change was almost simple).
- The feeling, "I don't want to be here anymore," is gone.
- My wife, who was a glass-is-half-empty person, now sees the same positives as I do!

To build trust in all your relationships, work in the quiet Empathizer or strong Instigator communication type of your talk cohort at home *and* at work. You'll see people change in front of your very eyes.

Wright

Are you saying that communication stress dims the light of Empathizers and drains the physical energy battery of Instigators?

O'Grady

Let me put it this way: *TALK2ME* is the key you put into the ignition switch of your blue Empathizer car or your burnt orange Instigator communicator car in order to get going down Talk Highway. Stick the wrong key into the ignition and your blood pressure is the only thing that's going to be revved up, that's for sure.

WRIGHT

Is relationship conflict or friction caused between the two communicator types due to prejudice, lack of awareness, or sensitivity?

O'GRADY

Absolutely, on all three David. People start honking their horns and using non-verbal gestures on Talk Highway when conditions are crowded or tense. Then the Blame Games begin, and, because all blame is lame, change avenues are shut down.

You are right, David, in that there is a great deal of conflict caused from the prejudices we carry around in our heads about how our opposite type simply doesn't "get it." A tall wall of resentment builds that you can't see over. I would guess that many of our readers here fail to understand what Empathizers need and what they dislike about Instigators, and what E-types admire about the inner strengths of I-types, and vice versa.

WRIGHT

I guess then, that E-types *feel* while I-types *think* about not listening to one another.

O'GRADY

Empathizers prefer open, two-way talks that include everyone. *Thus, E-types can be perceived as being wishy-washy.*

On the other hand, Instigators prefer narrow, one-way talks to get the job done. *Thus, I-types can be perceived as being too pushy.*

Neither type is better or worse, David, although each type works better in certain situations. Each type can blame the personality of the difficult person when, in fact, the confusion at this four-way stop is due to communicator type.

WRIGHT

Tell me a little about your research.

O'GRADY

In conducting research for *TALK2ME*, I found that about half the people you work with and love are Empathizer-type communicators and half are Instigator-type communicators. Neither talk type is better or worse. In fact, you *want* to look like either type, depending upon the situation, in order to gain results that will benefit all. You should not manipulate, but you should be in the driver's seat of your life!

TALK2ME co-creates peak communication experiences. Chances are, the person with whom you're having trouble talking—your boss, your wife, your kids, your neighbor—is probably your *opposite* communicator type and doesn't quite see the world through your preferred lens.

You've heard the old saying, "*You can't compare apples to oranges*," and that applies to the communication orchard as well. Empathizers are the apples and Instigators are the oranges in our metaphor today.

David, E-type communicators share many *strengths* and *traits*, as do I-types. Furthermore, I have learned over and over again that Empathizers benefit from adopting the inner strengths of their opposite communicator type—Instigators—with the reverse being true for Instigators and E-type strengths.

The main benefit of the *TALK2ME* system was recently touted by an I-type manager in this way:

> I can put up a barrier to block out negatives. I find it easier to talk to someone who isn't constantly complaining. I had a revelation of sorts—it just dawned on me. After you implement the strategies in *TALK2ME*, a light bulb comes on. In the past, I would have said, "I can't take it anymore, just quit complaining. I've got to move on." Now I take time to listen and come back with positives. It works better for everyone.

WRIGHT

Why adopt the strengths of my opposite communicator type?

O'GRADY

I strongly recommend that E-types *adopt the inner strengths* of their opposite communicator type—the I-type—and that I-types adopt the inner strengths of the E-type. Why? When they use their opposite type's strengths, they will get far better results when they're talking around the Communication Table—their opposites will be better able to understand the concept being presented, since it's in their own type of language. The following chart shows both E- and I-type strengths, so opposites, read, learn, practice, walk, and talk:

Empathizer Communicator Strengths	Instigator Communicator Strengths
• Willingness to listen • Really cares about a speaker's reality • More in tune with others' emotions • They seek the input and strengths of people around them; more willing to ask for input • E-types dare to care • More approachable • See things from others' points of view • More apt to change if necessary—not one-track minded • More open to change • Flexible—willing to take someone else's advice and utilize it • More caring and nurturing (you have a heart and soul) • Supportive (not as apt to crush someone) • Intuitive (gut checks in tune with others) • More laid back—easy going People persons	• Straightforward and blunt • Driven to produce • Fewer emotions • More analytical • Thicker skin • Focused • Ambitious • Demanding • Unwavering • Solutions people • Driving for progress • Stubborn—won't budge • Get to a decision and stick to it • Break problems down into parts • Don't take things too much to heart

The above chart depicts the more prominent strengths of each communicator type. Once you determine where you fit, it will be easy to decide which of your opposite type's strengths you want/need to adopt.

Wright

What secret inner strengths do Empathizers admire about Instigators and why?

O'Grady

Well, David, E-types perceive that their I-type counterparts possess characteristics that center around: 1) the appearance of confidence, and 2) the demonstration of personal power and communication prowess, both of which are core strengths that E-type communicators feverishly admire.

For instance, I-types can sell air conditioners to Eskimos, and they don't have trouble shrugging off stupid comments. I-types are a picture perfect example of, "I am confident about this, so follow me!" even when the I-type has some internal doubts.

Wright

What is it that I-types do to appear self-assured and powerful to E-types?

O'Grady

I-types have a way of exhibiting:

- An aura of dominance and competence
- An instantly high credibility factor
- A believability factor—the ability to really sell well, even when not sure of the details
- The ability to easily shrug off worry while flying high on the stress trapeze
- The ability to not worry about what happened during the day
- That they have bad moments but not bad days
- That they can move on down the road, not looking in the rearview mirror
- That they don't want to go back in time and change things—"It's over and I can't do anything about it now!"
- That they are able to keep their composure during emergencies or extremely stressful situations

- That they are able to hide emotions and keep calm
- That they are like the *Wizard of Oz*—able to maintain an image of power
- That they can control their jitters and pounding heart
- That they aren't afraid to take risks
- That they aren't afraid to give their opinions
- That they are more likely to be entrepreneurs
- Confidence in saying, "Hey, I can do this, just give me a chance."
- That they don't have to ask for everybody's opinions about a venture
- That they are quicker to go all in instead of fold with a good hand!
- An optimistic focus on "when" we do this or that rather than "if" we do this or that
- The desire to ask forgiveness rather than ask permission

What E-types usually fail to see is that they would make just as good leaders if they would just stick their necks a little further out of their fluffy wool coats. We need to ask them: confidence or competence—are you a lamb or a lion? While E-types are a naturally competent bunch of guys and gals who can err by not exuding an aura of confidence, I-types are a naturally confident bunch of gals and guys who can err by not valuing research and prudence.

To be an *Expert Communicator* in the *TALK2ME* system, a person must be a blend of E- and I-type strengths, one who can intertwine the powers of confidence and competence in centering and comfortable ways. No easy task, for sure, to combine the talents of the lion and the lamb!

WRIGHT

Is it really possible to have both the appearance of confidence and the reality of competence?

O'GRADY

I-types will tell you they're not so composed on the inside as you might think, much like the image from the *Wizard of Oz* when the curtains were pulled aside to reveal the smoke and mirrors tricks. In fact, I-types are surprised that you and I haven't caught on that they hide their emotions so well.

Yet, the single common denominator that radiates down each spoke from the hub of The Opportunity Wheel is *Confidence.* It is very possible to have both confidence and competence! Put loud confidence and soft competence together, and you will have an unstoppable team with high morale and creative staying power, and things *will* get done while profits soar.

WRIGHT

I know you aren't saying that one of the communication types is better than the other, just different. So what inner strengths of Empathizers *do* Instigators secretly admire that they would be wise to accommodate?

O'GRADY

I'm glad you asked! Both types have equally strong attributes which can benefit their opposite talk type. Thicker-skinned Instigators revere the high Emotional IQ of their sensitive Empathizer pals. *What the I-type admires about the E-type:*

- *Courageous:* The E-type's ability to show emotions
- *Talk Time:* Willingness to take time to talk with everyone
- *Passion:* Facial and hand gestures, octave changes in voice, show passion
- *Hugs:* Very "express-full and respect-full"
- *Fun-loving:* Are more fun and have more fun
- *Happy:* Eager, enthusiastic, happy-go-lucky
- *Expressive:* Are expressive
- *Tuned In:* Deep ability to interpret emotions
- *Radar:* With their spinning radar, they can usually read a person accurately
- *Warm Fuzzies:* Give "warm fuzzies" more easily
- *Patience Galore:* Have more patience
- *Teach Well:* Are natural-born teachers and teach about life
- *Quiet Leaders:* Are quiet and humble leaders and better listeners

- *Repeat Corrective Feedback:* Will take time to explain and will explain the lesson over and over again, without losing patience, until you get it
- *Seek Negative Feedback:* Stop to listen—they do not go through stop signs and red lights
- *Make Regular Relationship Deposits:* Will make a "time investment in listening"
- *Tender versus Tough Love:* Will take time to invest in a relationship
- *Approachable:* Are more approachable and approach-able
- *Accessible:* Will freely deliver or give emotionally-laden feedback
- *Ask:* Are more likely to initiate a feedback session with an E-type than with an I-type
- *Cautious:* Have all their ducks in a row before approaching an I-type

WRIGHT

Let me get this straight—the whole point of the *TALK2ME* system is to put an equal number of Empathizers and Instigators around the Communicator Table. Why?

O'GRADY

To brainstorm new solutions to old problems.

David, in workshops and couples communication coaching, I am always astonished and refreshingly amazed at the simple, creative solutions created when two or more *un*like-minded people are gathered around the Talk Table with a single purpose in mind.

When the *TALK2ME* system is used, you can bet that these predictable benefits will be recorded:

1. Everyone is valued for inner strengths shown
2. Respectful brainstorming occurs
3. Prejudicial "It's my way or the highway for you!" stops
4. Green lights of feedback occur
5. Positive changes are recorded, as both types team up to pull in the same direction
6. Pesky problems are solved

7. Communication confidence is strengthened
8. Increased profits result

WRIGHT

How will someone know when communication skills are improving?

O'GRADY

There are two obvious road signs on the two-way Communicator Highway that show you, through positive results, that communication skills are improving:

1. As an Empathizer communicator, you are heading in a positive direction when you don't take things so personally or literally.
2. As an Instigator communicator, you are heading in a positive direction when you don't wish you could take your just-spoken words back.

WRIGHT

Are we born as one type or does our family influence our type? Can't we be a mixture of types?

O'GRADY

"Well, I think I'm truly a combination of both communicator types," is a frequent I-type argument. But the answer is no, we aren't a mixture of both types. You are either an Empathizer or an Instigator, who, through the school of hard knocks *or* training in the *TALK2ME* system, can look-talk-and-walk like your opposite type. However, you will always go to your home base when you're under stress.

Now, it's true that men in younger generations appear more able to communicate sensitively, even when they're I-types, than those of my fifty-something generation. And it's also true, David, that women who work in traditionally male-dominated industries can look and sound like tough charging I-types in order to survive and be promoted. But, our basic communicator type is something we are born with—we are molded and fashioned like clay in our families of origin. Also, it's undeniable that you can look like one type at work—

say a bull-in-the-china-closet I-type—but then become quiet-as-a-mouse-in-the-house E-type at home.

We come into this world as one particular type, but hopefully, we will exit this world as a blend of types, respectful of the inner strengths of both types, at work and play.

Wright

Will you share keys that will sharpen communication tools so we can all receive high communication grades?

O'Grady

David, do you mean, "How can one achieve high performance rating scores of "A" on a Leadership or Couple Climate Survey?" The answer is by knowing how Empathizers and Instigators use unique viewpoints and different pencils (E-types) and pens (I-types) to score the measures.

Leadership/Couple Positive Communication Climate Survey Instigator versus Empathizer Communicators

Instigator	Empathizer
Less Talk	More Talk
Fewer Strokes	Lots of Love
Trusts Logical Facts	Trusts Emotional Relationship
No News is Good News	Needs Regular Reinforcement
Comes up with Own Suggestions	Gives Explanation for Direction
Control of Statistical Information	Control of Verbal Feedback
Respect is not a Lot of Close Supervision	Respect is a Lot of Close Relationship Interactions

Recognize Achievement	Demonstration of Caring
Recent Events	Past Practices
Physical Safety	Emotional Safety
Aggressive to Obtain Tools	Passive to Receive Tools
Training not Necessary	Education Extremely Valuable
External Customers	External and Internal Customers
Immediate Outcomes	Relationship-Based Outcomes
Direct Approach	Velvet Hand
Wants to See Results	We're Working on It
Needs Respect	Wants Appreciation
Monetarily-Based	Heart-Based
Job Benefits Very Important	Job Benefits Extremely Important
Enjoys Work If *Feel* Competent	Enjoys Work If *Think* Connected

David, imagine putting an industrial strength zipper over the mouth of the takes-things-too-personally E-type communicator, and then wondering why he or she doesn't ever tell you what you don't want to hear. You know the drill: "If *I* want to know what *you* think, I'll tell you!"

How do you turn off and shut up E-types or ice them instead of being (n)ice?

- Be very demanding: "This is how I want things done."
- Set unobtainable goals.
- Do not cooperate.
- Interrupt them when they're speaking.
- Disrupt their train of thought.
- Cut them off in mid-thought to hurt their feelings.
- "Your idea is really stupid!" (Use prescriptive pejoratives.)

- "Because I'm the boss" (this hurts most).
- Formal power: "Because I said so."
- Often pull rank: "Because I'm responsible to see that this gets done!"
- Do not listen at all, but instead, multi-task while the person is trying to talk with you.
- "We don't have time to socialize. We've got to get back to work."

WRIGHT

How do we open up lines of communication so that Empathizers will talk more?

O'GRADY

People who are E-types are starved for personal communication, but they will move sideways or even back away and withdraw into a shell when dinged.

David, if you really want to open up lines of communication with Empathizers:

- Give credit where credit is due.
- Use the "compliment sandwich" approach.
- Disallow team or family member's personal platform for complaining.
- Step out of your daily grind and take a minute to talk.
- Don't knock on people.
- Give and take positives.
- Make sure your E-type feels appreciated.
- Open and regular communication is key.
- Secrets are deadly, so share information regularly.
- Give others a boost.
- When you talk, ask more questions.
- Listen without a preconceived agenda.
- Fill up their energy tanks.
- Make weekly deposits in their Relationship Savings Account.

You have to remember, David, that Empathizers can be starved for acceptance, recognition, and energy validation—they need lots of love! You must overcome the hurdle of disbelief that sends the message: "You've got to shut up, get going, and put the past behind you!" If you really *do* want to be a better leader at home, work, school, or church, then open and regular communication is the key!

Wright

What would you recommend to get me started? Can I really just spend four minutes a day and learn the *TALK2ME* system? Is that all it takes?

O'Grady

Minutes, not years, are all that's required to provide you with the tools you need to drive down new change avenues, David. By studying these new talk tools just four minutes a day, you too can become a convert of positive communication.

As a couples communications psychologist and a corporate trainer, I've seen first-hand and up-close the miracles the *TALK2ME* system facilitates around the Communicator Table and the disasters that are prevented. How can you utilize strengths from both sides of Talk Street and make this week the beginning of a bright, positive, communicative future?

1. Learn how to turn on the strengths of both communicator types and to give and receive feedback, by talk type, at www.drogrady.com.
2. If you're an E-type, leave your comfort zone to give more feedback by speaking up!
3. If you're an I-type, leave your comfort zone to get more feedback by listening up!
4. Use the "accurate feedback in a minute or less" *TALK2ME* approach to become a better communicator.
5. Always ante up: Be full in, go full out, and be fearless. Know that good communication rules the work nook and home roost alike.

Apply all the tools in your communication toolbox.

Delivering and listening to quality feedback is key. Otherwise, David, how does anything ever change for long? How do you take communication training back to your home turf as you travel along the sometimes bumpy, always challenging, two-way Communicator Highway?

In fact, David, here are some gems of wisdom from a group of communication I-type gurus who were participating in a recent *TALK2ME* training session:

1. *Ease into the praise.* Realize that everybody's different—except that we *all* need praise. Your E-types will faint when you freely pass out more praise. Ease into the good stuff or E's will think you've been hitting the sauce.
2. *Make time.* Take time to talk *with* people, not *to* them. Minutes a day and small changes in habit patterns net huge rewards. Fine yourself ten dollars every time you interrupt an E-type.
3. *Listen when you talk.* Listen more and talk less. Ask open-ended questions. Ask more and more directive questions. By listening without a hidden agenda, it's easy to pull someone into your conversation.
4. *Listen better.* Listen to what you're saying for a change so you don't put your foot in your mouth. (Do you understand the difference between number three and number four?)
5. *A positive attitude toward feeling types never killed anyone.* You get a lot more out of your Empathizer people when you speak positively. Catch people in the act of doing a good job and never let them forget it.
6. *Respect everyone.* Pay attention. Everyone admires you, but your esteemed E-types might be too intimidated to speak up to you! Know the talk type (Empathizer or Instigator) of your life partner, your kids, and your grandkids.
7. *Go for genuine.* Teach Empathizers how to disagree and how to be disagreeable without fearing retaliation. Be more emotionally transparent to those people with whom you don't get along.

Remember: it is imperative that you be a precision communicator—don't barricade yourself in your office or always be on the go to avoid friction. Make yourself available and accessible—get out of your comfort zone more often.

Wright

To sum up, Dennis, will you give me some *TALK2ME* system communication rules that work wonders?

O'GRADY

Of course, David:

Rule1: Know your type (Instigator or Empathizer).

Rule2: Know your co-communicators' types (Empathizers or Instigators)

Rule3: Apply *TALK2ME* tools in a proactive way.

Rule4: Adopt the inner strengths of your opposite talk type.

Rule5: Ease into praise (stay relaxed when big changes happen fast and last).

If you still don't know your type, then you're causing yourself far more frustration than you deserve or need.

Check out your type at http://www.drogrady.com/type.php.

About the Author

Dennis delivers *TALK2ME*© effective communication workshops that provide a Communication Toolbox full of positive communication tools, to executive, managerial, and supervisory groups, to set people up for success. He also uses the *TALK2ME* system with his private, relationship communications-training clients. Dr. O'Grady is known as the "Talk Doc" since the advent of his positive and effective communication system, *TALK2ME*. He is president of the Dayton Psychological Association, founder of New Insights Communication, and is a clinical professor at the Wright State University School of Professional Psychology. His talk textbook, *TALK TO ME: Communication Moves to Get Along With Anyone,* received the 2008 Axiom Business Book Award Silver Medal. Please feel free to contact New Insights Communication at the phone number below to set up a time to speak with Dr. O'Grady. Your questions and inquiries are welcomed.

Dennis E. O'Grady, PsyD

New Insights Communication
7501 Paragon Rd., Suite 200
Dayton, OH 45459
937.428.0724
www.drogrady.com

AN INTERVIEW WITH...

JOHN CONG NGUYEN

IF YOU CAN SEE IT, YOU CAN HAVE IT

DAVID WRIGHT (WRIGHT)

Today we're talking with John Cong Nguyen. John Nguyen is a Vietnamese-American who arrived in the United States at the age of seven. A casualty from the Vietnam War, John lived the hardships of displacement to various refugee camps in Guam, growing up in "project" homes, and facing discrimination in America. These experiences seeded his "inner strength" to overcome his adverse environment.

Receiving his bachelor's degree in Engineering he later completed his formal "educational journey" with an MBA a PhD, and now as a Professional Certified Coach.

In 2002 John founded Lighthouse Leadership. The company's mission is to assist individuals to recognize their potential and bring focus to their life's goals.

During the last decade, John has positively influenced hundreds of business professionals in both the for-profit and non-profit business sectors. John was one of six global professional executive coaches for the Applied Leadership Program for Shell Global Solutions, a subsidiary of Royal Dutch Shell. John's coaching niche is in the area of Leadership and Emotional Intelligence development.

John, welcome to *Discover Your Inner Strength.*

The *American Heritage College Dictionary,* Third Edition does not have a definition for inner strength, how do you define it?

JOHN CONG NGUYEN (NGUYEN)

Inner strength to me is the intangible catalyst you possess that uniquely motivates you to overcome adverse environments and/or situations. It lies dormant within you until some factor—internal or external, perceived or real—comes into play that brings it to the surface. This inner strength can be positive or negative. You can be motivated to be constructive or motivated to be vindictive. It's something you can't buy, borrow, or beg for, but when you have it you can feel it and you know of its existence. This strength comes from deep within you. It is what you have remaining when everything is stripped away. It is a fervent inspiration or driving force that helps motivate you to achieve visionary goals, perform incredible tasks, or bestow a lasting legacy. It is your "nucleus" power plant that drives you.

It is imperative that we recognize our inner strength because for individuals to be effective and competitive in the landscape where skilled labor will be tight due to the Baby Boomers retiring in the next five to ten years, it will take more than just talent to rise to the top.

Inner strength is so important that Stephen Covey recognized it as part of his eighth habit. As Covey states, in order for us to move beyond effectiveness to greatness, which includes fulfillment, passionate execution, and significant contribution, the crucial challenge is to find our own voice and inspire others to find theirs. This is the eighth habit.

Others may identify this inner strength as conviction, a calling, fortitude, passion, and obsession. However they define it, the end result is that these people create their own future.

Wright

John, given the adverse journey you traveled, when and how did you discover your inner strength? What were the tipping points?

Nguyen

As one of millions of "unintended casualties" from the Vietnam War, I discovered my internal strength when I was around the age of nine years old. A series of events led me to the tipping point. My journey is not uncommon; in fact, it's very similar for those who enter America by way of immigration as refugees, persons in exile, and migrant workers.

My earliest recollection as a refugee was island-hopping from Guam to neighboring islands living in U.S. Army tents and hoping for a sponsor. One day the group I was with became the lucky few who were sponsored by a church in Minnesota. While we happily lived there for six months in Saint Paul, my parents could not endure the sub-zero winter temperatures and we transferred to Orange, Texas. There I grew up with the Texas summer heat, living in project homes, well seasoned by way of discrimination, prejudice, and surviving on government support programs.

One incident I vividly recall was being sent by my mom to our neighborhood grocery store to purchase a loaf of bread. When checking out I walked up and down the aisles looking for the shortest line. Without eye contact I handed the cashier a one-dollar food stamp coupon. I was embarrassed that we did not have any "money" and were in part dependent on government subsidies.

I soon realized that to get out of this rut my family was in, we had to do and be better then where we were. I told myself I could either be a victim of circumstances and accept my fate or use this painful situation as a fire to fuel my inner strength.

In general, most Asian values include family and education. In developing my internal strength I funneled my anger and negative energy to fuel the fire of hope that one day I would stand on the other side of the fence. Not long after that I promised myself to excel in school to achieve the highest level and pursue a doctorate, save enough money to purchase my parents a new home, and leave a positive legacy. Within twenty-three years, I achieved all of my commitments by using my inner strength to help bring focus, motivation, and direction. If I can do this, anyone can.

For others, inner strength has always been there, but they needed an external event to awaken it. The first tipping point for Ross Fava, Director of Sales & Marketing for Shell Global Solutions, was September 11, 2001. To him what happened that day made it seem like the world was coming to an end. In his wife's arms was their newborn son, only a few weeks old. All three were sitting on the sofa at home and witnessed the terrorist attack on the Twin Towers on their television. His mind was racing to find ways to keep his family safe, dry, fed, and clothed. Ross felt a surge of internal energy to rise to the occasion and do something with his life.

The second tipping point for Ross was the crossroad in his career. He was about to lose his job. In a traditional Italian household where the husband is the only breadwinner, this is a traumatic event. While mental chess games were playing out about his future employment, Ross's inner strength (his family) in both of these occasions, motivated him to navigate the turbulent water in search for a safe harbor. Today he has positioned himself securely doing something he enjoys.

For Linda Rimer, CEO Asia Pacific and the Americas Regions JA Worldwide, after serving 10 years as a missionary to a primitive Indian village in Mexico (Tarahumara tribe) returned to the US with four children without a job, earthly possession, shelter, food or transportation. Her inner strength came from having the responsibility for her family, to provide and care as sheer necessacity with no time to panic or thinking about her self.

Others may find their inner strength through the insight of a wise person. Kimberly Cornwell's mom noticed at an early age that her child had a gift for winning disagreements. Kimberly had never thought to be a lawyer, however with persistence and encouragement from her mom, she was the first to go to college, she graduated from Boston University, and at thirty-three years old is on track to become the VP of Legal Affairs for her company. Her natural talent and the drive to overcome poverty while growing up created her own luck in life.

Frank Glaviano, Sr., Vice President Production Shell Energy Resource Company, discovered his inner strength around the age of 40. At this point in life his career plateau at Shell and many times thought of leaving the company. After reflecting on his personal values and what he really wanted to do, Frank decided that he wanted to be a physician's assistance. For the next eight years he worked during the day, went to school at night to obtain the prerequisites and for a couple of years volunteered on Saturdays as a radiologist. What Frank did was removing himself from the victim mindset to creating a career option that he would enjoy doing with passion.

Discovering your inner strength can happen at any stage in life, under any circumstances, and to anyone. The message here is: Are you honest with yourself such that the best learning comes from your greatest defeat?

Wright

Would you share with our readers your process in developing your inner strength?

Nguyen

The heliotropism principle states that people and organizations are like living plants—they move toward light and energy. Our energy comes from life events we can control or seem to be in control of. However, there are times in our life when we seem to be disorganized and thrown in a state of disarray. We lose focus because of inconveniences, and from time to time there seems to be no reason or purpose for our existence. But, when we are able to sort out life's jigsaw puzzle pieces and can see the whole picture with clarity and focus, we tend to be more motivated, inspired, and willing to work harder to chase our dreams. Only on this journey will we discover our inner strength.

As with any growing organism, plants need water, sunlight, and soil to grow. We too must surround ourselves with positive people, a positive environment, and develop positive attitudes to overcome self-doubts and choke the weeds of negative thoughts. When we have a clear sense of direction in our life, we attract others with similar goals, thus providing a source of internal motivational energy to achieve our personal dreams. The first step in creating this personal portrait of our desired future or internal strength is to start with the end in mind—your personal vision.

"To begin with the end in mind means to start with a clear understanding of your destination. It means to know where you are going so that you better understand where you are now and so that the steps you take are always in the right direction"—Stephen Covey, *The 7 Habits of Highly Effective People.*

Empirical research indicates that visual and verbal images can be used as a tool to reinforce one's vision of the future to the present reality. Each individual has a preferred domain to learn, communicate, and express feelings, thoughts, and needs. While one domain may be more dominant, we express our feelings and desires most effectively and most creatively when we place ourselves in an environment that is in harmony with our center being.

The first step in discovering your inner strength is to create your personal mission statement. A mission is your core broad purpose and reason for existence. It defines your core values and reason for being and it provides a basis for the creation of your inner strength. Your inner strength draws from two core elements: Core Values—your core values guide you no matter what. A metaphor for core values is a compass. A compass always points north, no matter how disoriented the terrain can be. Core Purpose—your core purpose captures your idealistic motivations for why you exist. An example is teachers. Their core purpose is to teach and educate children.

There are many ways to create your personal mission statement. One effective way we have found is to complete a fun fill-in-the-blank writing exercise we call "Discovery Writing." In this center-based reflection exercise you: define your strengths and values, your motivators, reflect on events that influence your life, you recognize barriers that hold you back, and identify various people who are significant in your life. From the information obtained, the next step is to methodically structure it to develop your personal mission statement.

Based on the empirical research studies indicating that most individuals have a dominant learning domain, "EnFusion" is a workshop we pioneered in 2003 to incorporate all the learning domains, pulling together multiple ways to reinforce learning, enabling you to fuse your vision of tomorrow to the present reality of today. Starting with your personal mission statement we transform the work document into a stimulating visual art piece that is unique to you. A collage of motivating statements, personal pictures, encouraging captions, and inspiring aspirations will remind you of what truly is most important in your world. It is your road map for the successful life you want to achieve. It reminds you of your core values, the milestones you want to realize, the important people in your life, and the legacy you want to leave behind.

I created my EnFusion collage six years ago, today it still holds true as my compass to my inner strength. I have attained many of the milestones on my road map and I am looking forward to completing my journey. It is the only art piece that constantly centers me and refuels my inner strength. It hangs on my office wall as a constant reminder of what is important.

WRIGHT

Does everyone possess inner strength?

NGUYEN

There are two subtle disciplines of thought regarding this. One belief is that everyone has some capability or potential of possessing inner strength; while the other position is that everyone possesses inner strength.

The first position is that everybody has a certain level of potential for inner strength. Like innate intelligence, everyone has a certain level of potential that can be developed. The development of inner strength could be affected by work ethics, self-reliance, appreciation and respect for others, experiences, genetic motivation, or innate ability. It can be fostered and developed over time. One possible reason for the underdevelopment of inner strength is that many people live superficially and do not stop long enough to genuinely understand his/herself and anchoring their values. Society perpetuates the rush through life and does not pause for interspection to discover the priority, true values and purpose. There is a saying that whatever you brush under the carpet will trip you up later. On the other hand, the second discipline of thought is that everyone possesses inner strength. What you do with it when it surfaces is the differentiator. There are external factors that cause inner strength to come out in people, and what you do with it is up to you. Inner strength is limited and there are some people who are not talented, intelligent, or creative, but their inner strength helps propel them to realize their achievements.

I believe that inner strength lies in everyone. The problem is that most people have difficulty discovering their "true" inner strength. From the time of our first gasps of air at birth we fought innately to survive and for attention. As we grow older, society, academia, culture, and peer pressure taught us to conceal, stifle, and eliminate our internal motivator. Most of the time we deceive ourselves by the motivators that satisfy our temporary desires such as purchasing an expensive watch, keeping up with the latest fashion, owning the newest gadget, or the desire for affection from another person. Chasing these motivators leads us only down the rabbit trails in life without a sense of purpose or fulfillment.

Finding our true inner strength is easy when we have someone who can help us discover it or know of a methodology or process that can guide us. Our company's mission is to help our clients improve their ability to recognize their potential and bring focus to their life's goals—to believe in yourself, you have to believe in something worthwhile.

Over the years, Lighthouse Leadership has enabled hundreds of students to clarify their goals and ambitions in life. We have had students from almost every continent experience our EnFusion workshop.

The workshop's objective is to develop and capture the participant's personal mission and vision and transform it to a visual piece of art. Students who do not even speak English have been able to grasp the concept and create their own life's road map without pressure from their parents.

It is amazing to see a twelve-year-old student from Africa living in the United States driven to one day be a doctor so she can return to her country and heal her people. It's wonderful to witness an eight-year-old Asian child express her love for nature and talent for art without being pressured to live out her parents' dream. The biggest impact is when they share their personal vision with their classmates. This is when I catch sight of the internal drive, the passion, and the genuine human spirit to live a meaningful life.

Beside students discovering their goals in life, Lighthouse Leadership has also enabled hundreds of adults to build their life's road map and discover their inner strength through these workshops. John, an emergency responder, broke down in tears as he described how a picture of a set of golf clubs represents his strength.

Like a game of golf, there are bunkers, roughs, and false fronts set in your path once you tee off. In life there are obstructions and setbacks. How you react to each situation is like choosing the right golf club to help you overcome the obstacles. It has been seven years and John still has his collage up on his wall as a constant reminder of his internal strength.

People who are fortunate to find their inner strength find that it gives them direction, a purpose, and fulfillment in living. However, engaged in our inner strength sometimes means going against the social norms and going against the deeply ingrained habits and the environment in which we are placed. It creates consequences because, more than any other aspect, our internal motivation affects the choices we make and the way we spend our time. It provides tension between where we are presently and where we desire to be. Not having our unique internal strength, we tend to make choices based on what is in front of us. We react to whatever is urgent, the impulse of the moment, and our feelings and moods. We feel hopeless because we limit our options and are pressured by other people's priorities.

Our passionate inner strength—calling, inner voice—can empower us to transcend our fears, doubts, discouragements, and many things that keep us from accomplishment and contribution. A strong inner strength can transform us to be a better person from the inside out, raise us to the next level of excellence, and provide more opportunities for productivity.

In order to achieve it we must own it and when we do, it will give us a new independent will. Your personal inner strength incorporates your spiritual and mental well-being, your relationships, and core values. For some it is the cornerstone that they lean upon during times of adversity.

Wright

I have heard of emotional intelligence, but how does it contribute to inner strength and success?

Nguyen

According to Wikipedia, the online encyclopedia, Emotional Intelligence (EI), which is often measured as an Emotional Intelligence Quotient (EQ), describes an ability, capacity, skill, or (in the case of the EI model) a self-perceived ability to identify, assess, and manage the emotions of one's self, of others, and of groups. It is a relatively new area of psychological research. The definition of EI is constantly changing. Emotional Intelligence measures a core set of social and emotional abilities. How well we develop and use these abilities greatly affects how well we live our lives.

Reuven Bar-On developed one of the first measures of EI that used the term "Emotion Quotient." (Bar-On, R. [2006], "The Bar-On model of emotional-social intelligence (ESI)," *Psicothema,* 18, supl., 13–25. This reference can be accessed on the Web at: http://redalyc.uaemex.mx/redalyc/pdf/727/72709503.pdf. Last accessed, October 30, 2008.)

Bar-On hypothesizes that those individuals with higher than average EQs are in general more successful in meeting environmental demands and pressures. He also notes that a deficiency in EI can mean a lack of success and the existence of emotional problems. Problems in coping with one's environment are thought by Bar-On to be especially common among those individuals lacking in the subscales of reality testing, problem-solving, stress tolerance, and impulse control. In general, Bar-On considers emotional intelligence and cognitive intelligence to contribute equally to a person's general intelligence, which then offers an indication of one's potential to succeed in life.

EI is a learnable skill, unlike the raw intelligence (IQ) that one is born with. Those who lack it can acquire it; those who have it can enhance it. As a certified assessor for the Bar-On EQ-i, and a student in the emotional intelligence field, I have observed that a person's inner strength can be derailed or enhanced by the many factors in one's emotional intelligence space. My observations have revealed that achievement-oriented behavior is a solid foundation for individuals to have a robust inner strength. Using the Bar-On EQ-i Emotional Quotient Inventory (EQ-i), the composite scales that correlate to strong inner strength are: intrapersonal, which includes self-regard, assertiveness, independence and self-actualization, and interpersonal, which includes interpersonal relationship, adaptability, which includes reality testing and flexibility, and general mood, which includes happiness and optimism. (For an in-depth explanation of the Bar-On EQ-i, please visit www.eiconsortium.org or call me for assessment and insight development.)

Having the EQ-i assessment, combined with your personal mission and EnFusion collage, I can guarantee that your inner strength will be discovered, defined, and developed to its fullest potential.

An example of how EQ works in the corporate setting we turn to Ross. Ross works for a top tier energy company. He is very much in tune with his emotions. If something doesn't feel right he gets a very hard and deep reading, which allows him to gauge it internally. If a situation or an event does not pass the "sniff test," like fish, it may not stink today, but in three days it will, and you are already looking for it; this is where you have the advantage over others.

Some people have developed a tough skin to protect them against harsh conditions, however being callous and letting insensitivity roll off our back, we may be perceived as people without feelings who do not care or are aloof. Improving emotional and social skills increases our ability to become more productive and successful in the workplace, thus more effective for the organization and in our daily lives. We should embrace EI's contribution to enhance our intuition. Not mastering it may make you a lousy poker player.

Wright

Tell me more about your credo "If you can *see* it, you can *have* it!"

Nguyen

Based on the heliotropic phenomenon and positive psychology, I truly believe in the power of imagery and visualization. Sports athletes use these techniques to psych themselves in preparing for competitive events. Buddhist monks seek mindfulness and they envision peace and harmony in their daily lives. Artists conjure a vision of their masterpiece before they start. All provide an inspiring picture of what success looks like.

With so much evidence that includes the power of visualization in goal achievement, I believe that we can apply the same technique and learning to use pictures as reinforcement to our success. While logic and linear thinking come from our left brain, pictures involve the spatial and creative property of the right brain. Many times personal statements and vision statements involve our left-brain. Pictures of success, excellence, and achievement conjure emotions and feelings and involve our right brain.

In his book, *You've Got to Believed to be Heard*, author Bert Decker writes about the "First Brain," which is our emotional brain. The First Brain is directly affected by sensory input. What you see and hear is transmitted through the First Brain even before it reaches the cerebral cortex—our thinking brain. The First Brain is dominated by visual input, which is why visualizing can have an even more powerful impact. Facts and logic inform, they do not inspire nor excite. Paint a picture and you will have the power to encourage and arouse.

To harness the power of visualization, we have to define what success looks like for us. We need to honestly answer for ourselves the following questions and see the answers in vivid detail:

- What do I desire from my life?
- Where is my career taking me?
- What are my core principles and values?
- What excites me most in or about the world?

- What role do I play in this lifetime?
- What gift or talent do I possess?
- What legacy do I want to leave for my loved ones?
- If I could relive my life again, what would I do differently?
- If everything I believe and possess fell overboard, and I could only save five things, which five would I save?

When we can see what the whole picture looks like, then we will know what we want. When we know what we want, only then we can start working toward it and behave as though we own it. The potential of self-actualization is so powerful that our inner strength can live or die from it. If we do not believe in ourselves and see ourselves achieve success, then who will? Creating a better future starts with the ability to envision it today. That is why my credo is "If you can *see* it, you can *have* it!"

WRIGHT

How can one use his or her inner strength to be successful?

NGUYEN

"Success isn't money. Success isn't power. The criteria for your success are to be found in yourself. Your dream is something to hold on to. It will always be your link with the person you are today—young and full of hope. If you hold on to it, you may grow old, but you will never be old. And that is the ultimate success."—Tom Clancy.

This quote really resonates with me and helps define my coaching philosophy. My coaching clients are driven, ambitious individuals with a strong focus on career and business success. My purpose is to help them reach success in a compressed time period. In addition, I also help clients discover their inner strength through identifying their values, telling me more about what motivates them, and who are the significant people in their life, what legacy they want to leave behind. I also have them reflect from a point in the future to understand what they have achieved with the limited time they have in this lifetime. To view the total beauty of a painting, one cannot stand inches from the art piece, but at a distance to take in the whole masterpiece.

Inner strength helps propel success because it incorporates much more than a myopic view of the near future. Inner strength takes in the whole purpose for our existence. It completely incorporates all the rudiments of importance to encourage our travel in this journey in our life. The road to success is marked with many attractive parking places, tempting rest stops, and forbidden U-turns. My job as a professional certified coach is to help my clients create an accurate personal road map to their success.

When people define success in terms of wealth (accumulating money), fame, and power, these things do not last and will never be satisfying. Many people live their life consuming their health to build wealth and then desperately spend their wealth trying to hang on what's left of their health. Success may never come without a compelling personal commitment to something you care about and would be willing to do without counting on wealth, fame, and power. In fact, it is something you will do for free—something you will do because it matters to you. Success should aim to bring personal fulfillment, lasting relationships, and make a difference in the world in which we live.

In this day and time where the economy is volatile, job security is uncertain and retirement is postponed. The terrible truth is, if you don't love what you're doing, you will lose to someone who does. People who are fortunate to position themselves in a role where they give 110 percent each and every day will be the successful ones. What they do may not make them rich, but it helps provide a rich life to another human being.

Adversely, the persistent irritation of not loving what you do makes you a nuisance to be around; it will generate a demoralized work environment and chip away at your health. Making success last takes tenacity and passion; it must resonate with your personal value.

When you discover your inner strength, true success will be as clear as crystal, and the life you live will be much more meaningful. Your inner strength will give you energy to persevere in setting short- and long-term goals.

Wright

What model have you uncovered to help sustain or keep in balance your inner strength?

Nguyen

There are many models one can develop to help support inner strength. A Texas Instruments Senior Fellow, Duy-Loan Le, shared with me that her drive and success are based on three elements. These elements are balanced in a triangle configuration, one of the most stable geometric shapes. These elements consist of family, work, and community. When any one of these elements is out of balance it is a flag for her that success is imminently destabilizing.

For Linda Rimer, her model is called the leadership fitness. It includes three essential pillars: Spirit, Mind and Body. The spirit provides humility, servant to others and priority. Mind includes the discipline of life long learning, preparing and being ready for change and evolution. The body provides the vehicle to manage the stress in life so we can live to our full potential.

At around the age of ten, Paul Hamilton's parents were renovating their home. They hired a gentleman in his early fifties to replace the linoleum floor tile throughout the house. One morning Paul stood and watched with curiosity and then mustered enough courage to ask what the man was doing and why. The gentlemen stopped his work and started to cry. Paul was puzzled and thought he had offended him somehow. However, the gentleman stated that in his thirty years of employment Paul was the first person who had cared enough to ask him what he was doing and how he was doing it.

What Paul realized that day is that people, no matter what they do or how old they are, need acknowledgement. No matter what we are doing we contribute to the whole. Many people desire respect by others and confirmation by friends, family, and the community. Being somebody who acknowledges people in whatever they do can be a strong inner strength.

For engineers, scientists and left-brain logic driven thinkers, consider creating a picture of the future three to five years from now. Make milestones to achieve that future. Take those milestones and develop tasks. Break the tasks into 12, one for each month and develop goals one for each week to complete each task. As each week ends check off the action items. This format provides a structured way to accomplish important and urgent matters. Frank Glaviano, Sr. use this model for the last 20 years.

Others use self-realization and humility as bellwethers in their life. Ross, an Account Executive for Energy Company, shares that you have to know what you know and know what you don't. You may not have all the answers, but you have to be open enough and vulnerable enough to put yourself out there and seek help from others, even if their advice is something you would not act upon. You cannot count on someone else to carry you to the finish line. Life is not about connecting the dots—it is not linear. Theory is great in textbooks, but in life the world takes over and hard and fast rules do not apply. So be very self-confident of what you bring to the table. No one can be in charge of you better than you can. If you arm yourself as best you can and you have self-realization, then you have a better chance for success.

When we try to compete with the Jones we are inviting discontent and frustration in our life. We don't know the Jones's circumstances. The Jones may have a bigger house than you, but the roof may leak. They may have a better car then you, but their relationships might not be good. Everybody has some unseen, unrealized cross to bear. If you are happy with who you are and you make your situation as good as it can be for you, then you are going to be a happy person.

When you compare yourself with others, you're always going to feel inferior. Doing this is a big mistake. If you have internal strength and know that you have the best that you can have, independent of what is happening around you, then you have already won. This doesn't mean that you are arrogant, but your inner happiness will be evident and others will get the message. They will wish they had your attitude. When people stop playing the comparison game they will be a lot happier and they will realize more of their dreams.

The model that works for me consists of four elements. These elements are family, faith, career, and community. These four elements work for me because of the strong family values I have embraced and was brought up to treasure.

Family dinner is always an event we share together at the dinner table. We eat together, we pray together, we stay together. Individual members in the family are like twigs—alone it's easy to snap them, but together in a bundle they are difficult to break.

Faith was not crucially important to me ten years ago. However, as I grow closer to faith (thanks to my wife) I can remember many hollow and heartbreaking periods in my life that would have been impossible to get through without my faith in God. Accepting this fully has lifted my burden of responsibility. I have come to realize that some things are beyond my control. Living and practicing His teachings are also reminders of taking the high roads in life.

Career is the third element in my model. Career is more than just working for someone else. Career to me is about obtaining new skills, honing my talent, and enjoying the results I produce. I believe the work we do not only supports our living standards, but it is also about discovering our strengths.

"Never continue in a job you don't enjoy. If you're happy in what you're doing, you'll like yourself; you'll have inner peace. And if you have that, along with physical health, you will have had more success than you could possibly have imagined"—Johnny Carson, comedian and television host (1925–2005).

Community is the next element. In 2003 my wife and I raised a significant amount of funds to build a two-classroom building in Vietnam in collaboration with YMCA International. In 2007 we also worked with YMCA International to refurbish a large community clinic in a rural area. These structures will be there long after our lifetime, providing to thousands of individuals an opportunity to have an education and hope for better health care. Our community is global, not just the city we live in.

Sometimes my model is equally balanced to make it a square, while other times it's a rectangle or a diamond. Whatever the shape it has, I know that there are only four points that hold me true to my belief. These four pillars make up the model I go by in sustaining my inner strength. Whatever processes or methods you use to develop your model, be sure it can resist the changing environment and stand the test of time.

WRIGHT

How do beliefs and values factor in determining inner strength and do they change over time?

NGUYEN

Our values define our beliefs, our beliefs define our expectations, our expectations define our attitude, and our attitude defines our action. In physics there is a reaction to every action. In life there is a cost to every choice we make, whether it is in relationship, wealth, faith, etc. To win in the game of life we need to minimize the cost and increase the benefits.

Paul, a successful executive, once in a while pauses, steps back, and recalibrates his values and asks what matters most to him. Working for the same company for thirty-two years, his values of family, wealth (standard of living), education, hard work, accomplishment, religion, and respect have enabled him to make tough life and business decisions. Whatever matters most, it is important to have the element of integrity in our inner strength. It is holding fast to what we believe that will make the difference overall. There is nothing more personal than discovering your personal strength and how it is meaningful to you.

Kimberly, who has reached the pinnacle of her career in the law profession, decided to redefine herself and her definition of success. Overcoming her self-doubts and negative talk about not having entrepreneurship ability, she became the CEO of her company, Celadon Roads, an organization that holds at-home parties to sell eco-friendly, organic products. One year ago she concluded that being more socially responsible and using eco-friendly organic products was the legacy she wanted to leave behind for the world.

Some fortunate individuals have been able to discover their inner strength early in life. They felt their calling and knew exactly what their purpose should be in their lifetime. For others their inner strength is realized later in life. Sometimes a life-changing event may initiate this calling such as a loss of a child because of an accident caused by a drunk driver, experiencing breast cancer, child abuse, or certain miracles. Whatever path life takes us; we discover more of our inner strength overtime.

After assisting hundreds of individuals in EnFusion workshops, ranging from middle school students to those with established careers, my observation is that the inner drive and passion changes with little variance over time. Feedback from many participants states that motivation changes. However, for the vast majority, what they have adopted during their collage years will not change. This sample data tells me that the core motivators do not change drastically over time. As we experience life and accumulate wisdom, we adjust our reality to the ideal mindset we had when we were younger.

WRIGHT

What other characteristics do people need to enhance their inner strength?

NGUYEN

As noted earlier, the characteristics I observed that are needed to nourish inner strength are some of the composite scales and subscales from the Bar-On EQ-i emotional intelligence model (e.g., happiness, self-regard, etc.). Other characteristics that I believe are also important to possess are confidence and discipline.

Confidence matters more than anything else in determining success and in developing strong inner strength. Confidence is the difference that makes the difference. As humans we are naturally drawn to confident people. Being confident will immediately propel your inner strength to attract success in your relationships, business, career, and life. If you don't project that you believe in yourself, how are others supposed to believe in you? Your confidence level determines how others view you. Confidence is the biggest indication of how successful you will be in life and how strong your inner strength will develop. Studies consistently show that people with a high degree of self-esteem are more successful, well liked, and more effective in every aspect of their lives. Confidence also leads to a stronger inner drive.

Here are some things you need to remember that will help in developing your inner drive:

- Avoid comparing yourself to others.
- Surround yourself with positive, loving people.
- Smile often, laugh more.
- Walk as if you own the establishment.
- Dress confidently.
- Display confident body language.
- Be brutally honest with yourself.

Discipline is one of my four pillars for success. Anyone can have a dream, some may have the drive, but most do not have the discipline. Without discipline you can never deliver. Al Hirschfield, a caricaturist, once stated, "I believe everyone is creative and talented. I just don't believe everyone is disciplined. I think that's a rare commodity." Case in point is that a great majority of people who make a New Year's resolution on January 1 fail to stick to their commitment by February 1. Many reasons contribute to this failure, including unfocused, unrealistic, and immeasurable goals. In fact, a contribution to failure is not being able to see the benefits of achieving the goal.

"Discipline is the bridge between goals and accomplishments"—Jim Rohn.

People with strong inner strength will naturally have internal discipline and confidence because they know in their heart and they can feel it in their bones what it's like to attain their purpose, leaving that legacy, and affecting the people who mean the most to them. People who have discovered their inner strength know the benefits when they achieve their goals. This small, privileged population is very focused in doing what they need to do because failure does not sleep, tough times do not sleep, and stress does not sleep.

WRIGHT

Who do you go to for support during this process and in tough times?

NGUYEN

In tough times I go to our long-time friend and Catholic priest, my best friend (my wife), and various mentors for advice. In fact, for the last ten years I have been actively seeking mentors at work. So let me take a moment to share with you my rules of thumb about seeking out mentors:

Rule 1: Be proactive in seeking out a mentor. Rarely does a first-rate person drop into your life to share with you their mistakes, insights, and to give wise advice without being asked.

Rule 2: Seek out mentors where you work who are at least two job grade levels above you. Most of the time the conversation will revolve around career progression. It is human nature that there will be more discomfort for a person to help you to rise to their level where both of you will compete in the same arena. The two job grades will provide a buffer zone for your promotion, thus leaving your mentor still one grade level above you.

Rule 3: Seek a mentor who is outside of your business department and/or line of management. A mentor from another department will be neutral in providing more unbiased advice. You can also discuss your work issues. This usually involves colleagues, direct reports, or supervisors without affecting judgment or facing political repercussions. Having an outsider also helps you understand another business and develop a supporter in that business.

Rule 4: Be mindful of the chemistry in the first couple of meetings. If there is chemistry between you, continue the relationship. If not, cut the cord and politely bail out. Hanging on to a bad relationship only gets worse. And the sad part is that it's a lose-lose proposition for the mentee.

Rule 5: You as the mentee drive the relationship and agenda with the mentor. Always be prepared with a meeting agenda, schedule early, and do not be late or forget your meetings. Remember that the mentor's time is much more valuable than yours.

My last advice about mentors is to not limit yourself to the people around you. Stephen Covey, Jeffrey Fox, John Maxwell, and many authors have been my mentors over the years. From career, family, and relational insights, reading books written by these authors is a great way to learn and be mentored indirectly. For an investment of about twenty dollars per book, I have learned years of experience from the best in the world. Life is too short to make the same mistakes others have made; learn from others and the journey will be much enjoyable.

WRIGHT

What are some advises would you give to our readers to help them realize their inner strength?

NGUYEN

Some of the advices I would like to share come from the fortunate mentors I have had and the admired people in my life.

1. Know yourself and be a student of Emotional Intelligence. These are the fundamental skills that will make you stand out from the average. When you can develop high intrapersonal capacity, have strong interpersonal skills, and master the ability to manage stress, adapt to the environment, and be in a positive mood, people will treat you positively. From these skills you will distance yourself from mediocrity. There is a wise Chinese proverb that states, "Knowing others is wisdom, knowing yourself is enlightenment."
2. Live your life the way you want your kids to remember you. We live an average of eighty years, and that is a minute amount of time relative to life on earth. Be happy, laugh more, count your blessings, don't compare, and your journey will be much more rewarding.
3. Continually learn. Learn from others' mistakes. Learn how to do something new. Do something that is challenging to you. The more you learn, the more you realize how humble you need to be. See learning as a journey not a destination.

4. Have various role models. When we limit our self to one we tend to emulate that person and lose our uniqueness. Having multiple role models we can pick and choose the admirable characteristics we want to possess. Thus making us a better role model to others.
5. Watch a life affirming and inspiring movie by yourself. Nothing lifts the human spirit more than a perfect choreography of music, script and emotion in a movie scene. Let your subconscious mind soak up the idea and images to affirm your inner strength. Here are some of my favorites: A Beautiful Mind, Bucket List, Patch Adams, The Pursuit of Happyness, Joy Luck Club and Remember the Titans.

About the Author

John C. Nguyen, PhD, PCC, is Founder and Principle Partner of Lighthouse Leadership. Dr. Nguyen has over seventeen years of experience in the oil and gas sector. As a successful entrepreneur, public speaker, "crucial people skills" trainer, adjunct professor, and a professional coach, Dr. Nguyen brings his diverse experience and insight in leadership development together with his academic research and professional certified coaching to inform audiences through keynotes, workshops, and consulting. This unique combination of "experiencing the hardship" and leaving a legacy makes Dr. Nguyen qualified to help others discover, define, and deliver their dreams.

Dr. Nguyen is a speaker on the topics of Leadership Development, Emotional Intelligence, and Life Skills. His credo is "If you can See it, you can Have it." Dr. Nguyen's inner strength and joy in life comes from his blessed relationship with his wife Kirsten, son, Hunter, and daughter, Kirby.

John Cong Nguyen
Lighthouse Leadership
9234 Sandstone Street, Suite 440
Houston, TX 77036
713.384.5047
Win@LighthouseLeadershipCoaching.com

AN INTERVIEW WITH...

GARY LUNDQUIST

DEVELOPING YOUR INNER INNOVATOR

DAVID WRIGHT (WRIGHT)

Today we're talking with Gary Lundquist who speaks and consults in innovation. Gary is a *decision synthesist* who helps teams Pre-Plan™ both innovations and innovation processes through a combination of strategic identity, integrated strategy, and innovation culture. He focuses clients on creation of value for stakeholders rather than mere development of businesses and products.

Gary earned his BA and PhD from the University of Colorado, and then founded an INC 500 software business in the energy industry. He has twenty-five years' domestic and international experience in strategic, product, and tactical marketing of high technology for clients from start-up to units of Fortune 50. He applies his marketing to technology-transfer in both industrial and federal labs. Gary is developer and practitioner of Strategic Pre-Planning™ for innovation of businesses, products, processes, and markets. He chaired the Colorado Innovation Summits in 2003 and 2004 and authors the *Colorado Innovation Newsletter.* Gary is Director of InnoSearch™ Colorado and blogger at Innopinions™.com.

Gary, welcome to *Discover Your Inner Strengths.*

You were educated as a scientist. How did you become an advisor to businesses?

GARY LUNDQUIST (LUNDQUIST)

I joined a small government consulting company-doing work that was an extension to my thesis. While on a trip to Denver, I found an opportunity to apply our science to the energy industry. I started a software business inside that little company, and over a couple of years, software became our primary business, then our only business.

It turned out that I was the only person in that company with any natural talent for marketing. Today, I'd say it was a talent for innovation. For a while, I managed the software business, and then was moved into corporate marketing. It was the opportunity of a lifetime in a company with dramatic growth, but I didn't have the personal tools and knowledge that I needed to succeed. Later on, a venture capitalist brought in a new marketing strategy. I didn't like it, but I didn't have the marketing knowledge to articulate my concerns. Fourteen months after that strategy was implemented, we were bankrupt.

We'd had a great ride. We had received the INC 500 award and had sales all around the globe. Losing that company hurt like hell. Within three months, I'd made a conscious commitment to help other technical professionals to avoid the same pitfalls that I'd faced. I chose to become a strategic and product marketer with no academic training, just experience in the school of hard knocks.

My first major customer was Texaco. They wanted to license technologies from their labs to companies who would commercialize products. This was a great fit for me—working with scientists and engineers to move their inventions to market. Later on, I discovered that I'd been doing technology transfer. Today, technology transfer is a core driver of innovation in both entrepreneurial startups and major companies like Proctor and Gamble.

In 2003, I defined, designed, and chaired the Colorado Innovation Summit. Marketing two annual conferences forced me to formalize a language of innovation. Most people see marketing in terms of Web sites and trade shows. I was frustrated with efforts to connect with clients. After experiencing the conferences, I re-branded myself around innovation. Strategic marketing is business innovation. Product marketing is product innovation.

Today, innovation dominates corporate and government conversations. As scientist-turned-marketer, I bring a unique perspective.

WRIGHT

What a series of transitions! Is there any single lesson that stands out?

LUNDQUIST

Yes. Actually, I've based my entire approach on three simple yet powerful lessons. The most important to me came from Miller and Heiman's book, *Conceptual Selling*. I've shortened their words to an adage: *No one ever buys a product*. Let me repeat that: no one *ever* buys a product. You believe that, don't you? My signature routine as a speaker conveys this concept. It's not telephones, but connections to people and information. Not a compass, but a sense of direction. Not a pen, but ideas captured on paper. Not a necktie, but conformance to social norms. Not a mousetrap but fewer mice.

All you need do to understand this principle is to look again at those few examples. The implication of that one concept changes all of innovation. No one invests in new businesses or new products, no one ever licenses a technology, no one ever pays a salary, and so on. We buy the value of the product or technology, the potential returns of a business or product, and the good work done in exchange for wages.

And look a step further. Value exchanges are best when done in repeated cycles. As consumers, we pay for the value of the product, and the company gets the value of our payment. Value for value, win for win, over and over. The value mindset creates relationships, not just customers. Best of all, we can apply the value mindset to any relationship. We achieve and sustain strong relationships by exchanging gifts over time—friendship for friendship, work for salary, product for payment, and on and on.

WRIGHT

This sounds like it comes from your marketing days. How does your focus on value relate to innovation?

LUNDQUIST

That's a great question. You see, innovation implies something new. In innovation, we go beyond marketing to becoming practicing agents of change. Every marketing tool is still valuable, yet we now accept other challenges. As a process, innovation is development of ideas into "products" in use for the first time anywhere. To be used implies that we've gone beyond invention to introducing inventions to marketplaces. As a result, an innovation is a valuable "product" not previously available that meets needs not previously met. If markets of customers use our products, we've created compelling value

Please understand the word "product" here to mean everything from an idea to a whole company. We can innovate technologies, strategies, business models, facilities, products, product features, events such as trade shows, and more. We can innovate entirely new industries and new markets. We may even be able to innovate ecological balance on Earth and peace among humans.

So when I talk about innovation, I mean development of something new that has value great enough to have significant *impact* on targeted markets. Think of *impact* as the measure of importance of an innovation.

WRIGHT

As a practical matter, how does anyone apply innovation to meeting personal challenges?

LUNDQUIST

We've already talked about product for payment, value for value, and win for win. That's the single most important lesson in my own business life. To achieve impact on any market, we must produce and deliver value, over and over and over. Accomplishing that takes another level of awareness.

You've brought me to my second basic principle of marketing and innovation, and to another signature element in my speaking. As with the first principle, I state this as a negative. *"How" is not the most important question.* Think about the way our world works. Schools teach how, from kindergarten to graduate school, in every class from English to physics to physical education to music. It's the same in the military. And many companies train new employees in their particular corporate methods. Everyone has their ideas on *how* to accomplish this or that. We love to tell our friends *how* we would run a company or the country if we had a chance. *"How"* is a way of life. So when I say that how is not the most important question, I'm challenging the way civilization often works.

In innovation, the most important question is *"why?"—why* would customers buy this product? *Why* will investors support this business? *Why* should we put this product at higher priority than that product? How doesn't justify investment in development and launch of an innovation. Answering why does. It changes our entire perspective. To face personal or business challenges, we need to go way beyond how.

In spite of the dominance of how mindsets, asking why is a core necessity in innovation and in life—an essential survival tool. I'm waiting. Are you asking yourself, "Why?" Try it out loud.

WRIGHT

"Why?"

LUNDQUIST

See! You can do it! Now to my answer. Asking why is the core skill of strategists and leaders. Asking how is the core skill of tacticians and managers. I'll say that again. Asking why is the core skill of leaders and strategists. Asking how is the core skill of managers and tacticians. No matter what our challenges might be, leadership and strategy will enhance our chances of success. Certainly we need management skills, yet if we try to solve problems and grow opportunities with just management, we will fail as innovators.

Innovation is a leadership activity. We lead markets by leading change inside of our business while also leading change inside of ourselves.

Be careful, though. Asking why can be seen as an attack question—a clear statement of doubt. Asking why questions authority and challenges assumptions. Asking why makes people defensive and sometimes insulted. It helps a lot to soften the language—to not be blunt about it. For instance, you might say, "How did you happen to choose that approach?" instead of "Why the hell did you do that?"

To summarize just a bit, if we know that no one ever buys a product, then we will use our leadership and strategy skills in ways more likely to succeed. If we know that how is not the most important question, then we will leverage our strengths by questioning conventional methods.

Wright

You've mentioned two of your principles. What is the third? And, if you'll forgive the phrasing, *how* can that be applied to building inner strengths?

Lundquist

Principles change perspectives, and unique perspectives offer advantage. We may be highly strategic, seeing both short- and long-term priorities. We may manage our businesses well enough to compete in global markets. We may produce and deliver value so great that customers would buy in favor of alternatives, then ask for more. And we may blow it all away by misunderstanding the core purpose of our communications and interactions.

My third principle is this: "Product brochures are *not* about products." Not? What else could they be about? Football? My cousin's new job? Of course product communications are about products. Not so! And there is more. Business plans are not about businesses. Project reviews are *not* about projects. Sales calls are *not* about sales. Scientific papers are *not* about science. Darned hard to accept, isn't it. After all, most business communications *are* about the nominal topic (product, business, etc). Can all those authors have missed the point?

Look at it this way. Business itself is all about relationships. Businesses must build bonds of trust with their stakeholders. Customer loyalty alone delivers greater cash flow, more reliable cash flow, faster cash flow, faster time to payout, lower cost of sales, lower cost of capital, and higher share value. Communications are strategies for reaching those business goals just as much as products are.

All too often we fall into the trap of selling our stuff rather than creating and developing relationships. After all, we worked ourselves to the bone to define, design, develop, produce, and deliver our "stuff." It is our baby. Of course the world wants to know all about it and how we did it. And most of all, we want to tell them—in detail—in our business plans, project proposals, product brochures, user meetings, trade shows, and sales calls. But that style really doesn't work! Our audiences do *not* care about our product. (We just learned that above.) And they run powerful filters—less than half a second to reject an ad, less than six seconds to reject a trade show booth, and less than a minute to tune out of a sales presentation.

The difference is elegantly simple. It's about the "center." We can write self-centered communications that speak about what we care about or we can innovate audience-centered communications that speak about what our audience cares about. Simple. It's not about us or our stuff, but about them and their needs. It's not about our product, but about their concerns and fears and then how our product can resolve their frustrations.

To produce audience-centered communications, we need to know a lot about our audience. And it can be complex when the audience is a mix of personalities. Nevertheless, to gain attention and sustain interactions, we need to put our audience first. Value, as they define it, is a great connector. Strategies for delivering value over time sustain their attention.

WRIGHT

Value, strategy, communication—a neat package. Still, they don't provide a clear path to success. How do you apply your principles?

LUNDQUIST

Let's begin with opportunities. An opportunity is a chance to perform—to turn work into salary, products into profits, and investment into returns. It is also a chance to grow acquaintances into relationships and relationships into mutual respect. Opportunities open doors to innovate something new, better, and more desirable. The paths of our lives, personal or corporate, depend on opportunities—those we perceive, those we grasp, and those we leverage into greater potential.

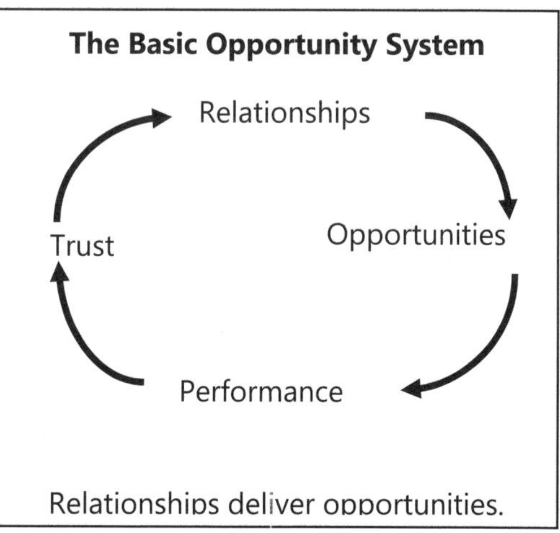

Chances we miss can have as much impact as those we seize. Chances tried but not realized make as big a difference as those we turn into dramatic reality.

If success is tied to opportunity, then what do *outrageously* successful people know about opportunity that we don't? I hadn't ever thought to ask that question until a Fortune 50 company asked me to find out. You see, their internal technical-services group was facing competition from outside contractors. They hired me to discover both opportunities for their services and how to leverage those opportunities. As I synthesized results of interviews of both service-group members and their business-unit clients, I used this simple figure to describe how customer-vendor relationships worked. It turns out to be a fundamental model for creating almost any kind of opportunities.

Relationships deliver opportunities. We tend to go to resources we already know. Successful performance builds trust, which strengthens relationships. The cycle can go on and on Of course trust works the other way, too. If our resource fails to perform up to expectations, then trust is compromised. That resource goes back on trial at best, and may never get another chance at worst.

The basic opportunity system integrates these parts:

- **Positive Relationships** are based on trust developed via interactions. Relationships build a core of loyalty able to stand many of the tests of time.
- **Opportunities** are chances to perform. Opportunities arise from relationships. We give opportunities to those we know and trust. (In the absence of relationships, good marketing can open doors.)
- **Performance** at or above expectations creates trust. Poor performance kills trust and loyalty.
- **Trust** strengthens relationships and improves the probability of future opportunities.

Each element influences and is influenced by all the others. This system is a whole that is broken when any part is missing—a color spectrum so important that anyone blind to one or more colors is disadvantaged. It is a tool kit so tightly integrated that working without all four tools means that jobs are never fully completed or done quite right.

To achieve a never-ending flow of the opportunities we most want, we must "*do the loop*," managing all four elements for optimum impact. That's it! Ultra simple. Relationships deliver opportunities. Opportunities enable relationships.

WRIGHT

It's a nice picture, but not in any way simple. Every step requires both knowledge and experience. Where do we start?

LUNDQUIST

First, we need to conceive of the skills needed to *do the loop.*

- **Marketing skills:** Abilities to generate opportunities. To create value propositions based on clear understanding of markets and customers. To speak to others from their perspectives and convey potential solutions. To open doors where none existed.
- **Performance skills:** Expertise and experience in one or more professional disciplines needed for the work we want to do. In many cases, related expertise such as leadership, management, project management, people management, collaboration, and communication. Abilities to perform at or above expectations of our stakeholders.
- **Character skills:** Integrity and authenticity. Abilities to choose core principles of business and life. To integrate what we believe with how we behave. To ensure that trust developed through performance is not compromised through blunders elsewhere.
- **Relationship skills:** People skills to initiate, sustain, and manage relationships. Abilities to network and then turn contacts into rapport. To relate to ensure durability of relationships. To properly leverage relationships for win-win.

We need all four skill sets to *do the loop:* marketing skills to generate opportunities, discipline skills to perform, people skills for relationships, and character skills to become and remain trustworthy.

Technical professionals, myself included, often focus on performance. We work at the bottom of the loop and exercise our technical excellence. We believe in our hearts that trust in that excellence is enough to create new opportunities. Though we continue to survive, a vast majority of us have very little idea of how to leverage good work into better opportunities.

The truth is that we simply can't achieve success—ordinary or outrageous—with just the tools of our technical profession. We may achieve high respect among peers and even gain the admiration of higher management, customers, and clients. Still, we'll never earn ten times the average in our professions. We'll never gain the most cherished opportunities and promotions. We'll never be seen as top performers—not until we learn to do the loop.

Wright

That makes sense, yet it seems static—just getting along.

Lundquist

Absolutely! To simplify initial concepts, I've left something out. Just a small detail: *opportunities are not all equal.*

The opportunity to do what someone else says is not the same as a chance to set strategies for a global company. The opportunity to work for $10 per hour is not the same as the chance to make $1000 per hour.

Doing the loop doesn't guarantee outrageous success. The loop only guarantees *more* success by delivering *more* opportunities. To achieve outrageous success, we need a system that delivers *ever better* opportunities.

Visualize the basic opportunity system as a two-dimensional loop lying flat on a table. Then visualize the *outrageous* opportunity system as an upward spiral—the basic system pulled up and up by higher expectations of ourselves. Visualize how excellent performance might build enough trust to create new levels of relationship that deliver new levels of opportunity. Seen edge on, the spiral can look like a ladder, so let's conceive of an opportunity spiral pegged to an "opportunity ladder." On our ladder, the bottom rung is where we started, and the top rung is the highest we think we could ever go.

The fifth skill, then, is visioning—it is the ability to see a potential future and describe it in enough detail to enable practical action. To, in this case, see a personal or team future as we work our way up our opportunity ladder, to look beyond what we know we can achieve to what we would love to do if only we had the chance. Opportunity visioning is not about sustaining our current position—it is about changing ourselves, over and over, to reach *outrageous success.*

Wright

And visioning like that would be the key to innovating ourselves or our products or our businesses!

LUNDQUIST

Precisely! Our success is up to us. Back in my market research project I asked those I interviewed how to get started with them. By far the most frequent answer was, "Be proactive! Come meet us. Come learn how we do business and what kinds of problems we face."

What marvelous advice. Proactivity fits all five skills. It fits all personality types. It changes the playing field, step by step. It's an ongoing practice as important as any of the five skills. Proactivity means innovating our own careers and innovating our own teams and companies. It means innovating a range of skills outside our normal comfort zone. Good "spiral skills" enable movement with greater confidence and flexibility. Those skills deliver power and control over our lives.

Climbing the spiral means moving on to achieve our potential, yet it need not deny our past. Each step upward opens new doors, yet doesn't necessarily close doors behind us. Perhaps the most important climbing skill is sustaining those key relationships that deserve to last a lifetime.

WRIGHT

But visioning itself is another skill. Do you have any advice on developing powerful visions?

LUNDQUIST

I'd like to preface that answer with a learning experience. Back in my software company, we worked to improve products, service, and marketing. As part of that process, I would introduce a potential marketing strategy. I would get the officers (mostly PhD scientists like myself) together in a conference room and present an idea. That turned out to be one of the most frustrating experiences of my life. You see, scientists are trained to test hypotheses. My colleagues had no problem at all with testing marketing ideas to death. Hey, it became a source of pride for them—and defeat for me.

My lesson learned, the hard way, is this: instead of presenting a solution, ask questions and facilitate development of powerful answers. Telling people answers is like stating a challenge. Asking, on the other hand, builds teams that develop buy-in. For teams below senior management, teamwork is much more likely to influence management.

When I began consulting, I based strategic and product marketing on questions asked in team environments—the leadership team of a business or a functional department, the product team attempting to move a concept from initial development into the product pipeline. I've now honed my questions into formal visioning tools called Strategic Pre-Planning.

Because I focus on questions rather than answers, I've been able to work in a wide range of industries and a range of products about which I knew nothing when I began, from little GPS systems that fit in your hand and cost $100 up to refinery systems that cover acres and cost half a billion dollars—services as well as products, businesses from startup to elements of Fortune 50, from bioprocessing facilities to space communications, and nonprofits as well. I don't need expertise in their business or product domains; I just need a suite of proven questions.

In each case, our objective as a team is always creation of the best vision this team can make of both the developing innovation and its competitive marketplace. When team knowledge is incomplete, market research has a better starting place. Business questions cluster naturally into three suites: Strategic Identity™, Integrated Strategy™, and Integrated Culture™. For product-like innovations, Identity is enough.

For Identity, I've settled on eight categories of questions: features/functions, markets/customers, needs, benefits, uniqueness, image, mission, and name. Strategy develops goals, objectives, strategies, and multi-strategy initiatives. Culture works on principles, core roles, choice of driving factor, and a compact vision statement. Most question categories achieve results through multiple sub-questions.

We are defining a guiding vision of an innovation that sets requirements for implementation. This is a big job, and it all applies to ourselves as both innovations and innovators. Just as important, the time spent in visioning accelerates development. Visioning pays for itself with high ROI.

WRIGHT

It certainly sounds like a big job, yet it seems you now have only a series of answers, not a vision.

Lundquist

True. Synthesis is a crucial step. First, I create a summary that shows the highest priority elements of lists and final wordsmithed statements. For team benefit, each summary entry briefly explains what that element is and implies. Next, I develop a one-page Statement of Identity to bring all dimensions of the innovation into a tight focus. Third, evaluate. When seen as a whole, is any critical element missing? Do all elements work well together?

Of course, we still have too much content for today's fast pace. The tightest version is the brand concept. We integrate name (identity), functional class (functionality), and slogan (personality) with the value promise (commitment to primary stakeholders). This is typically fewer than a dozen words. Clarity at a glance:

Name
Functional Class
Slogan
Value Promise

At this point, we meet as a team again. We go over every decision in context of all decisions. After all, questions around mission may have found new or refined perspectives on customers. To provide a guide for tactical marketing, we focus the identity down to a "core message" of about two hundred words." Tactical marketing can also combine brand concept and message with a logo mark and graphic presentation.

So we have brand concept (more than twelve words), core message (two hundred words), identity (six hundred words), summary (ten pages), and appendices (forty pages).

Wright

You promised to show relevance of this process to a person or team working to discover their inner strengths. Can we do all of that for a person?

Lundquist

Yes. It may be tricky to find an appropriate team, yet the questions all apply. Let's lay them out:

- **Features/functions:** What are my strengths? What can I do? What should I learn?
- **Markets/customers:** Whom do I want to serve? In what industry? In what geographic market?
- **Needs:** Why would they need me? What specific needs will I choose to meet?
- **Benefits:** What value will I offer? What solutions will I strive to deliver?
- **Uniqueness:** Why should they choose me over others? What are my strengths? My track record?
- **Image:** How do I want to be perceived? How will I be remembered?
- **Mission:** What is my sense of purpose? What do I really care about?
- **Name:** What is my name? Should I use my middle initial? My maiden name? A title such as Dr.?
- **Goals:** What are my long-term strategic directions? What do I want to achieve with my life?
- **Objectives:** What near-term results must I achieve to further my goals?
- **Strategies:** What methods will I use to achieve each objective?
- **Initiatives:** What multi-strategy actions will I take to achieve my objectives?
- **Principles:** What personal ethics guide my actions every day? What broader criteria will I use to focus my strengths on reaching my goals?
- **Core roles:** What higher functions will I choose to perform, as shown in my behaviors, in responsibilities accepted, and in commitments to action (e.g., leader, change agent)?
- **Driving factor:** What fundamental motivation to achieve will characterize the way I approach my markets (e.g., value-driven)?
- **Vision statement:** What phrase or short sentence captures my desired situation at some future time?

Then build your brand concept: name, functional category, slogan, and value promise. Here is mine:

Gary Lundquist
Decision Synthesist
The Accelerator
Innovation of Business and
the Business of Innovation

WRIGHT

Wow! I've never heard of anyone developing a personal vision with that kind of depth.

LUNDQUIST

It makes very clear sense in the business world. To get personal, all we need to do is think of ourselves as a business of one. Imagine answering these questions about yourself. Imagine getting three to five friends who know you well and asking them the questions.

WRIGHT

I notice you don't say "brand," but "brand concept." What is the difference?

LUNDQUIST

Brand and branding are typically misunderstood. Well, that understates the issue. Value is the single most important concept in business, and brands are used to build loyalty to the value delivered by particular businesses and products. If we don't manage our brands, everything else may be a waste of time.

Two camps exist: one relating to symbols and the other to value as defined by customers.

SYMBOL VIEW:

The American Marketing Association and marketing guru Philip Kotler, among others, define a brand as "a name, term, design, symbol, or a combination." With this kind of high profile reinforcement, many practitioners equate "brand" with words and symbols. They believe that companies own brands, that businesses and products should be developed first, then branded, and brands are built through advertising that connects names to products or businesses.

VALUE VIEW:

Today's best marketers see brands differently. Businesses own names, but markets own brands. We can write names on paper. Brands are written in the neurons of people's minds. Names can be brainstormed. Brands must be organically grown. Names are cognitive. Brands are emotional. Names are labels on mental file folders that help people remember information about a product or business. Brands are the relationships that fill those folders with trust, respect, loyalty, track records, and willingness to overlook mistakes.

Names enable recognition. Brands enable relationships. It's the difference between acquaintance and sweetheart, between, "I know that name" and "I know that person." A brand is a relationship, not a name. Forget the old definitions. Brands have *always* been relationships.

We build brands by relating to markets, not just by repeating names. Brands develop around trust. It's that simple and that complex. Brands grow around promises made and kept—the core of trust essential to any relationship. Businesses today carefully craft their value promises, then state those promises visibly and audibly. To make very clear who is stating that promise, they use name, logo, slogan, and jingle to connect brand to product and/or business.

Aside from that, why bother with brands? Why not settle for names? Brand equity—that's why. Don Schultz of Northwestern University has shown that brands are the single most valuable assets of any business—everything else changes, only brands can stand the test of time. Brand equity is the source of greater cash flow, faster cash flow, more reliable cash flow, lower cost of sales, lower cost of capital, higher share value, and durable corporate wealth. Powerful brands produce easier sales, repeat purchases, up-selling and cross-selling, lower barriers to competition, easier market expansion, and competitive platforms for higher market impact.

Well-developed brand equity is a business's single greatest asset and only truly durable source of wealth. People and products come and go. Facilities degrade and alliances change. Market evolution is dynamic. Only brands have the potential to survive change over time.

Thorough visioning can develop a unique, durable brand promise. Marketing then conveys the promise to target audiences. Or, said another way, everything the business (or person) does or says must reinforce the promise. Breaking the promise kills trust, which breaks down the basic opportunity system.

Wright

We started and ended this conversation with a focus on value. To me, that is perfect emphasis for developing our inner innovators.

As a parting thought, do you have a favorite quote on innovation?

LUNDQUIST

Perhaps you remember the dialog from Lewis Carroll's *Alice's Adventures in Wonderland.* Alice was lost and asked for directions. The Cheshire Cat, of course, asked her where she wanted to go. When she said she didn't know, the Cat suggested "If you don't know where you are going, then any path will take you there."

The Cat is too smart to suggest that our path to innovation begins with a vision of where we want to go. You see, we need to envision our innovation being chosen over competitive alternatives and now in use by its logical customers who are so pleased with its performance that they gladly deliver market loyalty and repeat business. Now that takes quite a vision! The Cat would be impressed. Or maybe he would call it all just wind in the trees until that vision is put into action in the real world. The real world will decide whether our multi-faceted vision has any real impact.

About the Author

Gary Lundquist is a "synthesist" who helps innovation teams develop their strengths via combination of strategic identity, integrated strategy, and formal culture. He targets creating value for stakeholders rather than merely developing businesses and products.

Gary earned his BA and PhD from the University of Colorado, and then founded an INC 500 software business in the energy industry. He has twenty-five years' domestic and international experience in strategic, product, and tactical marketing of high technology for clients from start-up to units of Fortune 50. He applies his marketing to technology-transfer in both industrial and federal labs. Gary is developer and practitioner of Strategic Pre-Planning™ for innovation of businesses, products, processes, and markets. He chaired the Colorado Innovation Summits in 2003 and 2004 and authors the Colorado Innovation Newsletter. Gary is Director of InnoSearch™ Colorado and blogger at Innopinions™.com.

Gary Lundquist
Market Engineering® Inc.
12006 N. Antelope Trail
Parker, CO 80138
303.840.9929
www.Market-Engineering.com

Chapter 21

AN INTERVIEW WITH...

NINA PRICE

INNER STRENGTH

A Core Assumption of Professional Competitiveness

DAVID WRIGHT (WRIGHT)

Today we're talking with Nina Price. Nina grew up in New York City and earned a bachelor's degree and her MBA from the University of Michigan. After business school she moved to the Silicon Valley to be a high tech professional. Twenty years later she realized that it was time to do something else; she quit her corporate job and trained to be a life coach and a message therapist. After practicing these disciplines for several years, she realized that she wanted to do be able to do more for her clients. She studied acupuncture and Traditional Chinese Medicine at Five Branches University in Santa Cruz, and now is also a Licensed Acupuncturist. Recently she created "Sharpen Your Competitive Edge: How to Stay Professionally Competitive in a Rapidly Changing World," an information product and workshop to help high tech professionals deal more effectively with the stresses, strains, and professional challenges of working in an industry where constant, rapid change is a daily fact of life.

Her new business venture is called RESET! It is a new model for integrative medicine practices, which includes complimentary, alternative, and integrative medicine (CAM) under the same roof as fitness, wellness, and business/wellness coaching. With corporate trendsetters like Cisco Systems Inc., setting a precedent by offering CAM and fitness together on a new facility on their San Jose campus, RESET! is poised to offer the same services and more to smaller, high tech companies. Nina Price helps high tech professionals reduce their stress, look and feel better, and stay professionally competitive.

Nina, welcome to *Discover Your Inner Strength.*

NINA PRICE (PRICE)

Thanks! I'm pleased to be here.

WRIGHT

So I know you're the "professional competitiveness coach," but what exactly is "professional competitiveness"?

PRICE

Well, David, "professional competitiveness" is having the professional life you *really* want. Creating the professional life you really want is a process of constantly understanding and improving your value in the marketplace, while at the same time taking incredibly good care of yourself so you can be resilient to the stresses and strains of a work environment defined by constant change. Let's paint a picture of what professional competitiveness looks like. It involves staying employed and growing professionally, no matter what happens in the economy or in your industry, in your company, or even in your work group. It involves staying attractive to your current employer or to other potential employers. It means having the skills and attributes that employers pay top dollar for.

Professional competitiveness means having the professional opportunities that you really want—the jobs you want, the promotions you want, the raises, the assignments, and the stock options. It means avoiding career stalls. It also involves working for as long as you want to and retiring when you choose to, as opposed to when you have to.

We're hearing a lot about layoffs and we're hearing a lot about ageism these days. I'm judging by what I'm hearing from my clients that folks over forty are having a lot harder time staying employed the way they want to rather than the way they were some years ago, so I address this as well.

The components of professional competitiveness are:

- Stress Management—Understanding what underlies your stress and how you can best respond to your stressors so you can be resilient.
- Health and Wellness—Since you're the author of your own level of health or disease, learning how to be in charge of your own health and/or enlisting the assistance of others you believe in, if and when you need it.
- Managing Others' Perceptions of You—Like it or not, first impressions count, especially in your professional life. Making the best first impression you can and being aware of stereotypes that could affect you.
- Interpersonal Skills—Communicating your ideas, your knowledge, and your value effectively, through both written words and conversation, and knowing how to negotiate for what you need.
- Business Savvy—Understanding how the organization you work in really works so you can be more effective as a part of it.
- Business and Technical Skills—These are probably the reason you were hired in the first place. Maybe it's what you studied in college, and it's usually how you make your living. If you haven't kept them up to date, others who may cost your employer a whole lot less may be better qualified to do what you do.

Those are the components of professional competitiveness.

Wright

It's easy to see why up-to-date business skills or business savvy and excellent interpersonal skills are important to staying competitive professionally, but why include health and stress management?

PRICE

Well, David, my early experiences of coaching taught me that many of my coaching clients were dealing with health and stress management issues along with business and career issues. In fact, health and stress issues were often either the underlying cause of the business and career issues they were dealing with, or side effects of the business and career issues. Here are a couple of examples.

The first one is about stress as the underlying cause. I was working with Mary, a single woman in her forties. Mary had an elderly mother who required her constant attention and support. Mary was her mother's only child. Mary's resume was solid—she'd worked for good companies and she'd done well at the various assignments she'd been given.

As her mother's health deteriorated, Mary spent more and more time making sure that her mom was well cared for. The quality of her work suffered a bit and her boss suggested that she get some coaching from me to help her manage the balance between the job and her mom's needs.

When her mother died, Mary had already spent all her vacation and sick days for the year dealing with her mother's needs and wellbeing. After the funeral Mary was exhausted and she was depressed. She was having migraines and she was having trouble sleeping. Her boss was really concerned about her, but she needed her back in action at work. So Mary and I talked about what her options were. She really needed some time off and she really needed to take care of herself. She loved her job and she didn't want to lose it. But in the end, Mary decided that her most important priority was herself.

This is a case where stress—family stress—was the underlying cause of a problem at work. I'm sure you can think of other similar situations such as divorce, or parents having to deal with problems with their teenage kids.

Let's also look at stress as the side effect of a work problem. When I was an intern in acupuncture school, a patient named John came in complaining of intense low back pain. What was most puzzling was he had no idea what the cause of the back pain was. He hadn't fallen, he hadn't had an accident, and he hadn't been injured playing sports. He just woke up one morning in excruciating pain. He had even gone to the hospital and had some x-rays taken, which he showed me. There was no evidence of an injury. There was no broken bone. There was no disc problem.

John was in his fifties and I asked him whether he had hypertension, and he did. He admitted that he hadn't been taking his medicine regularly, and of course, I encouraged him to be diligent in taking his medication regularly.

I asked him whether anything in his professional life or his personal life had changed in the last week or so. He told me that his boss had significantly cut back his work hours and he was worried about how he would be able to pay his bills. I explained to him that low back pain can be a very common symptom when a person has been hit by a layoff or when a person's pay has been significantly cut, as John's had. I proposed an acupuncture treatment strategy for the pain, and I coached him about the next steps he wanted to take to deal with his job situation.

These are two examples of why it's important to include health and stress in professional competitiveness, because very often they are key factors.

WRIGHT

When I introduced you, I mentioned your new workshop and product, "Sharpen Your Competitive Edge: How to Stay Professionally Competitive in a Rapidly Changing World." Will you give us more details about this program?

PRICE

I'd love to. I think of "Sharpen Your Competitive Edge" in two ways. I think of it as an in-depth professional competitiveness checkup. The people in the workshop, or who are working on their own with the information product, take a close look at themselves in five areas—the key areas of professional competitiveness that I mentioned earlier—and they find out where their blind spots are. Honestly, I think we all have blind spots. These are areas where we don't like to admit we've got a problem, and maybe we're a little stuck. Then they develop an action plan for getting themselves to be where they really want to be.

I also think of "Sharpen Your Competitive Edge" as an emergency preparedness kit for a person's professional life. We've all been taught that we should prepare our homes and our families for natural disasters. Out here in California we have earthquakes; in other parts of the country you have snowstorms, power outages, and droughts for which you put together a household emergency preparedness kit. I think that since we're dealing with times of economic uncertainty, the analogy is pretty clear—it's probably a good idea to have an emergency preparedness "kit" for your professional life so that you can continue to work no matter what happens. It's all about being proactive and addressing the issues so you can be prepared.

WRIGHT

So once your clients have identified what needs to change, how do you work with them?

PRICE

Well, it depends what they're asking me to work with. Very often people come in looking for coaching or they'll come in for an acupuncture treatment or for a massage and I look at the whole picture. I look at the presenting issues and even the underlying issues—the symptoms, the lifestyle, and what's really going on in their life—to get the whole picture. We talk and we come up with an action plan and the client makes it real.

I have many tools that I use; sometimes it's coaching, sometimes it's treatments like acupuncture or Chinese herbs, sometimes it's energy coaching like the Emotional Freedom Technique (EFT®). There's a new technique I'm working with called ETHOS (http://ethosmethod.com). We just proceed with our action plan working on the whole picture and zeroing in on what needs to be done.

WRIGHT

Nina, you've mentioned that when you're working with people you're always looking at the whole picture and the underlying issues, but how do you get people to share the truth of the matter—to "spill their guts"?

PRICE

I've found that all my life people have always told me things, often more than what I really wanted to know. When I first started doing a radio show I noticed that people would call and talk to me as though they'd known me their whole lives. They would tell me the deep dark secrets of their souls.

On the second date with the man who is now my husband, I got some insight as to why people tell me all about themselves. As we were about to say goodnight, he said to me, "What I like about you is that you're so easy to talk to." No one had ever told me that before. But since that time many people have told me that I'm "easy to talk to." I've learned that what they mean is they perceive I genuinely care about them and they can feel safe being themselves, which allows them to share what needs to be shared.

Now, I jokingly say that I make a living by "being easy to talk to," and I feel honored that my clients can see that I genuinely care about each one of them.

WRIGHT

You're a licensed acupuncturist and practitioner of traditional Chinese medicine, so how does that allow you to do more for your clients?

PRICE

Well, as you mentioned earlier, David, I studied acupuncture because in my coaching and massage practice I kept noticing that my clients always seemed to have underlying health and stress issues. I wanted to be able to help them with those issues as well, so people may come for acupuncture treatments and they might end up getting acupuncture as well as some coaching, or people come for coaching and we may decide that they need to do some health related treatments as well.

I'd like to talk for a minute about some of the key benefits. I think most people know about acupuncture and traditional Chinese medicine. More and more folks in the United States have actually tried them, but I think people don't always realize some of the key benefits they should be considering.

Traditional Chinese Medicine is Holistic. It looks at the whole person and what's happening in his or her whole life, as we talked about in the back pain example earlier. John was noticing that he had back pain, but the real problem was his job situation. He really needed to be working to address the problem with his job and what his next steps should be there. We treated the back pain with acupuncture. He also needed to spend some time coming up with an action plan for the job situation.

Pain is usually your body trying to get you to pay attention to something, whether it's a physical injury or arthritis or other problems.

Mentioning arthritis made me think of a patient I worked with by the name of Bill, who had very painful arthritis. The man had been a professional athlete. He was retired now and had arthritis in his hips and in his legs. It was so bad that he could hardly walk.

When I met and worked with him, I asked Bill about his diet, because I had a hunch that maybe there was something in his diet that was an underlying cause or issue. I asked him if he ate a lot of sugar or a lot of dairy products or if he drank alcohol. It turned out he did drink quite a bit of alcohol, and he asked, "Do you want me to cut back?"

I said, "As a matter of fact, I'd like you to try an experiment here. I really would like you to cut back on your alcohol and see what happens." So he cut back on his alcohol intake very significantly, and he noticed that the more he cut back on his alcohol intake, the more the pain and the swelling went down in his leg and hips. He was a wonderful person to work with because he was willing to make changes. He was also wonderful because he saw the link between his behavior and the outcome he didn't want. He ultimately chose to change his alcohol intake on an ongoing basis so that he would have less pain and be able to walk.

In addition to looking at the whole person, *Traditional Chinese Medicine (TCM) offers more specific diagnoses and taxonomies of disease.* What I mean by this can be illustrated when you think about catching a cold. Have you ever noticed that everyone catches a cold their own way? Most of us catch colds. From the perspective of Western medicine we say, "I have a cold." In Traditional Chinese Medicine there are many kinds of colds and they're all different. You could have a "Wind Cold," or a "Wind Heat," or even "Lung Heat." To the TCM practitioner they look different and are treated differently. You use different acupuncture treatments and you prescribe different herbal remedies for each one of the ten or twenty kinds of colds. It's a much more precise diagnosis and a much more precise remedy.

My client Nancy is a teacher. Most teachers dread catching a cold, but since they work with lots of young people they're exposed to plenty of colds. She says, "As a teacher I can't afford to be sick. When a cold or flu is going around at school I'm careful to take preventative measures. Nonetheless, every now and again I get sick. I've learned that the best way to recover from a cold, cough, or flu is to make an appointment with Nina for an acupuncture treatment and then follow it up with Chinese herbal remedies. The amazing thing is that with acupuncture and Traditional Chinese Medicine I always get better faster than all of my colleagues who are relying on Western medicine, and I actually feel stronger after I have fully recovered."

My clients are always amazed to discover that there are Chinese diagnoses that don't exist in other types of medicine that precisely describe their problems.

One of my clients, a very health conscious lady, went to visit her older sister in another state. When she returned home after a week at her sister's house she was glad to be home, but found that she had a very unusual cough. She mentioned that visiting her sister was often trying and this visit was no exception. The cough she had puzzled her because it felt as though there was something in her throat, but she couldn't cough it up or get it to descend from her throat. I explained that in Chinese medicine this is a textbook case, and I showed her the description in my textbook for what's known as "plum pit throat." She was amazed that Chinese medicine had a name and a remedy for this problem and sure enough, it worked.

Another case of a Chinese diagnosis and treatment that worked involved a young graduate student who had very unusual stress-related digestive symptoms. She had had every test that Western doctors could think of for her symptoms, including an endoscopy to make sure that she didn't have stomach cancer, but no one could come up with a conclusive diagnosis. One of my teachers treated this young woman for "blood stagnation" with acupuncture and two Chinese herbal formulas. The symptoms, which had plagued her for eighteen months, completely disappeared.

Chinese herbal formulas offer non-pharmaceutical solutions that are often more effective. One of my clients had a very high stress (high tech) job and noticed that she was getting a lot of urinary tract infections. When she relied on antibiotics to treat her symptoms she would get a secondary infection because the antibiotics killed off the good bacteria in her system. When we treated her with acupuncture and Chinese herbal antibiotics, she got better faster and never got a secondary infection.

Bottom line: I use Traditional Chinese Medicine for any problems that I wouldn't take to an emergency room.

As one of my teachers says, "Traditional Chinese Medicine: clinical trials for over 1,000 years and more than 1 billion people served."

WRIGHT

Ageism keeps coming up as an issue when you talk about professional competitiveness. How prevalent do you believe it is, and what can people do about it?

PRICE

I actually did some research about this. Ageism is a term coined by Robert Butler in 1969 to describe discrimination against seniors, and I was really amazed that ageism isn't a new problem. I kept hearing stories from my clients about how they weren't getting hired, they weren't getting rehired, they weren't getting jobs, they weren't getting promotions; in fact, they were getting laid off because they were considered old. I was somewhat surprised by that.

I think the reason that it's a problem right now is because of the fact that there are so many Baby Boomers. There were actually 76 million people born in the Baby Boom Generation and that represents about 31 percent of the American population right now. So there are people turning fifty in that population at a pretty fast rate. Because there are a large number of people in their forties, fifties, and sixties who still want to work, we're seeing this phenomenon in the workplace. I think it's ironic that the Baby Boom Generation who followed Bob Dylan's advice of "never trust anybody over thirty," is now well over thirty and on the other end of the distrust of their younger colleagues.

Part of what we talk about in "Sharpen Your Competitive Edge" and *Professional Competitiveness,* which is the book I'm writing based on the same topic, is how to deal with ageism. Honestly, one of the things you can do about ageism is to be proactive. You must constantly strive to understand and improve your value in the marketplace, while at the same time, taking really good care of yourself. You can also work on your appearance.

I had one client named Ed, who wasn't getting what he wanted from his job interviews. I ended up telling him that what he needed was a makeover because he looked tired and older than he was. I actually sent him to a hairdresser, an esthetician, and a style consultant who worked with him. He was really wonderful about this because he was willing to go along with it. I think a lot of men are resistant to the idea of a "makeover." But Ed was really terrific and he looked so fabulous after the makeover that both he and his wife were thrilled with the results. Best of all, he got a job within the next month.

So it's about looking younger, being energetic, and defying the ageism stereotypes that pigeonhole you as you get older as obsolete, ineffective, and maybe even incompetent. You're also considered expensive. There could be the perception that you don't work as hard, or won't work as hard as a younger person.

Some might consider you difficult to manage. One friend of mine was even told that he "wasn't a cultural fit." As with all stereotypes, you don't actually have to be any of those things. In fact, once you realize what the stereotypes are, you can be proactive about preventing that perception.

WRIGHT

Tell me, what does inner strength mean to you?

PRICE

Well, that's what this book is about. Inner strength means that you can deal with whatever life hands you—whatever happens in your life. Inner strength is knowing what you're made of.

For me there are really three components to inner strength. One is your life experience—what you've learned. I always think of that as my invisible Kevlar or flak jacket—it's what makes me bulletproof. Sometimes when things don't turn out the way I want, or when I feel like things are kind of difficult, I say to myself, "Let's get some perspective here; you've dealt with harder stuff than this, you can do this." I think it's that kind of perspective that allows you to have the confidence and the inner strength to deal with whatever happens.

The second element is to be in the moment—it's that creativity and resourcefulness we all have that allows us to think on our feet, be confident, and handle a situation in the moment, no matter what.

The third component has to do with faith—knowing that no matter what happens, you'll have what you need. Maybe the outcome doesn't look like what you thought it would look like, but it's the belief in yourself and in the divine, and that the divine will be with you no matter what. It's believing that you'll learn what you need to learn or what you're supposed to learn from all of the experiences of your life. I've always told my children that "any mistake you don't learn from wasn't worth making in the first place," and I really believe that. The experiences of our life are here to teach us things, and when we don't learn the lessons, typically we will re-experience them. So sometimes it's good to pay attention to the lessons we're supposed to learn from a given experience. Learning those lessons contributes to our inner strength.

WRIGHT

So how does inner strength relate to professional competitiveness?

PRICE

Professional competitiveness is a process of constantly understanding and improving your value in the marketplace, while taking incredibly good care of yourself. Inner strength is an underlying factor or core assumption in being professionally competitive. Becoming professionally competitive at the same time most likely causes you to discover your inner strength.

To get to professional competitiveness you have to be open to feedback and willing to look at your challenges, your bad habits, your blind spots, and the places where you get stuck. Then you need to learn more effective ways of handling those situations or addressing the issues. In order to do this, you've got to have faith that even though looking at your issues may not be pleasant, the end result is worth it. It's about realizing that you have a particular issue and then learning what you really need to learn to address it.

Ideally your life experiences have taught you that you can learn anything you need to learn, and you've done so in the past. In the case of professional competitiveness, it means keeping your eye on your larger goal of staying in the game professionally.

For the second piece of inner strength—the resourcefulness and creativity in the moment—it's using that resourcefulness and creativity when you're in a situation where you can promote yourself, like meeting someone new or a job interview. It's being crystal clear about the value you offer as an employee or a consultant or whoever you need to be in that situation. Inner strength allows you to be able to communicate your unique value in a way that the listener can understand.

Finally, inner strength means always having the faith that by being proactive and learning what you need to learn, constantly improving yourself and your skills, and taking incredibly good care of yourself that the outcomes you want will come to pass.

WRIGHT

Tell us a little bit more about RESET!, your new business adventure.

PRICE

I like that you call it a business "adventure." I think it is an adventure. In fact, my life is definitely an adventure. RESET! is a new model for an integrative medicine practice, where we're going to include, as you mentioned earlier, integrative medicine, Eastern and Western medicine, fitness, business and wellness coaching, and workshops all under one roof. We'll also have a network of affiliates and associates. We are going to primarily serve high tech professionals and work with their companies to act as a partner providing health, wellness, fitness, and coaching to help employees take better care of themselves. In the end, everyone wins. Employees are healthier and better able to do outstanding work for their employers. Employers can recruit talented employees because they're offering benefits the employees want.

WRIGHT

It's interesting that corporations today are viewing their employees' health as a strategic asset. What do you say to those companies who aren't ready to see that?

PRICE

Typically I tell them a story. There's a great model of small businesses in Jackson, Michigan. It was the subject of an article that ran in the *New York Times* in October of 2008. The article is called "Building Better Bodies." There was a group of several dozen small business owners in Jackson, Michigan, who joined forces to put together a wellness campaign for their employees because they noticed that some of the key wellness metrics in their city were significantly worse than the national average. For example, occurrences of obesity and type-2 diabetes were both greater than the U.S. national average. They felt that their employees' health was a crucial part of their corporate strategy, not just a cost cutting or cost management problem, which I think was very forward looking.

We've seen the larger trend-setting corporations like Cisco Systems are already addressing these issues. However, the example from Jackson, Michigan, shows that you don't have to be a giant corporation to offer your employees incentives and opportunities to take better care of themselves.

Wright

You're located in Northern California in the Silicon Valley; clearly other professionals in other parts of the United States could also benefit from your work. What are your intentions for sharing your work with others elsewhere?

Price

Well, David, I started with a target market I knew well. I was a high tech professional myself for twenty years, so I had done the jobs, I'd learned the skills, I'd sat in the next cubicle or the next office, I'd been the manager of high tech professionals, and I'd lived the lifestyle. So I know how to talk to people who are high tech professionals. I'm a peer—I'm the person they used to sit next to and work with or work for, and I speak their language, I know their world because I've lived in it rather than looked into it. So I felt that I needed to start with what I knew. I saw what happened to me and to some of my friends after twenty years of working in a high stress job and industry and then the impact of aging on top of that. It was just a perfect setup for all manner of stress related disease. So I'm starting in the market I know well. I'm sure that other people will benefit from RESET! I certainly intend to grow it into other target markets and other geographic markets over time. This is just the beginning.

Wright

Well, this has been a great conversation, and I wish you the best of luck in your new venture/adventure, RESET!

Today we've been talking with Nina Price. Nina spent twenty years working in high profile, high tech firms in Silicon Valley as a software engineer and a marketing executive. She's a radio personality and motivational speaker, a teacher, and a creative problem-solver. She is nationally certified as both a life coach and a therapeutic message practitioner, and has practiced both of these disciplines since she left the corporate world. She completed a graduate degree in Traditional Chinese Medicine, and is also a licensed acupuncturist. She is now completing her new book, *Professional Competitiveness: Creating the Professional Life*

You Really Want. It's coming out in early 2009 and I think I'll be standing in line for this one.

Nina, thank you so much for being with us today on *Discover Your Inner Strength.*

PRICE

Thanks David, it's been my pleasure.

About the Author

Nina Price grew up in New York City; she earned a bachelor's degree and her MBA from the University of Michigan and moved to the Silicon Valley to be a high tech professional. Twenty years later she realized that it was time to do something else; quit her corporate job and trained to be a life coach and a massage therapist. After practicing these disciplines for several years, she realized that she wanted to do be able to do more for her clients. She studied acupuncture and traditional Chinese medicine at Five Branches University in Santa Cruz, and now is also a licensed acupuncturist. Recently she created Sharpen Your Competitive Edge: How to Stay Professionally Competitive in a Rapidly Changing World, an information product and workshop to help high tech professionals deal more effectively with stresses, strains and professional challenges of working in an industry where constant rapid change is a daily fact of life.

Her new business venture is called RESET!, a new model for integrative medicine practices which includes complimentary alternative and integrative medicine under the same roof as fitness, wellness, and business coaching. With corporate trend setters like Cisco Systems Inc., setting a precedent by offering CAM and fitness together on a new facility on their San Jose campus, Reset is poised to offer the same services and more to smaller, high tech companies. Nina Price helps high tech professionals reduce their stress, look, and feel better and stay professionally competitive.

Nina Price
RESET!
Mountain View, CA
650.493.0354
nina@ninaprice.com
www.ninaprice.com

AN INTERVIEW WITH…

MARY BETH HARTLEB

DEFINING SUCCESS ON YOUR TERMS

DAVID WRIGHT (WRIGHT)

Today we're talking with Mary Beth Hartleb. Mary Beth has worked in the human resources field for twenty years. Five years ago, she started her own management consulting practice called PRISM Human Resource Consulting Services, LLC. She has a master's degree in human resource management and a law degree, and she earned the Senior Professional in Human Resources designation, as well as a specialty certification in California employment law. She is also a licensed insurance broker in life, health property and casualty insurance lines. She has owned and operated an international import/export business and previously worked in marketing and retail sales. She has authored two books, *Market Your Job Search*, and the *Las Vegas Employment Guide* available in English and Spanish.

Mary Beth, welcome to *Discover Your Inner Strength.*

How do you define success?

MARY BETH HARTLEB (HARTLEB)

To be successful in business and in life, one needs a peaceful co-existence in both worlds. We are often told that work is work and there is no place for a personal life in the office. Yet, as more and more people are working harder, not necessarily smarter, it is impossible not to have overlap in both work and personal life. To be truly successful means understanding the difference and achieving fulfillment in each area of life. If one area is not in harmony, it will negatively influence other areas.

WRIGHT

What suggestions do you have for those who want to be successful in the workplace?

HARTLEB

The most important thing to do is be honest with yourself. Sometimes we need to work for a paycheck. However, if you find a way to make money in a field you are invested in, the money and success will follow. By investment I am referring to passion—something you have an affinity for or desire to do.

WRIGHT

How do you discover what you're passionate about?

HARTLEB

I often ask the question "what is your dream job?" Most often, the description I receive is not a match for what that person is currently doing. I answered this question six years ago while I was working full time and attending law school. As thankful as I am for my legal education, I also knew I would need to apply my education in a non-traditional sense. My two main criteria for a dream job was working for myself and being able to work anywhere in the world so I could combine my passion for travel with my work. Clearly, working eighty hours a week as a new attorney in a law firm was not a good fit.

It is interesting to me how many people have never taken the time to ask the question. I often interview candidates for jobs and I usually ask this question to find out if the type of work, and the work environment, will mirror the candidate's idea of a dream job. Many candidates have a difficult time responding because they focus on pay and benefits and never ask if the job is something they want to do or if they want to work for that particular employer.

WRIGHT

What else can a person do to discover their inner strengths and passion through work?

HARTLEB

A career assessment tool is an excellent way to determine your strengths and translate those strengths into a job where you can excel. Many times, we try to focus on fixing what is broken—our weaknesses. Focusing on what you are good at and designing a career around those strengths is a much better way to go and will lead to success in the workplace. Think about what you love to do when you are not working. If it is something you can build a business around, it may be worth exploring.

I also tell job seekers that an interview is a two-way street. The working relationship and environment needs to be a good culture fit. Interview a company as they interview you, and base employment decisions on the entire package, not just the paycheck or benefits.

WRIGHT

What do you mean by "culture fit"?

HARTLEB

Many people strive only for the job without considering whether the position, the hours, the responsibility, or the type of industry is in line with their personal work ethic, morals, and values. For example, living in Las Vegas there are many businesses revolving around gaming. If a person is interviewing for a position in a casino environment, but has a strong aversion to gambling, it is likely that neither the employee nor the company will have a positive, long-lasting working relationship.

WRIGHT

How does success in one's personal life translate to success in the workplace?

HARTLEB

This is more difficult for people. Many times, we don't want to admit that we need to end a relationship, be better at saving money, or lose twenty pounds. But, it is important to remember that when one area of your life is out of balance, it will negatively affect others.

Consider an issue many of us are facing today—personal debt. If you are working for a paycheck so you can pay your bills on time, instead of seeking fulfillment in your career, you are working in a job that in the long-term is not going to be rewarding for you. As a result, you may be experiencing a tremendous amount of stress that will show up at the workplace in a negative way. I also understand and agree that in difficult economies, people need to work to support their families; however, the long-term goal should be to find work that is financially rewarding and personally fulfilling.

WRIGHT

You say it is very difficult to separate work from personal life. How are companies working through this issue?

HARTLEB

Many progressive companies have now realized the importance of providing work/life balance. The newer generation of workers is demanding this, and it translates to simple things such as work-at-home arrangements to more complex benefit offerings such as elder care, credit counseling, employee assistance programs, and leaves of absence. Companies are now starting to acknowledge that workers who have their personal life in balance are more productive, miss less time at work, and are often more successful.

WRIGHT

What are some of the mistakes you see individuals make in the workplace that prevent success?

HARTLEB

Many individuals stay in a job out of fear of failure if they try something else. I once worked for a telecommunications company that had employees who had been with them thirty or more years. On one hand, the loyalty is admirable. I often wonder, though, what prevented these employees from pursuing growth opportunities within or outside the company. We had a saying, "there is life after (Company X). I went through the same feelings when I decided to leave the company, but I knew I had to for my professional growth.

The most troublesome mistake I see is a failure to maintain perspective. We talked earlier about the difficulty in separating work from personal life. Keep perspective on what is important, keep emotions in check, and remain professional at all times. I have lost count of how many times I have witnessed erratic displays of emotion from crying to yelling, cursing, screaming, threats, and even violence at the workplace. I have witnessed this behavior from hourly employees to the executive ranks. This is the easiest way to lose credibility, respect, and the ability to motivate others. If you are unable to maintain a professional demeanor in a variety of situations, step aside so someone else can.

Wright

How can one come back from such a mistake?

Hartleb

It is difficult to earn respect and credibility. It is even more difficult once it is lost. If it was an unusual circumstance or a one-time occurrence, an apology with an explanation is a good way to start. This type of behavior is toxic to everyone surrounded by it and results in poor morale and lost productivity. People ultimately base their opinions on the actions of others, not what they say. Make a commitment to treat all individuals with respect and dignity and over time, you will earn credibility.

Wright

What recommendations do you have for someone who is working for a difficult individual?

Hartleb

I think we have all had co-workers we did not get along with or a boss we did not respect. Perhaps we thought we knew more or that we should have that person's position. It is best to keep these thoughts to yourself. If you cannot respect the person, respect the position and act accordingly. You are probably not the only one who feels this way and it may just be a matter of time before you are the boss.

It is also important to be honest about the situation. For example, if this is a family business, it may be that the person you are reporting to is a relative and he or she will probably be there for the long haul. Your best option may be to seek other employment.

WRIGHT

How do you position yourself for advancement opportunities?

HARTLEB

Take on highly visible, difficult projects. Learn a variety of tasks, jobs, and responsibilities. Do not complain, never gossip, be genuine, support your words with actions, be honest, ethical, non-threatening and make valid suggestions.

WRIGHT

What should individuals do before stepping out on their own?

HARTLEB

Starting a business is a tremendous undertaking. You will never work so hard or wear so many hats, but it is worth it if you are an entrepreneur at heart. My best advice is to come up with a transition plan while you are still working for someone else.

A transition plan includes a review of your budget, determining how you will support yourself and meet financial obligations while building a business. Determine if you have any potential clients now or if you have time to start taking on some clients and projects while you are still working. You may need to devote nights and weekends to building a clientele.

When you plan to leave your organization, don't burn bridges. Leave on good terms, provide adequate notice, and if you have a non-compete, a confidentiality, or non-disclosure agreement, comply with it. In many cases, your first and sometimes best client will be a former employer.

Wright

What have you personally done to ensure success in your personal and work life?

Hartleb

After years of working for a variety of large corporations and smaller, entrepreneurial ventures, I realized that I was not a very good employee. It took a lot of introspection for me to figure out that I am very creative, I do some of my best work at three o'clock in the morning, and I was stifled by the regimented nine-to-five schedule sitting in a cubicle. I work very hard; however, it needs to be on my terms. I wanted to be able to work on projects that I was interested in and choose how, when and where I would do the work. I am a gypsy at heart—an avid traveler—and one of my criteria is that I have the capability to work with a phone line and Internet connection anywhere in the world. After acknowledging my work-style preferences and setting goals, I was able to turn my strengths into a thriving consulting practice.

Wright

What final words can you offer to our readers to help them achieve success in the workplace?

Hartleb

Always be true to yourself, your ideals, and your ethics. Understand how you work best and seek out a company or a business that will support you. Focus on your strengths, not weaknesses. Understand the affect that both a positive and negative experience can have in different areas of your life and strive to achieve balance and harmony in both.

About the Author

Mary Beth Hartleb founded PRISM Human Resource Consulting Services, Inc., www.PrismHRC.com, in 2003. The company offers the full spectrum of human resource services, products, and technology across all industries. Mary Beth's career spans almost twenty years in the human resources field working for Fortune 500 companies while also developing human resource departments for smaller, entrepreneurial ventures.

With a diverse background in human resources, she has worked in the areas of organizational development, recruiting and staffing, training, compensation, benefits design and administration, policy and procedure development, mergers and acquisitions, OSHA compliance, and employee and labor relations. She has worked in various industries including gaming, restaurant, telecommunications, broadcasting, and non-profit organizations. Mary Beth also founded an international import/export business working with the countries of Turkey and Morocco, and has previously worked in marketing and retail sales.

As Business Development Chair for NAWBO Southern Nevada, she created and implemented the first Women Mean Business Expo, which allowed women-owned businesses to showcase their products and services to the Las Vegas business community. She serves in a voluntary capacity for the governor appointed committees of the Business Development Advisory Council and the Regional Business Development Advisory Council in Nevada. Mary Beth adjuncts at UNLV, University of Phoenix, Regis University and has taught at the University of Southern Nevada. She previously served in a voluntary role as President of the Southern Nevada Human Resource Association.

Mary Beth holds a Juris Doctorate degree from the William S. Boyd School of Law, a master's degree in Human Resource Management, and a bachelor's degree in Marketing and Business Administration. Her credentials include the Senior Human Resource Professional (SPHR-CA) designation from the Society for Human Resource Management with a focus on California employment law. She is a licensed insurance broker in health, life, property and casualty insurance lines.

She is a contributing writer to Gaming & Leisure Magazine; she has published articles on Ezine.com, and has authored several articles on human resource topics. She is frequently quoted as a subject matter expert in business publications.

Mary Beth is a member of the International Speakers Network. Recent speaking engagements include the Public Broadcasting Association, World of Concrete Conference, Recharger Magazine Conference, the Southern Nevada Human Resource Association, National Association of Women Business Owners, the International Association of Management Professionals, the Employer Resource Institute, and Marketing Research Association.

MARY BETH HARTLEB

PRISM Human Resource Consulting Services, LLC

701 N. Green Valley Parkway, Suite 201

Henderson, Nevada 89074

702.990.3344

hr@PrismHRC.com

www.PrismHRC.com